RETURN OF THE WOLF

RETURN *of* *the* WOLF

Conflict & Coexistence

Paula Wild

Douglas & McIntyre

DOUGLAS AND MCINTYRE (2013) LTD.
P.O. Box 219, Madeira Park, BC, V0N 2H0
www.douglas-mcintyre.com

Edited by Pam Robertson
Indexed by Allie Turner
Jacket design by Anna Comfort O'Keeffe
Text design by Shed Simas / Onça Design
Printed and bound in Canada
Printed on FSC-certified stock

Endsheets: Wolf track at Howse River Flats, Banff National Park. Photo by Shutterstock/Autumn Sky Photography
Title page photo by Paula Wild. Photo on page vi by Dan Stahler, US National Park Service.
Photo on page viii by John Cavers.

Douglas and McIntyre (2013) Ltd. acknowledges the support of the Canada Council for the Arts, which last year invested $153 million to bring the arts to Canadians throughout the country. We also gratefully acknowledge financial support from the Government of Canada and from the Province of British Columbia through the BC Arts Council and the Book Publishing Tax Credit.

LIBRARY AND ARCHIVES CANADA CATALOGUING IN PUBLICATION

Wild, Paula, author
        Return of the wolf : conflict and coexistence / Paula Wild.

Includes bibliographical references and index.
Issued in print and electronic formats.
ISBN 978-1-77162-206-6 (hardcover).--ISBN 978-1-77162-207-3 (HTML)

        1. Human-wolf encounters. 2. Wolves—Social aspects. 3. Wolves—Effect of human beings on.
4. Wolves—Folklore. 5. Wolves—Ecology. I. Title.

QL737.C22W55 2018   599.773   C2018-903821-7
                                        C2018-903822-5

To my brother, Doug, and sisters, Kelly and Kim,
the best packmates a human could ask for.

CONTENTS

The study of wolves is actually one of discovering how the human mind works.
—VALERIUS GEIST

CHAPTER 1

THE WOLF AT THE DOOR

Their ears are like radar. They can smell a man from three to four kilometres away. And their eyes ... they can see through everything.
—ION MAKSIMOVIC in *Wolf Hunter*

AT FIRST GLANCE I THOUGHT IT WAS A GERMAN SHEPHERD. THE COL-ouring was just about right but the extraordinarily long legs ended in huge paws, the muzzle was long and blocky, and the head seemed too large for the slender body. It was beautiful and totally still. The dead wolf lay in the back of Gordie Boyd's pickup. Boyd had been hired by the British Columbia government to trap and kill wolves on northern Vancouver Island. He had told me about the carcass and I'd asked to see it. Even so, I wasn't prepared for the fascination I felt at my first close-up view of a wild wolf, and my confusion about why it had to die.

I never dreamt that thirty years later, just down the road, I'd be sitting within a few steps of a young white wolf. It lay on the grass, head on front paws, staring at me intently. Barely daring to breathe, I returned its gaze. Minutes passed, then—*poof!*—it disappeared. It felt like the wolf had stared straight into my soul, and I wondered what it had seen there.

Seconds later, the small hairs on the back of my neck stood on end. I turned my head and there, on the side of the deck, was the white wolf. As silent as fog, it was creeping up behind me.

Nahanni isn't a purebred wolf, but pretty darn close. His owner, Gary Allan, who operates the education and advocacy program Who

1

Speaks for Wolf, figures Nahanni's DNA is 95 per cent or more *Canis lupus* (grey wolf). Weighing in at 23 kilograms (51 lbs), Nahanni is an Arctic wolf, and Allan says they have a reputation for being particularly wary of humans. Nahanni definitely fit that profile. Of the two four-month-old high-content wolf-dogs I met at Allan's in August 2014, Nahanni always kept his distance, yet was the one that watched me the most closely. On my first visit, every time I went into the house, he jumped up on the deck to sniff the spot where I'd been sitting. Once he squatted to leave a small brown turd at the former site of my derrière. A sign of welcome or a warning to stay out of his territory? At the time, I had no way to determine the nature of his calling card.

While researching my previous book, *The Cougar*, I came across some intriguing information about wolves and knew I wanted to write about them. I'd spent a day at Cougar Mountain Zoo observing the fluid body movements of three young cougars and the ways they related to each other and zoo visitors. I was after something

more with wolves. I wanted to watch the way their muscles tensed and relaxed; touch coarse hair; peer at big teeth; and observe pack dynamics. To do all that meant interacting with captive animals. Allan's four almost-wolves were perfect: they were of varied ages and degrees of familiarity with humans, and close enough that I could visit numerous times.

I've often wondered how people and wolves initially related to each other and when those first encounters took place. Recent estimations of the appearance of early humans and wolflike canids indicate that some version of human and wolf may have shared the landscape for one to nearly three million years. While those dates are speculative, a set of foot and paw prints confirms that a wolf and a child, estimated to be a boy around eight years old, explored the same cavern long ago.

Rediscovered in 1994, the Chauvet-Pont-d'Arc Cave is located on a limestone cliff above an old riverbed about a two-hour drive northwest of Marseille in southern France. Although there are other caves in the area, Chauvet-Pont-d'Arc is by far the largest—and, more importantly, contains hundreds of some of the oldest known and best preserved figurative cave paintings in the world. These ancient illustrations depict at least thirteen species of animals, as well as two partial human bodies. Fossilized bones and skulls of a variety of ungulates and predators litter the soft, claylike floor, which retains the impressions of human and animal tracks, as well as what are believed to be cave bear sleeping areas. Radiocarbon dating taken from prehistoric hearths and smoke residue from torches places the oldest art and mammal remains at approximately 30,000 years old.

The foot and paw prints of the young child and wolf are pressed into the dusty floor in a smoke-smudged chamber of the cave.

Nahanni, a high-content wolf-dog, is four months old in this photo. He gets his white coat from his Arctic wolf ancestry and, like many wolves and high-content wolf-dogs, is wary around humans, especially strangers. Photo by Paula Wild

According to "Dog Story," an August 2011 article in the *New Yorker*, the tracks of the child and wolf are side by side with their strides evenly matched. Near the end of the documentary film *Cave of Forgotten Dreams*, the narrator wonders if the wolf was stalking the child, if the two were walking together as companions or if the prints were made thousands of years apart.

Although there is much we don't know or understand about wolves in the past, there are also many misconceptions about their behaviour today. A few are that they howl when hungry, kill for pleasure and always live in packs. A huge fallacy is that healthy North American wolves do not pose any danger to humans. While those beliefs are not true, science continues to reveal intriguing information about the canids. For instance, each wolf has a distinct howl that is as unique as a human fingerprint and those in northern climates have temperature regulation systems that prevent their toes from freezing. Wolves can trot at around eight kilometres (five miles) an hour for much of the day or night in search of prey and, along with birds, worms and other creatures, use the earth's magnetic field to find their way. Some contemporary scientists believe that wolves' complex social structures and intimate family bonds are more humanlike than those of any other mammal, including primates. New data and concepts are important but so are the misconceptions, as a great deal of how people relate to wolves has nothing to do with science at all.

Mystical and mysterious, the wolf has influenced the culture, art and legends of human societies since early times. Perhaps more than any other animal, it has become embedded in the human psyche, even affecting our language. *A wolfish grin, wolfed down his food* and *keep the wolf from the door* are common phrases, joined in more modern times by *lone wolf* to indicate a solitary terrorist. But there is no single vision of the carnivore. Depending on the time and place, it has been portrayed as ruthless and evil or a majestic icon of the wilderness. And, although few people ever see this elusive creature in the wild, its photograph has graced countless calendars, and generations of parents have coaxed children to bed with promises to read "The Three Little Pigs" or listen to *Peter and the Wolf*.

In Japan, where wolves are now extinct, farmers created shrines to worship the canids and took food to their dens, hoping successful litters would keep deer and wild boar out of grain fields. The Lithuanian goddess Medeina is described as a bosomy, beautiful she-wolf who excels at hunting, while Serbian poets use the wolf as a metaphor for fearlessness. Some Indigenous peoples in North America, including the Tsimshian along BC's mighty Skeena River and the Dzawada'enuxw First Nation from the remote coastal fjord of Kingcome Inlet, view the wolf as a symbol of intelligence, leadership and family values. Not all, however, look upon the predator so kindly.

Most human-caused animal extinctions have been inadvertently provoked by ignorance and short-sighted values. But wolves were different: they were targeted. In many areas of the world they were—and often still are—known as killers of children, livestock and pets, as well as competitors for game. As such, they were systematically hunted for bounty and revenge. Aside from humans and their livestock, wolves were once the most widespread large land mammal in the world. By the early twentieth century, however, populations in most of North America and Western Europe had been drastically reduced and, in many areas, completely eradicated from the landscape.

Nevertheless, since the 1970s, wolves have been navigating mountain passes and forested areas to re-establish their ancestral territories in Western Europe and are now found in much of Eurasia and in parts of North Africa. By the late 1980s, or perhaps even earlier, North American wolves—sometimes with human assistance but often on their own—began repopulating their former habitat. Wolves currently roam northern portions of the Americas from coast to coast, as well as the Arctic, with a few populations as far south as northern Mexico.

Wolves are versatile creatures capable of surviving in a variety of landscapes and climates, including barren arctic tundra, open grasslands, parched deserts and lush temperate rainforests. And since they share genetic links with other members of the Canidae family, they can mate and produce fertile offspring with domestic dogs and coyotes. There's been an increase in both hybrids' populations, with most wolf-dogs being domesticated animals and wolf-coyote hybrids remaining wild.

More wolves means unexpected surprises. The reintroduction of the carnivore into Yellowstone National Park in 1995 contributed to a dramatic regeneration of the landscape that affected everything from woodlands and streams to bugs, bears and beavers. In BC, scientific evidence shows that coastal wolves differ from their interior cousins in numerous ways, including some who primarily feed on fresh salmon and seafood instead of deer. And the increased quality and use of trail cameras and GPS collars is revealing previously unknown interspecies relationships, such as wolves chasing cougars off their kills.

A wolf is both hunter and hunted. Working together they are capable of taking down a muskox or buffalo that is more than 10 times their size. Yet a single human armed with a gun, poison or traps can wipe out multiple packs of wolves. Recent studies indicate that the random killing of wolves disrupts pack dynamics, destroys family networks and can lead to increased predation of livestock and possibly aggressive behaviour toward humans. And yes, contrary to popular opinion, healthy North American wolves have attacked people, at times appearing to view them as prey. Human reactions to the return

Tofino is a tiny community on the rugged west coast of Vancouver Island. It borders Pacific Rim National Park Reserve, where wolves, cougars and bears are common. Wolves often pass through human residential areas in the middle of the night, but this wolf was acting unusually bold. Its photo was taken behind the Common Loaf Bake Shop one morning around nine. Photo by Kim Evans of the carnivore tend to be highly emotional, running the gamut from fear and anger to awe and excitement.

The concept of carnivores lurking in the woods often causes a primal uneasiness. To complicate the issue, these new generations of wolves don't always play by the old rules—or at least what people perceive the old rules to be. The shy wolf found in some parts of North America and Western Europe during the last 50 to 100 years is now appearing in human-use areas. In 2015, a wolf on the greens interrupted a round of golf in Norway, a pack of wolves was photographed less than a half-hour drive from Hamburg, Germany, and a young wolf was found wandering the outskirts of Loutraki, a seaside spa and resort town just west of Athens. Trail cameras in Tofino on the west coast of Vancouver Island show wolves taking nocturnal strolls in residential areas and a healthy wolf was discovered living in a small city in Minnesota.

All predators carry the baggage of their past and present reputations but the wolf seems to stir the strongest emotions. For some, it has shifted from being the Big Bad Wolf to being the number-one poster animal for the wilderness and all that implies. But for others,

the resurgence of wolf populations has rekindled fears and concerns that have never completely disappeared. When I began researching wolves I was astonished at the polarization of opinions. Scientist, rancher, photographer, wildlife worker, camper and calendar buyer all have passionate feelings about wolves and their place in the environment. Often, it's a love/hate affair, with city dwellers on one side and rural residents on the other. In a bizarre juxtaposition, 2015 saw three conservation groups suing the United States Fish and Wildlife Service for failing to protect critically endangered red wolves in North Carolina, while more than 11,000 Norwegians registered for licences to shoot a total of 16 wolves—estimated to be half the country's population. Biologists forced to climb trees to escape wolves are reluctant to tell their stories for fear of ridicule. Wildlife officials are threatened for doing their jobs. University professors and government employees are gagged or forced to jump bureaucratic hoops before speaking to the media. Even I was encouraged—strongly at times—to stay away from particular topics and interview sources, and not to write about wolves in certain locations. The degree of animosity, petty possessiveness and dissension dismayed me. It also made me curious. And determined to discover the "real" wolf.

Why, I wondered, was there no—or scant—middle ground? It seems difficult for many to see the wolf for what it is: an important part of a balanced ecosystem, a mammal with incredibly strong family ties and a predator that goes after wild prey—but also livestock, pets and, on rare occasions, humans. Why do so many people pull up a soapbox to proclaim wolves all saints or all sinners? Is it something in us that can't accept the concept of so-called good and bad behaviour

Although wolves are often seen on their own, they are very social animals and love spending time with their packs. In the wild, a pack is usually composed of a breeding pair, their offspring and sometimes extended family members or other wolves who have joined the pack. Photo by iStock/dssimages coexisting in a wild animal, even though we encounter it in human culture every day?

Faced with strongly diverging opinions, my gut instinct is always to go with the science. But even biologists disagree about wolves. Of course, science is not static. New information or ways of perceiving animals and the natural world bring fresh perspectives and new hypotheses all the time. Still, it's difficult to understand how some biologists can declare a wolf cull to save endangered caribou necessary, while others consider it an outrage.

In many regions of the world, wolves have existed for a century or more only as creatures in fairy tales and movies or as residents of zoos and sanctuaries. But now the wolf is at our door, standing in the soft shadows of moonlight, howling to his kin on the ridge. Inside, clutching their bedcovers, humans shiver with fear and fascination. Is it possible to untangle the complex web of myth and misconception, truth and terror that surrounds this carnivore? One thing is certain: just as wolves have affected human actions, attitudes and cultures for centuries, human perceptions will continue to shape the destiny of the wolf.

CHAPTER 2

THE BIG BAD WOLF OF THE OLD WORLD

The wolf Fenrir was so large that when he yawned, his upper jaw touched the sky and his lower jaw rested on the ground.
—NORSE LEGEND

THE RUSSIAN WEDDING PARTY PILED ONTO SEVEN HORSE-DRAWN sledges to attend a banquet at the nearby village of Tashkent, about 1,500 kilometres (932 mi) east of the Caspian Sea. According to newspaper accounts of the day, halfway to their destination, they saw a huge "black cloud" racing toward them and, within minutes, were surrounded by "hundreds of yelping wolves." The terrified horses strained to outrun the predators but the combination of overloaded sledges and only two horses to a harness, instead of the usual three, meant first one sledge and then another tipped over. Screams filled the air as more upended. In the only sledge pulled by three steeds, the newlyweds and two male members of the wedding party outraced the carnage only to find more wolves ahead of them. Maddened by fear, the men pushed the newly married couple overboard in an effort to lighten the load. They reached Tashkent soon after, leaving behind a body count of 118 people and 12 horses.

Stories about the 1911 tragedy were published in newspapers worldwide and were even the basis of a memorable passage in American author Willa Cather's 1918 novel *My Ántonia*. Which brings up a good question: Is the wedding party massacre fact or fiction? The story ran in the March 19, 1911, edition of the *New York Times*, which gives it some credence, and Russian wolves *do* have a reputation for attacking humans. But even though members of a wedding party may have been killed that winter, it's likely the number of wolves and humans was mistranslated or grossly exaggerated.

Accounts similar to that of the wedding party massacre, and there are many, make it easy to understand humans' age-old fear of wolves. And the wolf, usually portrayed as wicked and dangerous, is a character many children meet early on in bedtime stories such as "Little Red Riding Hood" and "The Boy Who Cried Wolf." People like to be scared—but safely—and what better way to experience a shiver of fear than cuddled up with mommy or daddy?

Historically, wolves in the Old World ranged from Portugal to Japan and Russia to India, and that's where the majority of frightening stories about wolves originated. Most people associate fairy tales with Aesop's Fables, stories supposedly told by a Greek slave in ancient times, or with the German siblings Jacob and Wilhelm, known as the Brothers Grimm, who published collections of oral stories in the 1800s. But the genre goes back thousands of years and can be found in most languages throughout the world. Early fairy tales catered to adult audiences and were rife with dark elements. Rapunzel, the young woman with the long golden hair, became pregnant out of wedlock and her prince was blinded by thorns trying to reach her, while Cinderella's wicked stepsister cut off a toe in an effort to cram her foot into a dainty party slipper.

Over time, fairy tales became more child-friendly, and popular ones have been rewritten many times with modern versions (some adapted as movies by Disney and others) eliminating the gruesome deaths, sexuality and discrimination. In a contemporary adaptation of "Little Red Riding Hood," instead of eating Grandma, the Big Bad Wolf abandons his predatory ways to become head baker at her pastry shop.

A fascination with wolves spans many cultures and time periods. Long ago, Greeks wore wolf teeth and tails as good luck charms, while eating the canid's heart was believed to instill courage on the battle-field. In some areas of Pakistan, wolf fat is considered an aphrodisiac, and Joseph Stalin, leader of the Soviet Union from the mid-1920s until 1953, frequently sketched wolves in the margins of his papers.

The wolf holds pride of place as national animal in several coun-tries, including the Chechen Republic of Ichkeria, located in Eastern Europe approximately 100 kilometres (62 mi) west of the Caspian Sea. The nation's folklore includes a loving wolf-mother and all Chechens are considered equal and free like wolves. In 1992, Chechen separatists created a series of improvised submachine guns that they named *Borz*, the Chechen word for wolf. And contrary to elsewhere in the world, Chechen legend states that sheep were created for wolves but humans stole them for their own use.

Turkic peoples, comprised of various ethnic groups spread throughout parts of Eastern Europe and Asia, traditionally thought that ingesting body parts from wolves imbued a person with magical powers. They also believed that a she-wolf with a sky-blue mane

found and cared for an abandoned human baby and later gave birth to wolf-human cubs that created the Turkic nations. Stories about feral children being raised by wild animals have intrigued people throughout the ages. The good-hearted kindness of the animals, and the children's ability to survive and adapt, bridges the gap between animals and humans. Goats, monkeys, gazelles and even an ostrich are said to have filled the role of mother to a human child. Wolves are particularly popular as surrogate parents and it's said their adopted human children can run on all fours for long distances, howl like real wolves and often try to escape back to the wilderness and their canid family if rescued by humans. Well-known stories about wolves raising children include Rudyard Kipling's *The Jungle Book*, featuring Mowgli, an infant boy suckled and raised by a female wolf, and the legend of Romulus and Remus. These infant twins were also saved by a wolf. One was later credited with founding Rome.

But the wolf, perhaps more than any other animal, has a long history of being perceived as cunning, ruthless and evil. The Bible portrays wolves as killers and employs the word metaphorically to describe deceitful people who attempt to lead others astray from true Christian values and beliefs. Many view Christ, the good shepherd, as being on one end of the spectrum, a flock of steadfast or hoped-for followers in the middle, and the devil, often portrayed as a wolf, at the other. Prior to the twentieth century, most of Eurasia was plagued by wolves—often rabid—that frequently attacked livestock and humans. And in some countries, even today, there are people who believe that those who die in mortal sin are occasionally resurrected as werewolves

Like many fairy tales, an early version of "Little Red Riding Hood" focused on morals. The story was intended to warn girls and young women about the dangers of strange men and encourage them to remain virtuous no matter what the circumstances. This image is one of several illustrations French artist Gustave Doré created around 1892 for Charles Perrault's version of the story.

instead of being sent to hell. Stories about werewolves originated in Europe and eventually spread to the New World. These men, women and children could transform themselves into wolves and back at will and, while in canid form, were obsessed with killing and devouring people and domestic animals.

A person could become a werewolf by being bitten by one, as divine punishment for a transgression of faith, by being excommunicated from the Roman Catholic Church or by pledging allegiance to Satan in order to satisfy a craving for human flesh. While there are some references to werewolves in ancient Greek mythology—for instance, Zeus turning King Lycaon into a wolf—belief in the phenomenon didn't become prevalent in Europe until the latter part of the fourteenth century.

In 1573, more than 50 witnesses testified that they had seen French hermit Gilles Garnier appearing sometimes as a man and others as a wolf, killing and devouring children in fields and vineyards. At his trial, Garnier confessed that while hunting for food one night, a "spectre" appeared and offered an ointment that would allow him to transform himself into a wolf, thus making his nightly forays for food easier.

One of the most famous werewolf trials took place in 1589 when, while being tortured in Bedburg, Germany, a wealthy farmer named Peter Stumpp confessed to practising black magic. According to a pamphlet published in London the following year, he'd done so since the age of 12, when the devil gave him a belt that allowed him to change into "the likeness of a greedy, devouring wolf, strong and mighty, with eyes great and large, which in the night sparkled like fire, a mouth great and wide, with most sharp and cruel teeth, a huge body, and mighty paws." When Stumpp removed the belt he became a man again. Some historians suggest that the concept of werewolves was an imaginative explanation for the disease hypertrichosis, an abnormal, copious growth of hair over all or much of the body, and for serial killings, especially those that involved cannibalism.

Numerous legends mention Viking "berserkers" who drank wolf blood before battle and fought with a tenacious, trancelike fury. According to Hilda R.E. Davidson in *Animals in Folklore*, "men went without their mailcoats and were mad as hounds or wolves, bit their shields ... they slew men, but neither fire nor iron had effect upon them." Vikings considered wolves battle companions and their word for the canid translates as "corpse troll." Poor burial practices in medieval times, and the casualties of war, plague and famine throughout

In the Middle Ages, it was common to believe in werewolves. Fear of wolves was rampant and those suspected of transforming from human to wolf and back again were often tortured violently until they confessed and were killed.

the centuries, all drew wolves in and contributed to their taste for human flesh. They, along with ravens and vultures, were often called the "beasts of battle."

Stories shape and define human culture and beliefs, so it's no surprise that the Big Bad Wolf, a hairy, dangerous creature that many considered the most terrifying predator in Europe, assumed the persona of an evil shapeshifter in folklore. The combination of actual experience, fear, biblical references and the telling of fairy tales led to the wolf being seen as the ultimate enemy of humans, livestock and God. How's that for a bad rap passed down through the ages?

As humans shifted from a nomadic lifestyle to an agricultural one, the resulting changes to the landscape, as well as the keeping of livestock and killing of wolves' natural prey, led to more interactions between wolves and humans. Most people in the Old World were ill-equipped to defend themselves or their livestock, as it wasn't unusual for governments to forbid commoners from owning firearms in order to prevent uprisings due to social unrest, and to reserve big game hunting for the upper class. István Türr, a Hungarian nationalist who fought in the mid-nineteenth-century Hungarian and Italian revolutions, witnessed the hardships his unarmed compatriots faced first-hand. Their plight so moved him that he mentioned it in an autobiographical account he published in 1856 titled "A Narrative of the Arrest, Trial and Condemnation of Colonel Türr." He wrote, "... since the restriction of the liberty of hunting and the seizure of all arms in Hungary, wild beasts have so multiplied, that, besides an enormous damage done to the crops, the flocks, and the poultry, the wolves venture, not only into villages, but into the very towns, and besides doing fearful depredations, attack even people." Rural residents in Russia have been plagued for centuries by wolves entering villages at night to prey on dogs, break into outbuildings after livestock and sometimes attack humans. And as recently as 1993, a Romanian newspaper urged people living in the countryside to smear garlic over their windows and doors during an upcoming national holiday to protect themselves from werewolves, which were believed to be active at that time of year.

People had good reason to fear wolves. An attack meant the risk of severe injury, infection and death, as well as rabies, which was common prior to the twentieth century. Even after French biologist Louis Pasteur invented the first vaccine in 1885, most people died after being bitten by a rabid animal because they lived too far from sources of the vaccine to receive it in time. Rabies is a very serious disease, usually fatal if not treated soon. It can affect any mammal, including humans, and is transmitted primarily by an animal bite or occasionally an infected animal's saliva. As the virus spreads through the central nervous system, victims experience swelling of the brain, agitation and often a fear of water due to throat spasms when swallowing. Animals with rabies sometimes become aggressive. Wolves can experience an especially "furious" phase of the disease and may race around biting living and inanimate objects, even the ground, for a day or so. Due to their size, stamina and ability to cover large distances, they can infect many before dying or being killed.

"The Fear of Wolves: A Review of Wolf Attacks on Humans" was published by the Norwegian Institute for Nature Research in 2002. Compiled by 18 international wildlife officials, the report focuses on verified attacks during the eighteenth century to the end of the nineteenth. France is interesting as during that time period, residents experienced a nearly equal number of attacks by rabid (1,038) and non-rabid (1,076) wolves. Two case histories are notable, both for the number of confrontations and the clear delineation between rabid and predatory attacks.

In April 1851, a rabid wolf ran through nine villages in northern France biting 41 men, women and children, as well as 96 domestic animals. It's believed that most, if not all, of the victims died. The wolf's journey took seven hours and covered 45 kilometres (28 mi). It did not feed on any of the humans or animals it attacked.

The second incident involves what is perhaps the most famous series of wolf attacks in Europe, which took place near the mountains and plateaus of Massif Central in southern France from June 1764 to 1767. Depending on the source, one or several wolves attacked more than 200 people, killing and partially eating over half the victims. King Louis XV called on the army and nobles, as well as conscripting local residents, to kill what became known as the Beast of Gévaudan. Nonetheless, the attacks continued until two especially large animals were killed in 1765 and 1767. Even though rabies was common at the time, the lengthy attack period ruled out the disease as the cause, and the fact that many victims were consumed indicates predatory behaviour, with the wolves viewing humans as prey. During the attacks and to this day, controversy abounds over whether the marauding beasts were wolves, wolf-dogs, an escaped hyena, a serial killer or a supernatural being. In 2001, the French film *Brotherhood of the Wolf* presented yet another possible explanation for the Beast of Gévaudan—a lion covered in armour and controlled by a secret society attempting to overthrow the king. Altogether, it's estimated that more than 1,100 people died from wolf attacks in France during the eighteenth and nineteenth centuries, approximately half the total number of attacks.

Statistics for wolf attacks in Asia are negligible prior to the nineteenth century. "The Fear of Wolves," however, notes numerous accounts in India obtained from official records kept by the British colonial administration during the late nineteenth century and into the twentieth. While the records do not differentiate between rabid

When many people think of aggressive wolves, they picture snarling animals with teeth bared. That is often the case when a wolf confronts another wolf or bear, but body language also says a lot about what's going on. The fact that this wolf has its ears pinned back indicates that it may feel threatened. Photo by iStock/twildlife and non-rabid attacks, in 1878 alone, 624 people were killed by wolves in India's Uttar Pradesh region, most being children under the age of 16. Figures for older attacks in what's now known as Russia are also scarce but Will Graves's *Wolves in Russia: Anxiety Through the Ages* fills in a lot of blanks. Government records for European Russia show that 1,445 people were killed by wolves from 1870 through 1887, a not uncommon body count in parts of Russia throughout the nineteenth century.

"Winters in Russia can be very harsh and when prey is scarce wolves move near villages," Graves explains. "Even today wolves will surround small villages and people will be afraid to go out at night. Often all they have to defend themselves is a shovel. If they do have a gun, they might not have any ammunition. The Soviet government was notorious for suppressing information about the number of wolf attacks." Graves, who has degrees in the Spanish and Russian languages and is fluent in German, lived and worked as an assist- ant consular officer at the US Embassy in Moscow from 1993 to 1995.

His interest in wolves and hunting led to expeditions to Kazakhstan, Siberia and Karelia, where he collected data and made valuable contacts with wolf experts. Graves is very clear about one point: "Unless they're a rancher, when most folks hear a wolf howl in North America, they're thrilled. When people in Russia hear wolves howl, especially in rural areas, they're terrified."

At times, European governments took vigorous steps to slaughter wolves and eliminate or at least reduce the fear and destruction they caused. It's possible the first bounty on wolves was offered around AD 46 to 120 by Solon, a magistrate of Athens. Throughout the middle ages each country dealt with the scourge of the wolf in its own way. During the ninth century in France, a select force of wolf hunters called "Luparii" was dedicated to decimating the beasts, while Magnus IV, king of Sweden during part of the fourteenth century, declared wolf hunting a national duty from which only landless women and religious officials were exempt. While common folk killed wolves for survival or to collect a possible bounty, it was often a privilege reserved for the aristocracy. Prior to becoming extinct in England around the early 1500s, wolves were considered one of the five royal beasts of the chase.

By the early to mid–nineteenth century, the wolf-devil, curse of farmers and fearsome beast of the woods, was essentially gone. No more paw prints in soft earth, no more howls echoing from the hills, no more silent shadows glimpsed from the corner of an eye. The British Isles and most of Western Europe were, for all intents and purposes, wolfless. But robust packs thrived in Russia and Romania, as well as other areas of Eastern Europe, with the Carpathian Mountains providing a refuge to many. Although equally feared and despised, most of the smaller wolves of southern Asia also survived. From the frozen tundra to arid plains, wherever the wolf remained, a single paw print or glimpse of its sinewy form was enough to haunt the dreams of humans.

CHAPTER 3

GOOD AND EVIL IN THE NEW WORLD

The wolf is a monstrosity of nature ... possessing the cruelty of Satan himself.
—*THE DILLON EXAMINER*, 1921

"TWO WOLVES ARE FIGHTING INSIDE EACH PERSON ALL THE TIME," SAYS the old man. "One is filled with anger, hate, jealousy and everything negative. The other wolf is pleasant, cooperative and an embassy of peace and goodwill."

"Which one wins?" his grandson asks.

"The one we feed," the old man replies.

Numerous versions of this ancient Cherokee story, also known as "The Tale of Two Wolves," pop up on Facebook pages and websites on a regular basis. But it, like nearly everything to do with wolves, is controversial. As it turns out, Grandpa's wise words might be based on a tale written by evangelical Christian minister Billy Graham in his book *The Holy Spirit: Activating God's Power in Your Life*. Or maybe Graham based his fable on a Cherokee legend. Similar stories about nurturing good and evil are present in many cultures, making it impossible to identify the original source.

Either way, most, if not all, Indigenous peoples in North America have intimate, complex relationships with wolves. The canids are honoured for their close family bonds, hunting prowess and ability to move through the woods in total silence. They're considered spiritual and powerful, and respect is accorded to anyone owning the rights to wolf regalia or rituals. The Wolf Clan has traditionally been the largest of the seven Cherokee clans and, in times past, was always the clan of the war chief. The wolf is highly respected as a hunter and protector by all Cherokee, who avoid killing the animal if at all possible.

While the roots of many beliefs about wolves can be traced to Eurasia, the wolf has played a significant role in the cultures and ideologies of North America. Perhaps the oldest reference to this was found in a 1552 Aztec manuscript, which lists wolf liver as an ingredient to cure the "black blood" of depression. The Aztecs, who reigned in central Mexico from the mid-1300s to the early 1500s, revered wolves as emblems of war and the all-important sun. In April 2017, an archaeological dig at an Aztec temple near Mexico City's central square revealed a stone box containing the corpse of a young wolf adorned with large pieces of gold. Archaeologists believe the wolf's heart may have been removed prior to burial as part of a sacrificial ritual. Farther north, Cheyenne medicine men used wolf fur to protect sacred arrows, while Hidatsa women, in what's now known as North Dakota, rubbed wolf skin on their abdomens to ease the pain of a difficult childbirth.

The Tlingit and Tsimshian, whose combined territories span Alaska, the Yukon and northwestern British Columbia, carve and paint wolves on their totem poles and longhouse walls, and incorporate wolf pelts, teeth and tails into ceremonial regalia. The wolf is held in high regard for the way it looks after and protects its young and is considered a role model for family values. Both peoples have highly respected Wolf Clans that trace their origin to a family group descent story. Also considering the wolf an ancestor are the Ojibwa, who currently occupy land surrounding the Great Lakes in Canada and the US. Their creation story says that man was the last creature placed on earth. He had a wolf as a partner, not a woman, and as the two walked the land, they named everything they saw. The man and wolf were like brothers. At the end of their journey, the Creator told them that, although they must separate, they would be forever connected.

To this day, many Ojibwa believe that what happens to the wolf—good or bad—will happen to their people.

Stories about transformation are common across many cultures. Whereas the Old World has werewolves, in the US southwest the Navajo word for "wolf" is synonymous with "witch," a term used to signify a shapeshifting skin-walker that bodes ill for any who encounter it. Numerous stories from BC coast First Nations recount wolves becoming men, orcas or even sea wolves—half-whale, half-wolf beings—such as Wasco, a creature of Haida lore that can hunt in the water and on land. Transformation stories are part of a complex belief system that emphasizes the intimate connections between Indigenous peoples and their non-human ancestors, including animals, as well as a strong relationship with and kinship to place.

Winter ceremonials have always been an important part of Indigenous culture along BC's West Coast, as well as in the villages linked to the sea by fjords and rivers that cut deep into the mainland. German anthropologist Franz Boas conducted extensive fieldwork in this region, collecting hundreds of oral histories. One described how a wolf created the first Kwakwaka'wakw winter ceremonial for the people who traditionally lived on northern Vancouver Island, the adjacent mainland coast and the islands in between. In it, the Chief of Wolves announced he would create an event to dispel the darkness of winter. An unnamed informant told Boas that at the end of the Wolf Dance, "all the animals and birds took their skins off, hung them up, and became men and women ... When they finished the winter dance, some of the myth people put their blankets back on, while others stayed behind and retained the shape of men." Some say that this dance signified the final separation of animals and humans, meaning they could no longer speak to and understand each other, or change from one form to another.

The Skidi, a tribe of the Pawnee Nation, originally located in what's now called Nebraska and Kansas, are referred to as the Wolf

People. Their sign for *Pawnee* and *wolf* is the same: two fingers held in a V shape by the right ear moving forward. The Pawnee believe that the recurring appearance and disappearance of Sirius, which they call the Wolf Star, indicates a wolf loping along the Wolf Road (Milky Way) as it travels to and from the spirit world. The Blackfoot refer to the Milky Way as the Wolf Trail or Route to Heaven. A powerful tribe that once occupied the Great Plains of North America, the Blackfoot traditionally dressed in wolfskins during certain ceremonies and hunts in order to become brothers to the wolf and benefit from the canid's knowledge.

Many North American Indigenous groups have strict taboos against killing wolves, while others traditionally hunted them on a regular basis. Their fur was highly valued in Alaska and Canada, where it was used for clothing and as a trade item. Indigenous people trapped wolves in a variety of ways, sometimes luring them to their death by howling, which possibly led resident wolves to think another pack was infringing on their territory. Oral histories of Athabascan peoples in Alaska, Yukon and the Northwest Territories mention attempts to reduce wolf predation on game by raiding wolf dens to kill pups.

Although not a mainstay of the menu, it's said that some western North American peoples considered wolves, especially pups, a delicacy. In 1913, Isaac Cowie, a Hudson's Bay Company official based in Fort Qu'Appelle in southern Saskatchewan, wrote that wolves were "generally fat, and yielded a large proportion of the grease eaten by the Indians and made into the finer kind of pemmican by them."

As well as hunting wolves, Indigenous communities of the Prairies and Great Plains on both sides of the Canada-US border disguised themselves in wolfskins to sneak up on enemy tribes and to hunt bison. Both people and wolves depended on the shaggy ungulate for food. Now extinct, the Plains wolf, sometimes called the "buffalo wolf," had smoky white fur and was said to be similar in size to a St. Bernard or Newfoundland dog, but much stronger. They could hamstring a mature bison but, as opportunists, often followed hunters and patiently waited for any scraps left behind after a kill. The almost sacred trinity of humans, bison and wolves created a symbiotic circle of benefit with each contributing to the well-being of the other. The hunters used virtually every part of the bison, including the meat, hide, horns, hair and tail. Even the stomach served as a water container. The bison benefited too, since by primarily targeting the old, weak, injured and young, wolves and humans kept herds from overpopulating, and selective burning of the prairies prevented overgrazing, ensuring there was always new grass for them to eat.

The 500- to 730-kilogram (1,100–1,600 lb) ungulates were used to wolves cruising the periphery of a herd to check for animals that would be easy to take down. As long as they weren't guarding young and

Many North American Indigenous groups respect wolves for their hunting abilities and close family relationships. Some have Wolf Clans, societies and special ceremonies. This wolf mask was carved in 1979 by John Henderson of the Wei Wai Kum First Nation in Campbell River. It is unique in that a wolf pelt is attached to the carving. Courtenay & District Museum 983.68.5

didn't feel vulnerable, most bison ignored them. In 1849, in *Adventures of the First Settlers on the Oregon or Columbia River,* Alexander Ross described how hunters used wolf disguises: "An Indian concealed in a wolf's hide, pulls the skin of the wolf's head, with the face, eyes and nose entire, over his own head, the ears erect, the tail in proper place, then will walk, run and frisk about on his hands and feet, so that he can scarcely be distinguished from the real animal itself." To mask their human scent, hunters smeared themselves with wolf fat.

As the bogus wolves approached the bison, one or more hunters draped in bison hides, complete with horned heads, placed themselves between the herd and a steep cliff, commonly known as a "jump." Once the bison were close to the cliff, the men dressed as wolves would stand up and charge full tilt toward the bison, whooping and hollering.

Startled, the bison would stampede, naturally following the pseudo bison in front of them. By the time they reached the cliff, the lumbering beasts could be running up to 64 kilometres (40 mi) per hour, too fast to avoid falling to their deaths or being sufficiently injured that the people waiting below could easily finish them off. As for the men camouflaged as bison? They ran like hell then grabbed carefully placed ropes so they could swing over the cliff to shelter in narrow overhangs until the ruckus was over. After the bison had been processed and the people headed for home with their dogs (and later horses) pulling travois laden with meat, the real wolves feasted on the leftovers.

An early wolf in the prehistoric Americas was *Canis dirus*, which translates as "fearsome dog." Some dire wolves were huge, others were about the size of a large grey wolf, but all were stockier, had bigger heads and teeth and much smaller brains than contemporary grey wolves. Fossils of this formidable creature have been found from southern Bolivia to Canada. When the dire wolf became extinct, *Canis lupus* was the only large species of *Canis* that remained. In *The Carnivore Way*, Cristina Eisenberg, chief scientist at Earthwatch Institute, explains that the early ancestor of all wolves, coyotes and dogs appeared in North America about 10 million years ago. Around 8.5 million years later, coyotes and wolves experienced a genetic split, with the latter loping across the Bering land bridge, a strip of land exposed by falling sea levels during the Pleistocene era that connected what are now known as Alaska and Siberia. Beginning approximately 700,000 years ago, wolves migrated back to North America in three

Even though a bison is 10 times the weight of a wolf, packs can and do kill them. The wolves will look for a lone bison or harass a herd until they start running and then watch for old, weak, young or injured animals to isolate from the others. It is dangerous though, as bison can gore and throw wolves with their horns, injuring and sometimes killing them.
Photo by Doug Smith, US National Park Service

separate waves, one including the predecessor of the grey wolf we know today.

For many years, it was believed there were three wolf species in the Americas—grey, red and eastern—and up to twenty-five sub-species. This was eventually whittled down to two species (grey and red) and four or five subspecies, all distinctly separate from the dire wolf. But it seems that not all wolves are created equal. The results of a 2016 DNA study by researchers in the US, China and Israel suggests that the only true species of wolf in North America is the grey, and that red and eastern wolves are wolf-coyote hybrids. Although scientists agree that red and eastern wolves possess some coyote genes, how much and when they acquired the genes—a crucial factor in determining species—is still up for debate.

The grey wolf is the only species of wolf to inhabit both the Old and New Worlds and a recent theory claims it is the only true wolf species worldwide. But scientists disagree about that too. In 2015, a DNA study led by Klaus-Peter Koepfli of the Smithsonian Conservation Biology Institute in Washington, DC, and Robert Wayne, professor of ecology and evolutionary biology at UCLA College, determined that the Egyptian golden jackal in north and east Africa is actually a wolf (now called the African golden wolf). And not just any wolf, but a new species closely related to grey wolves and coyotes but distinct from them and unrelated to other golden jackals found in Eurasia. To further complicate matters, even canids that are called wolves don't always have the genetics to back up the name. In South America, the maned wolf, an exceptionally leggy animal with striking reddish-gold and black markings, is neither wolf nor fox, or even closely related to other canids. Instead, it has the distinction of being the only species in the genus *Chrysocyon* (golden dog). Ongoing studies and evolving theories mean the definitive title of "real wolf" (or wolves) awaits a later chapter in the annals of *Canis* genealogy.

Of all wolves, the grey has the widest range and is the largest. Grey wolves in northern areas, such as Alaska, Canada and Russia, can weigh up to 80 kilograms (175 lbs). But that's at an extreme. According to the Alaska Department of Fish and Game, an average-sized male wolf in Alaska usually weighs about 45.5 kilograms (100 lbs), stands 81 centimetres (32 in) tall at the shoulder and can measure 1.8 metres (6 ft) or more from tip of nose to end of tail. Females tend to be 10 to 15 per cent smaller. And don't let the word *grey* fool you: their fur can be white, black or any shade in between. Red and eastern wolves have smaller, slimmer bodies and are somewhere in between the size of a grey wolf and a coyote, with the red being the larger of the two. Red wolves are brown or tan with some black and noticeable red markings, while eastern wolves generally have tan-coloured coats with a reddish overcast. Prior to the early twentieth century, red wolves were found in south central and eastern portions of the US, while the eastern wolf primarily inhabited southeastern Canada and the northeastern US.

For many early explorers and European settlers, North American wolves were sometimes heard, seldom seen and certainly didn't seem as dangerous to humans as those in the Old World. In *New English Canaan*, a three-volume memoir of his time in a New England colony, Thomas Morton wrote that wolves were "fearfull curs and will runne away from a man (that meeteth them by chance at a banke) as fast as any fearfull dogge." As the Lewis and Clark Expedition made its way from St. Louis, Missouri, to the Pacific Northwest from 1804 to 1806, William Clark noted in his diary, "the wolves are fat and extremely gentle."

Many settlers generally believed that a lone wolf was a coward, two wolves were dangerous and a pack meant danger of imminent death should a person be out alone or even with others if travelling by foot. There are many old-time stories of solitary travellers or sometimes two or three people being killed while walking from one place to another, with searchers finding their partially consumed remains, a broken rifle stock and a few dead wolves. No one knows if these accounts are fact, fantasy or gross exaggeration but there's no doubt a pack of wolves generated fear. Even so, records suggest there were nowhere near as many attacks in North America as in Eurasia. That could be due to poor record keeping, an adequate amount of wolves' natural prey or because the majority of settlers had firearms and didn't hesitate to use them.

As time went by, settlers made their mark on the land. Forests were cut, fields plowed and homes and communities built. And humans hunted, for both food and sport. Barrels of salted meat from deer, moose and other ungulates, augmented by strips of dried, pickled or smoked meat from wild and domestic animals, saw many a bachelor or family through the winter. Apart from providing food for the table, a day of hunting provided a diversion from clearing land and other chores, as well as a sense of adventure and accomplishment.

Whereas hunting was often a privilege reserved for royalty in Europe, in the New World it was a pursuit open to any and all. And the abundance of wildlife was like a starscape in the sky—something that could not be counted and would never diminish. In fact, Clark eventually stopped recording in his journal the vast numbers of bison, elk and wolves they came across as he didn't think anyone would believe him. Unfortunately, settlers gave little or no thought to the long-term consequences of unregulated hunting. Beginning in the east and moving west with development, populations of deer, moose and bison were drastically reduced and, in some regions, nearly eliminated in a shockingly short time.

Settlers further altered the dynamics of the Americas by introducing cattle, pigs, sheep and other livestock. As their natural prey became scarce, wolves turned to these animals to fill the void. Part of the problem was accessibility: often the animals roamed free on the periphery of a settlement or on a farm where grassland butted up against the wilderness. The only real protection against predators was the farmyard hound and the family rifle. If someone was close enough and responded quickly, injury or death could be averted. But the stealthy and primarily nocturnal wolves usually arrived when settlers were curled up under the covers, exhausted after a hard day's work. And compared to their wild, hoofed cousins, domestic animals were the equivalent of today's fast food—easy and quick to pick up.

And so the North American war on wolves began. Reinforcing the fairy tales and memories of the Big Bad Wolf in Europe were personal experiences with what many referred to as the scourge of the land. Youngsters grew up witnessing the angst wolves brought their families due to livestock predation and the seeds of loathing were planted deep in the generational psyche. Farmers trapped and shot wolves whenever they could. Sometimes their efforts turned into a blood sport, with entire communities joining in a circle hunt to kill any predators they surrounded. An account in *The Wolves of North America* by Stanley Young and Edward Goldman describes an 1830 event in New Hampshire when 600 males, age 10 to 80, armed with rifles, shotguns, clubs and pitchforks, put an end to their "siege of wolves."

Killing wolves was a bonding experience sometimes used to accomplish other goals as well. In *The Wolves of North America* the authors write, "Efforts to destroy the wolf ... were instrumental in the formation of Oregon." Pioneer, author and budding politician William H. Gray called a series of "Wolf Meetings" in 1843 as a ploy to get settlers to organize some sort of government. He suspected the topic would unite settlers—and he was right. Within two months, a bounty of fifty cents for a small wolf and three dollars for a large one was set and attendees had agreed to form Oregon Country's first provisional government.

If wolves were persistent in killing livestock, humans were devious—and relentless—in their retaliation. A common way to capture wolves was a pit trap. This was a hole in the ground about 2.5 metres (8 ft) deep with inward-sloping walls. The pit was hidden at ground level by a precarious platform of sticks and grass, with the aroma of meat at the bottom of the hole wafting out to entice wolves to investigate. While travelling through Indiana in 1814, John James Audubon, a naturalist known for his lifelike paintings of North American birds, described watching a farmer enter several pit traps to hamstring the wolves he'd caught, sling a rope around their necks and drag them out for his dogs to kill. At the time, Audubon, a future conservationist, was not shocked; after all, wolves were just animals, and devilish ones at that. And people were used to killing animals then, as many settlers slaughtered their own livestock and wild game for the table.

Both newcomers and Indigenous people employed various methods to dispatch wolves, in addition to the pit trap. One involved three large codfish hooks tied back to back, baited with meat and then suspended by rope from a tree limb 1.5 metres (5 ft) from the ground. Once a wolf took the bait, it was unable to escape. A shotgun or rifle could be rigged up along a wolf runway (a path created by and regularly used by wolves) with bait on the muzzle linked to a cord that pulled the trigger when an animal tugged on it. Tidewater sets involved anchoring a seal with rocks and ringing it with traps that remained hidden at low tide. Snares, a loop of light cable rigged to tighten as a captured animal struggles, were also used. Unfortunately, neck snares, like most other means of killing wolves, don't always execute animals quickly. Many wolves and other animals have been found still alive with snares deeply embedded in their necks, legs or even midsections from their struggles to escape.

Steel leghold traps were popular (and are still used in some countries, including Canada and the US, today) but, to be successful, need to be carefully set. Lone wolves tend to be more cautious than a family group and all but very young pups are wary of human scent. A bonus of the tidewater trap was that high tide washed away any human smell. Various scents were used to disguise land traps. These included mixtures of wolf urine and pulverized wolf gall and anal glands combined with glycerine or the meat of an oily fish such as carp or sturgeon that had rotted to mush. Some trappers used a wolf tail attached to a wooden handle to smooth the dirt around a trap as a way to erase their tracks and scent. According to *The Wolves of North America*, "The wolf's tail was to a real wolfer what a good saddle is to the cowboy."

But the best way to exterminate wolves was poison. And the poison of choice in Canada and the US from around the mid-1800s on was strychnine. The fruit of the Southeast Asian nux vomica tree contains greyish-green, flat seeds that resemble irregularly shaped buttons, and it's these small discs that are the source of the potent poison. Young and Goldman quote E. Carney as saying, "In the days when the early pioneers pushed their way into the forest of the eastern States, grey wolves were found in great numbers ... They are, of all the larger North American animals, among the swiftest runners, the hardest to trap, the hardest to get sight of in the forest ... There is no doubt that poison was the chief means of their destruction."

Strychnine was the number-one tool in the arsenal of the professional "wolfer." This term generally applied to US bounty hunters who killed wolves following bison (called "buffalo" by early US settlers) herds on the Great Plains. It's estimated that as many as 30 to 60 million bison roamed the vast sea of grass that made up the Plains during the time of European settlement. The shaggy brown shapes seemed to stretch to the horizon, an endless bounty just waiting to be harvested. Bison were hunted for trade by trappers who had pretty well eliminated the beaver. Bison were hunted for sport by those journeying on the recently completed transcontinental railroad, with trains advertising "hunting by rail" and slowing when a herd was sighted to ensure an accurate aim. And bison were hunted as part of the US government's plan to eradicate Indigenous people during the Indian Wars spanning the late 1860s to the 1870s by removing their primary food source. Aside from the hides, tongues and bones, the carcasses were left to rot. Eventually, the wolves that gathered for the feast of leftovers became the next targets. The centuries-old holy trinity was under siege.

Wolfers, working alone or in small groups, mixed strychnine sulphate crystals with water to create a slurry that wouldn't blow away in the prairie winds. Then they'd shoot a few bison, peel back the skin, liberally apply the paste and cover it with the flap of hide. Sometimes they cut bison meat into small pieces and slit them to hide the strychnine inside. After employing the latter method, two men working in the Santa Fe, New Mexico, area around 1864 reaped a harvest of 64 wolves in one night, all found within 2.5 kilometres (1.6 mi) of their camp. In Kansas, a man who had shot several bison returned to harvest the hides and saw numerous wolves feeding on the carcasses. He killed four with his rifle, injuring others. That night he salted the dead bison with strychnine and found 84 dead wolves in the morning. Results like that were not uncommon.

As European settlers spread across North America, wolves became public enemy number one, especially for the livestock industry, which heavily lobbied the government to exterminate them. The first official US wolf bounty was declared by the Massachusetts Bay Colony in November 1630 and was followed by others throughout the land. In 1905 the Montana legislature gave the go-ahead for mange, a debilitating skin condition caused by mites, to be introduced to wolf and coyote populations as a cheaper alternative to bounties. Nonetheless, official government wolf bounties continued in some US states until 1965. But even before then, wolf populations in the lower 48 had been eliminated or severely reduced due to the predator control programs and loss of habitat. Grey wolves were found only in Minnesota and on Isle Royale in Lake Superior, with possibly as few as 20 red wolves surviving in the south. A small population of Mexican grey wolves, a subspecies of grey wolf traditionally inhabiting parts of Arizona, New Mexico, Texas and northern Mexico, also remained. Wolves were hunted just as ruthlessly in Alaska but fewer people and more wild places meant the overall population was never threatened. Today, Alaska has the largest population of grey wolves in the US.

The decimation of wolves in Canada followed a similar pattern. Trapping, particularly of beaver, but later also of other fur-bearing animals, was an integral part of early settlement. From the late 1600s, the Hudson's Bay Company (HBC) controlled the fur trade throughout much of North America for centuries, even serving as the local government in some areas. Later the North West Company (NWC), based in Montreal from 1779 to 1821, provided some stiff competition until the two forces merged. Rather than attempting to eliminate Indigenous

These Mexican grey pups were photographed in their den in the Gila National Forest in New Mexico. They are part of the small, endangered population of Mexican grey wolves.
Photo courtesy of the US Fish and Wildlife Service, Interagency Field Team

people, the HBC and the NWC worked with them to obtain the choicest furs possible. Many HBC employees and Indigenous women entered into marriages *à la façon du pays* (according to the custom of the country) and at times Indigenous women made up close to half of the population at HBC forts.

For much of the seventeenth and eighteenth centuries, beaver pelts were king of the trade. Although wolf fur wasn't valued as highly as beaver or mink, the animals were abundant. Most wolf pelts were shipped overseas to the European garment industry. Wolves have two types of hair: a stiff outer layer, often referred to as guard hairs, and a soft undercoat. Guard hairs, which can be up to 127 millimetres (5 in) long, are waterproof, while the up to 63-millimetre (2.5 in) undercoat provides a downy insulation against the cold even when temperatures plunge far below freezing. Wolf pelts from colder climates tended to fetch higher prices as they were larger and the fur was longer, thicker and said to have a silkier texture.

The first Canadian wolf bounties were introduced in Ontario and Quebec (previously known as the Province of Canada) in 1793, and eventually spread throughout the country. Within a little more than

100 years, the eastern wolf was scarce and grey wolves had disappeared from the Maritime provinces, southern Ontario and Quebec. By the mid-1950s, aggressive eradication programs involving bounties and the use of poison had wiped out wolves in the lower mainland of BC and reduced their numbers to perhaps as low as 500 in Alberta. In the early twentieth century, predators weren't protected in Canadian or US national parks. Many had active predator control procedures, often founded on the misguided concept that a lack of predators would protect ungulates. The last wolf was killed in Yellowstone National Park in 1926, and as late as the early 1950s, a warehouse in Saskatchewan's Prince Albert National Park was filled with wolf pelts stacked like cordwood.

Although Canada's last true bounty didn't end until 1991, Canadian wolves have been lucky in a perverse sort of way; as in Alaska, a smaller, more spread out human population living on less of the land meant that, although populations fluctuated or were extirpated, many escaped the radical extermination that occurred in the continental US. Even so, the widespread slaughter of wolves in North America removed the predators in greater numbers and with far more speed than anywhere in Eurasia. Some municipalities and private organizations in Canada and the US still offer compensation programs to reduce wolf numbers.

Of course, it was inevitable that the war on wolves would result in folk heroes on both sides. There are scores of stories about "outlaw" wolves that lost toes in traps, had their tracheas partially blocked

In North America, wolves were ruthlessly hunted for their fur, for bounties, and to prevent them from killing wild ungulates and domestic livestock. This photo was taken near Bozeman, Montana, in the early 1900s and shows "wolfers" G.W. Brown (left) and F.A. Scheytt with a collection of wolf pelts, as well as some smaller animal pelts in the upper right-hand corner.
Photo courtesy the of Gallatin History Museum

due to a snare or were otherwise disabled, yet were still able to slay a slew of livestock and evade capture for years. The tales reach mythic proportions when it comes to size, pedigree—part dog or part cougar—and longevity. One of the most famous of these wolves is Three Toes. It's said the wolf got his nickname from losing three toes to traps. He wreaked havoc on livestock in North and South Dakota, as well as Montana, for 13 years. Three Toes is credited with killing $50,000 worth of livestock, slaying 66 sheep in two nights and being hunted by more than 150 men before being trapped in 1925. At the time of his death, Three Toes was estimated to be 18 to 20 years old. That part of the tale is tall for sure, as a wolf in the wild is considered old at eight.

Rags the Digger, another male wolf, reportedly killed at least $10,000 worth of livestock near Meeker, Colorado, in the early twentieth century. Rags was famous for his ability to walk traplines and dig up every trap without being caught. In 1917, a female wolf in southern Arizona is said to have run through rugged country dragging a wolf trap attached to a 2.5-metre (8 ft) length of steel chain and a 20-centimetre (8 in) gas pipe pin, which hit her in the rear every time she jumped. Despite this obstacle and the pain she must have been in, stories claim the wolf evaded a pack of hunting hounds and three men on horseback for 8 kilometres (5 mi) before being shot.

Another wolf, Lobo, trotted through the Currumpaw Valley in New Mexico killing livestock at will during the 1890s. Stories say he removed poisoned sections of meat from carcasses and ate the rest, sprung traps that had been set to catch him and, on one occasion, removed and buried baited meat that was meant to kill him. Part of the Lobo legend traces back to the man who wrote about him. Ernest Thompson Seton, author, wildlife artist and early supporter of the Boy Scouts of America, grew up in Canada and later moved to the US. When a rancher friend asked for help getting rid of Lobo, Seton accepted the challenge. The $1,000 reward didn't hurt either. But Lobo foiled Seton's attempts to kill him at every turn. Desperate to outwit the wolf, Seton concocted a special bait. The ingredients included melted cheese stewed with kidney fat from a freshly killed heifer, cooked in a china dish and cut with a bone knife to prevent the taint of metal. The cooled mixture was cut into lumps, which were filled with large doses of strychnine and cyanide. The holes were sealed with more melted cheese. As a further precaution, it's said Seton wore gloves steeped in the blood of the heifer and avoided breathing on the baits. He put his poisoned treats in a rawhide bag and dragged the liver and kidneys of the heifer in a 16-kilometre (10 mi) radius, depositing a lump of bait about every half kilometre (quarter mile). Lobo, as Seton had nicknamed the wolf, picked up four of the baits, placed them in a pile and pooped on them.

After four months of frustration, Seton discovered Lobo's weak link: the white wolf that was his mate. Seton successfully trapped and killed the female, taking her back to the ranch where he was staying. In the story he wrote about the incident, Seton said Lobo followed and howled from a distance for two days until he finally approached the female's dead body and was caught in several traps. Seton said Lobo died a few days later from a broken heart.

Not all who hunted wolves did so for fur or the bounty. John Reeves Abernathy was born in Bosque County, Texas, in 1876 but gained his fame as "Catch-'em-alive Jack." US president Theodore Roosevelt didn't believe it when he heard Abernathy caught wolves with his bare hands. So in 1905, Roosevelt joined Abernathy on a wolf hunt in southern Oklahoma to see for himself. On horseback and accompanied by three hounds, Abernathy would chase a wolf until his dogs could pull it down. He'd then dismount, throw the dogs off and grab the wolf. As it lunged toward him, he'd grip the wolf's tongue or grasp its lower back teeth with one hand and hold the upper jaw open with the other. Either way, the animal couldn't bite him. At least one wolf that the 59-kilogram (130 lb) Abernathy caught outweighed him by 3 kilograms (7 lbs). Abernathy credited his success to his good physical shape and the strength he'd gained from wrestling. Record has it that he caught more than 1,000 wolves in this manner, selling them all to zoos or travelling road shows. Roosevelt was so impressed he appointed Abernathy marshal of Oklahoma and later requested that a movie be made of "Catch-'em-alive Jack" in action.

Although other men captured wolves alive, most killed them. Until the mid- to late-twentieth century, it was considered the right, even honourable thing to do. But sometimes, after the rush of adrenalin had worn pale and thin, another feeling took hold. In "Pioneers in Paradise," a story published in *Raincoast Chronicles First Five*, Roy Padgett reminisces about the time three wolf packs moved onto the family farm, located on the BC mainland just across from Texada Island. For years the Padgetts and a neighbour had run their sheep free range but that was now providing a 24/7 buffet for wolves. Padgett and his mother were on a walk one day when they discovered 200 gorged turkey vultures on snags and stumps surveying the blood-soaked carcasses of 20 to 30 sheep and goats.

The families set out traps, as well as strychnine and cyanide. "With strychnine they tend to run for water," Padgett writes. "It gives them an uncontrollable thirst, whereas with cyanide they just run till they drop. It works on muscle tissue, pulls their muscles up in bunches. An agonizing death, both of them."

Within a few months, the wolves were gone. Padgett wasn't sure if the families had killed them all or if the wolves had left the area. They'd made him nervous but also fascinated him. "You can't help getting quite the feeling for them, even when you're just trying to exterminate them," he explains. Once they trapped a little white female wolf. "As we walked up with our guns, she threw her head up and let out the longest, most mournful pathetic howl right there in our sights. And perhaps two or three hundred yards off there was another long mournful howl, almost human, the feeling in it. It was her mate I guess."

Padgett goes on to say, "It didn't stop us, we went ahead and shot her, you know, we were so sure of our mission there to make this country safe for sheep. But that howl, it lingers in a person's memory."

As Padgett and others have learned, there's something about wolves that gets into a person's soul, that evokes wonder and sometimes respect, even if they don't want a single wolf anywhere nearby.

CHAPTER 4

THE LIFE OF A WOLF

For the strength of the pack is the wolf, and the strength of the wolf is the pack.
—RUDYARD KIPLING, "The Law for the Wolves"

THE HELICOPTER KICKED UP A TORNADO OF SAND AS IT LIFTED OFF. AS the *whap, whap, whap* of the rotor blades faded into the distance, there was a moment of that profound silence that's only heard far from human habitation. Then everyone started talking at once as we lugged our packs into the shelter of the treeline. It had taken two helicopter trips to transport the ten of us and our camping gear from Port Alice, a small community on northern Vancouver Island. Our destination: the first sandy beach on Brooks Peninsula. This squared-off, giant thumb of land, now a provincial park, juts out into the Pacific Ocean and is the only part of Vancouver Island that wasn't covered during the last ice age.

Our home for the week was a stretch of beach bordered by the rocky promontory of Orchard Point dotted with wind-twisted crabapple trees and a densely treed patch leading to Cape Cook Lagoon. The sand was pockmarked with the heart-shaped hoofprints of deer, hand-sized paw prints of four to six wolves and a dizzying array of feather-light marks left by wee creatures, one of which would wake me up rustling along the edge of—or perhaps inside—my tent several nights in a row. For some time we debated if the solitary track discovered halfway between our sleeping area and a small freshwater creek belonged to a cougar.

Mornings we huddled near the warmth of a driftwood beach fire, mugs of grounds-thick camp coffee dispelling the fog-damp air. Then, together or in small groups, we beachcombed, bushwhacked our way through the woods and even launched a blow-up dinghy to cross the lagoon. One afternoon some of us returned to camp to laze in the sun, sweat in our makeshift sauna and make quick dashes into the frigid surf.

Our heads snapped up simultaneously when we heard the lingering, melancholy howl. The primal call sparked wonder, as well as a tiny frisson of apprehension. When the wolf sang its short song again and was answered by a chorus of others—and then two shots—we all ran, fully clothed or not, down the beach. By the time I panted up to the source of the sound, all that was left of the wolves was some scuffed-up sand on the other side of the lagoon indicating they'd left in a hurry. The wolves had been howling but not acting aggressive so I wondered why a member of our group had shot at them. No one else said anything, so I never asked.

At the time, none of us knew that each wolf's howl was as distinct as a human fingerprint and that wolves in different regions howl in their own dialects. A wolf's howl is a magical, melodious sound. To the human ear it often seems sad and lonely but to a wolf it can mean anything from "Where are you?" to "I'm looking for a mate" or "Hey, we're all together and everything's cool!" Wolf communication is a complex repertoire of sounds, postures, scents and activity that influences everything from pack life to dominance, breeding and establishing and maintaining territory.

Many people believe that wolves howl at the moon, especially when it's full. From ancient times, Indigenous peoples of North America called the first full moon after the winter solstice the Wolf Moon. This was often the coldest, darkest month of the year, when hungry wolves could be heard howling outside villages. Wolves howl, hunt and travel at any time but are most active around dawn and dusk, as well as throughout the night. And whether they're sitting, standing or lying down, they lift their snouts to howl. But, rather than focusing on the white orb in the sky, some believe they're simply taking advantage of the extra light it provides. "I know from sleeping near the Sawtooth Pack for eleven years that wolves do howl more during a full moon," Jeremy Heft writes in the summer 2009 *Sawtooth Legacy Quarterly*. A wildlife biologist, Heft has worked at the Wolf Education and Research Center in Winchester, Idaho, since 1998. "They tend to be more active then because it's easier to see prey and hunt."

Wolves vocalize in a variety of ways, including snarls, growls, whimpers, whines and occasionally barks. But it's the howl that fascinates humans the most. In 1917, author Henry W. Shoemaker quoted a Pennsylvania wolfer as saying, "I wish I could describe this howl, but the best comparison I can give would be to take a dozen railroad whistles, braid them together and then let one strand after another drop off, the last peal so frightfully piercing as to go through your heart and soul …" Writer, naturalist and minister William Joseph Long spent

time in the wilderness of Maine and Nova Scotia during the early twentieth century. In *How Animals Talk: And Other Pleasant Studies of Birds and Beasts*, he writes, "When you open your ears among the beasts you hear precisely the same story ... that certain cries apparently have definite meaning ... Of all the beasts, the wolves are perhaps the keenest, the most intelligent, and these seem to have definite calls for food, or help or hunting or assembly."

People who live near wolves or study them are often able to distinguish one animal's howl from another, and that's what past research relied on—subjective interpretations by humans. But Dr. Arik Kershenbaum at the University of Cambridge, along with a team of researchers from the United Kingdom, US, Spain and India, took howl analysis to a new level. In the largest study to date, they created a database of 6,000 howls from wolves, coyotes, domestic dogs, jackals and other canids from around the world. They fed the recordings into a computer programmed to classify the howls into types. The findings, published in the March 2016 issue of *Behavioural Processes*, revealed that not all howls—even within the same species—are the same.

Analyzing the data from 700 wolf howls, it was clear that not only did each wolf have its own personal calling card of a howl but that wolves from different areas "speak" different dialects. North American grey wolves change frequencies often and have a fast tempo. Their Bavarian cousins send their voices skyward in a low flat voice with few changes in frequency, while Iberian wolves howl in a higher pitch. As well as singing in a different key and tone, European wolves hold

Each wolf has a howl as distinct as a human fingerprint and wolves in different regions howl in their own dialects. People often think wolf howls sound lonely or sad but, while they can be, howls are also used to communicate over long distances, to rally for a hunt and just to celebrate being together.
Photo by iStock/Waddell images

their notes longer than those in North America. During a 2016 CBC Radio interview, Dr. Holly Root-Gutteridge, a scientist involved with the study, compared North American wolves to jazz musicians and European wolves to classical ones.

Different dialects within the same species aren't unusual. First-generation English speakers in Britain, New York, Alabama, British Columbia and New Brunswick all speak the same language yet sound quite different and sometimes have trouble understanding each other. Studies indicate that wolves, humpback whales and dolphins possess similar levels of intelligence, hunt cooperatively and often travel in family groups that "speak" distinct dialects that can be heard for long distances. Like wolves, whales have been recorded "singing" in unison with other whales or changing their pitch to harmonize with them. And it's believed that each dolphin possesses a unique identifying whistle that it uses to communicate with others. Researchers discovered that if a dolphin's whistle is slowed down about 30 times, it sounds just like a wolf howling.

Howling reflects the seasons of both climate and life. In the spring, when newborn pups are in the den, howls are often softer, less frequent and made only when needed in order to avoid letting nearby packs discover where the defenceless pups are. As the pups become more active, howling picks up. In the fall, when the pups are fully mobile and the wolves are moving through more of their territory, howling becomes more pronounced to let neighbouring packs know where they are and what territory they're claiming. The howling cycle peaks early in the year when the mating season begins.

A wolf's song can resonate with loneliness or jubilance, or be a call to other pack members. It's a four-part harmony (more or less) that unites, laments and celebrates. It sends shivers down human spines or lifts the spirit, keeps other packs at bay and helps pack members keep track of each other. But howling has the potential to be so much more. As well as cracking the code of wolf howls, scientists are looking at ways the sound can be used. Kershenbaum's team is using recording devices and triangulation technology in Yellowstone National Park to see if they can determine differences in howls meant for family members and rival packs. He wonders if recordings of territorial howls may be a way to deter wolves from domestic livestock. In northern India, where wolves are endangered, the Wildlife Institute of India and Uttarakhand State Forest Department are attempting to estimate the number of wolves in the area by recording howls.

A few species, such as coyotes and endangered red wolves, possess similar high-pitched, whining howls. In fact, the first time I heard the *yip, yip, yip* part of a red wolf howl, I thought, "That sounds like the coyotes *kiyi*-ing up the creek from Mom's!" And I was right. Red wolves have a genetic relationship to coyotes and sometimes breed with them. What's unknown is if red wolves and coyotes began mating because they have similar-sounding howls or if the howl is a result of the hybridization. According to Regina Mossotti, director of animal care and conservation at the Endangered Wolf Center in Missouri, in early 2018 there were only about 30 red wolves in the wild and approximately 230 in captive breeding programs. Coyotes have migrated into the red wolf recovery area so, in an effort to conserve red wolf species integrity, the US Fish and Wildlife Service has sterilized some coyotes in that region. Kershenbaum speculates that in the future it may be possible to use subtle differences in howling to discourage these liaisons.

Humans tend to focus on the howl but wolves also have a variety of ways of communicating through body language and smell just like domestic dogs. They sniff, rub and lick each other as signs of affection, cock their ears to indicate alertness, aggression or playfulness and perform the yoga pose known as *downward dog* when inviting play. A wolf that stands tall with head and tail raised and ears erect is showing its dominance, while one with its head and tail tucked that crouches or rolls over to expose belly or throat is being submissive. A dominant wolf's steely-eyed stare is said to be enough to stop a submissive wolf in its tracks. Eyes, ears, mouth, hackles, tail and posture all convey mood, status, sexual interest and intent. Scent glands in the hackles, feet, vaginal and anal regions, as well as carefully placed deposits of urine and feces, all send clear messages.

Like humans, gorillas, elephants and many other mammals, wolves are highly social animals. They mostly live in family groups with a clearly defined hierarchy, inhabit a certain territory, care for their young beyond birth, often use babysitters and mourn the loss of loved ones. While the term *a pack of wolves* may sound like a rowdy bunch bent on mischief and mayhem, in the animal kingdom it refers to a territorial family group composed of parents, their offspring from one or more years and sometimes grandparents and aunts and uncles and the odd outsider who live, hunt and travel together. They look after each other, functioning much like traditional human families that live together and support one another.

The affection and loyalty between pack members can be profound. In *The Wolves of North America*, Danish author and explorer Peter Freuchen recounts an incident that occurred north of Hudson Bay in 1935. He and the men he was with heard wolves howling and discovered two adults and three pups nearby. "They were sitting on the ground, noses in the air and howling ... Shortly afterwards, we discovered a fourth pup caught in a steel trap close by ... The others had made great efforts to set it free by overturning large stones from the cache at which it had been caught," he writes. "And they had scratched at the frozen ground around the stone to which the chain was made fast; the trapped wolf could not have done it, for it was caught by the forelegs." The account doesn't say what happened next, but the pup would have been gravely injured, and was surely killed by the trapper, despite the devotion of its pack.

Early research focused on captive wolves that were often from different family groups. Scientists observed wolves fighting for dominance and dubbed the top wolf the *alpha*. But thanks to remote cameras and diligent fieldwork, we now know that the breeding pair are the leaders of the pack that guide, teach and reprimand the others as necessary to keep order. And the discipline can be vigorous. Due to different age ranges and the fluctuating memberships, there may be more than one male and/or female of breeding age in a pack. In most cases, the dominant male and female will do everything in their power to ensure that they're the only ones that breed. This includes intimidating the other wolves with growls, or a fearsome show of teeth, nips or even bites. In some cases wolves are run off or killed. And in a form of hormonal bullying, the dominant female may stress other females so severely that they don't come into heat. Even in a family unit, wolves form personal alliances, so if a fight breaks out, others may join in. Some say the dominant female is the real leader of the pack, deciding who to mate with, where to den and when to travel.

Occasionally more than one pair will breed, but only if there's enough prey to support multiple litters. Although wolves generally mate for life, the dominant couple may breed with others, and just like dogs, the female may be impregnated by more than one male. There are flirty females and male playboys, as well as lower-ranking wolves that sneak in a quick sexual coupling when the dominant pair aren't looking. At times a wolf will mate with a first-degree relative but that's usually due to a dwindling population, meaning there are few if any other options.

Depending on location and climate, North American wolves typically breed anywhere from January to April, with the female giving birth two months later. Most, if not all, of the pack will help dig a den, or the female may use an old den or a cave. Ideally, dens are located near the centre of the pack's territory, as far away from neighbouring packs as possible. They need to be close to fresh water and easily accessible prey, and a high spot with a good view that allows them to see who or what is approaching is a bonus. The area around the den usually includes hiding and resting places, as well as a series of trails. In *Among Wolves*, the late Gordon Haber describes dens with networks of tunnels as long as 6 metres (20 ft) with several sleeping chambers measuring around 2 to 2.5 metres (6.5–8 ft) in diameter and around 1 metre (3 ft) high. It's not unusual to find clusters of dens within a short distance of each other and for the wolves to move from one to another. Haber, who studied wolves in Alaska's Denali National Park for 43 years, and his predecessor, Adolph Murie, suspected that some of the dens they discovered had been used for centuries. Dating of bones found in one Arctic den indicated wolves had probably used it for more than 700 years.

Newborn wolf pups are about a half kilogram (one pound) of fuzzy dark fur that can easily be cupped in an adult human's hand. They're deaf and blind, making them totally dependent on their mother. Most litters average four to six pups. Although some females successfully raise pups on their own, a team of packmates that provide her with meat makes life much easier. Sometimes females with pups will take turns bringing each other food, as well as watching and even nursing each other's litter. At first, the squirming, squeaking youngsters alternate between feeding and sleeping while huddled together. They open their eyes around two weeks, begin to hear after three and by six weeks have been partially weaned and are venturing out of the den. At this point, they're fed semi-solid food in the form of regurgitated meat from other pack members. Pups trigger this by robustly licking and poking older wolves' muzzles. A unique digestive system allows wolves to regurgitate multiple times at will. One wolf usually stays behind to "babysit" while the others may travel up to 40 kilometres (25 mi) a day to hunt. Occasionally pups are left on their own for short periods. While studying wolves in Alaska, Adolph Murie wrote that one female with pups left the den and "ran as if in high spirits, seeming happy to be off on an expedition with others."

As pups grow, they're moved to rendezvous sites, places where adult members of the pack return to from hunts. These areas function as a daycare centre run by family members and make for serious playtime for pups. They explore the surrounding area, wrestle, mock fight and engage in vigorous games of tug-of-war over bones and hunks of meat brought back by older wolves. Even adults join in the fun. The exuberance provides an opportunity for the pack to bond and allows pups to rehearse skills they'll need later on. This is also where each pup begins to show its unique personality, be it bully, clown, grouch or fearless leader. In *Beyond Words: What Animals Think and Feel*, Carl Safina describes two such wolves from Yellowstone National Park: Twenty-one, a pack leader who never lost a fight yet never killed an opponent, and Casanova, a younger male who just couldn't restrain himself around females. Entire packs are even known for distinctive traits, such as being accomplished hunters or fighters.

The biggest threats to pups are disease, not getting enough to eat and predation by other wolf packs, cougars and bears. A study published in the October 2012 *Journal of Animal Ecology* notes that the mother's body weight and the size of the pack can up the odds of pup survival considerably. But what if something happens to the mom?

Fortunately, adoption is not uncommon in the animal world. Cougars, elephant seals, ravens and numerous other animals adopt orphans of their kind and sometimes other species as well. Once my former husband found a young swallow alone on the ground. He brought it home and put it in a swallow's nest in our carport. The newcomer was larger by far than those already present and, due to the shrill cries and pecking of mama bird, the orphan was shoved in upside down. We watched from the kitchen window until, eventually, the oversized interloper bearing human scent righted itself and the mother bird plugged its mouth with food, treating it just like the other chicks.

It turns out that wolves are excellent foster parents but timing is everything. Habitat destruction and persecution by ranchers and others means that wolf populations have become nearly extinct in some areas. Severely low numbers can lead to inbreeding, resulting in a lack of genetic diversity and vulnerability to diseases and physical abnormalities. This all makes healthy litters unlikely even if breeding occurs. Red wolves were successfully reintroduced into the wild via cross-fostering in the early 1990s and in 2006, the US Fish and Wildlife Service decided to attempt a similar experiment by exchanging two nine-day-old Mexican grey wolf pups that had been raised in a Missouri conservation centre with two pups from a litter of wild Mexican grey wolves in New Mexico. Mexican grey wolves were nearly extinct in the 1970s, when a few were caught and became part of a captive breeding program. It's estimated there are around 150 in the wild today and about 250 in breeding programs. Some of the original wolves' offspring were released into the wild in 1998, but this was the first time cross-fostering had been attempted. It's a tricky business, as both litters have to be born around the same time and the captive-born pups transferred to their new home before they're 14 days old. Special care was taken to ensure that the newcomers didn't look—or more importantly, smell—too different from the mother wolf's natural pups. People involved in the transfer wore gloves and the crew member who squirmed down the tunnel rubbed the tiny pups in the dirt of the den floor, against their new litter mates and even in their

In April 2016, two captive-born Mexican grey wolf pups found a new home. They were less than 14 days old when they left the Endangered Wolf Center near St. Louis and were placed in the den of a wild Mexican grey wolf high in the mountains of New Mexico. Vida, one of the pups in the cross-fostering project, is held by Regina Mossotti, director of animal care and conservation at the Endangered Wolf Center. The goal of the project was to increase the genetic diversity of the small number of Mexican grey wolves in the wild. Photo courtesy of the Endangered Wolf Center urine. Most adult wolves—even large grey wolves that can take down an adult elk on their own—usually leave a den site when humans approach and pace and bark at the intruders from a distance. That's what this particular mother wolf did, so she saw the new pups being introduced, or at least knew a trespasser had entered her den. No one knows if she noticed the strangers, but it didn't seem to matter as she fed and cared for them along with the pups she had given birth to.

What's even more amazing is that wild wolves appear to be willing foster moms even if they've murdered the pups' mother. In early 2000 researchers observed the dominant male of the Druid Peak pack in Yellowstone National Park mate with three females, which all produced litters. In the winter 2000 issue of *International Wolf Magazine*, a naturalist and field technician for the Yellowstone Gray Wolf Restoration Project, Rick McIntyre, recounts how the two subordinate female wolves killed the bullying dominant female, perhaps with the help of other females, and moved their two litters and hers into one den. There, they and two other female wolves cared for as many as 21 pups.

Most wolves head out on their own at anywhere from eleven months to two years of age, although some may remain with their parents for much longer. Availability of prey is probably the main factor determining dispersal but the urge to breed also plays a part. Unless a wolf can usurp the dominant male or female—parental respect only goes so far—they must leave the pack. Some wolves, possibly viewed as a threat to one of the dominant wolves, may be chased off and forced to disperse whether they want to or not. If lucky, dispersing wolves meet a wolf of the opposite sex and form their own pack or join another one, perhaps overthrowing a dominant wolf. Although the introduction of new blood ensures genetic diversity, dispersing is a dangerous endeavour. A single wolf isn't familiar with prey locations in new areas, isn't as efficient at hunting as a pack and may be more likely to be killed by humans or other wolves.

It's not uncommon for wolves to disperse 300 kilometres (186 mi), but some go much farther. A radio-collared male from Banff National Park in Alberta headed north in 2016, travelling 500 kilometres (311 mi) before turning around and going back home. The same year, a two-year-old male from the Huckleberry pack in northeastern Washington took a walkabout through Idaho, headed north into British Columbia and then into Montana, where he was shot for killing sheep. He'd covered more than 1,100 kilometres (684 mi) between June and September. In 2011, a 47-kilogram (104 lb) black wolf headed north from Yukon-Charley Rivers National Park in Alaska and passed through the Arctic Circle a couple of times before heading south. He had a mate for part of the time but she died of starvation near a picked-clean moose carcass. The male wolf's collar stopped working in October and his emaciated dead body was found curled under a tree. He'd lost more than 15 kilograms (33 lbs) on his 3,356-kilometre (2,085 mi) expedition.

Some wandering wolves achieve celebrity status. The fall of 2014, a three-year-old female travelled at least 1,200 kilometres (746 mi) from Cody, Wyoming, to northern Arizona. She was nicknamed Echo—as in "she came back like an echo"—and made international news as the first grey wolf to be seen at the Grand Canyon in more than 70 years. She was shot and killed later that year by a hunter who mistook her for a coyote. OR-7, also called "Journey," turned into a media star when he became the first wolf to set paw in California in 90 years. The two-year-old left northeastern Oregon on a 1,600-kilometre (994 mi) trip that took him through Oregon and into California before he headed back to Oregon. In 2015, OR-7 and his mate had pups in the Rogue River area of southern Oregon. Now a grandpa and possibly the most famous wolf in the world, OR-7 is featured in a book and a documentary film and has his own Facebook page and Twitter feed.

Wolves seem unfazed by any obstacle nature puts in their path and frequently use human structures to their advantage. DNA tests conducted by Memorial University in Newfoundland and the University of Idaho confirmed that an animal shot on the Bonavista Peninsula of Newfoundland in 2012, initially thought to be a large coyote, was actually a grey wolf. Government officials think the wolf—and possibly others—reached the island by travelling on ice floes. Barbara M.V. Scott was researching wolves on northern Vancouver Island in the late 1970s when she used telemetry to track one wolf from north of Sayward on the northeast coast of the island to Victoria on its southern end. The wolf covered at least 300 kilometres (186 mi), most of it on the BC Hydro right-of-way.

But the wolf that scores the highest for surmounting geographical challenges is Slavc from Slovenia. His GPS collar was set to send in locations every few hours, allowing researchers to get detailed information about where he was and when. Slavc's meandering route eventually took him to Italy, with his collar recording a journey of 2,000 kilometres (1,243 mi). Along the way he crossed two major motorways, using an overpass for one and a lengthy viaduct for the other. He swam across a 280-metre (306 yd) section of the Drava River and crossed formidable mountain ranges, including one where the lowest pass was 2.5 kilometres (1.6 mi) high and the snow was estimated to be 6 metres (20 ft) deep. Slavc also navigated some high human-use areas, with one GPS reading showing him in the backyard of a house in the middle of a small town. Other readings revealed that he spent three days near the international airport of Ljubljana, the capital of Slovenia, before crossing the Alps into Italy. There, in Lessinia Natural Regional Park, Slavc found what he was looking for:

Wolves are highly social animals and it's unusual for a wolf to live most of its life alone. But a male wolf has been living by himself on a group of small islands about a nautical mile from Oak Bay near Victoria, BC, since 2012. He can hear dogs in Oak Bay barking and sometimes sits looking in that direction. Photo by Cheryl Alexander a female that the researchers dubbed Juliet. In 2012, remote cameras showed the pair with two pups.

Experts estimate that lone wolves make up about 10 to 15 per cent of the population and that many of those are dispersing wolves that will eventually join or form their own pack. But sometimes circumstance means that isn't the case. In 2012, an approximately two-year-old male wolf suddenly appeared on Discovery Island, less than one nautical mile from the densely populated municipality of Oak Bay on southern Vancouver Island. He'd likely dispersed from an area north of Victoria looking for a mate and territory to call his own. Somewhere along the way, he made a wrong turn and found himself in an urban area, which prompted a swim though challenging ocean channels with extremely strong currents. He ended up on a group of small islands with no other wolves, no year-round source of fresh water and no deer or other ungulates to hunt.

Since wolves are highly social, no one thought he'd stay long. He did attempt to leave at least once, swimming strong currents to Trial

Island and then continuing west, but was possibly spooked by a large fishing vessel and ended up back on Discovery. About two-thirds of Discovery Island is a marine park; the rest includes a small piece of property owned by Fisheries and Oceans Canada and land belonging to the Songhees First Nation. The Songhees feel protective of the wolf as he appeared three months before their elected chief, Robert Sam of the Wolf Clan, died. Cheryl Alexander, a conservation photographer, also feels a spiritual connection to the wolf she calls Takaya, named after a local Indignenous word for *wolf*. "I was curious about the wolf as soon as I heard about him," says Alexander, who lives a 15-minute boat ride away. "Then the spring of 2014 I saw him. He came out of the water onto the beach and disappeared into the trees, where his howls filled the air. It was a very poignant, yearning sound and touched me deeply."

Alexander began tracking and studying the wolf's behaviour from her boat and with motion-sensor cameras. When she walked around on the island she kept her distance from the wolf as she didn't want him to become habituated to people. Habituation means an animal has lost its natural caution around humans, no longer fears them and is willing to come close, as it doesn't associate their presence with a negative experience. It's a process that occurs over time. "Even so, it seems that we've developed a relationship," she says. "He lifts his nose and sniffs the air when I arrive, I'm sure he recognizes and trusts me." Through observation and by collecting scat (feces) and having it analyzed, Alexander was able to answer the question of how Takaya survives on about 2.5 square kilometres (1 sq mi) of land total. During much of the year, fresh water is available in marshes and collects in

There are no deer on Discovery Island so the lone wolf living there primarily hunts and eats seals. He carried this approximately 11-kilogram (24 lb) seal pup a long way around the shore, up and over logs and bluffs, before eating it. Photo by Cheryl Alexander tarns during rains. Alexander suspects he obtains enough fluids from his prey during dry periods. "His primary prey is seal but he also eats otter, mink and geese," she says. "The tests show that his diet is ninety-five per cent marine mammal." It's believed that most coastal wolves scavenge seal carcasses that wash ashore but Alexander has seen Takaya actively hunting seals. "He kills lots of pups during pupping season and also kills very large adult seals. This is interesting as he might not have been familiar with hunting seals so had to figure it out on his own. He appears healthy and his fur is very glossy, I think from all the seal fat." As a strong, healthy wolf that has lived on his own for at least six years, Takaya is an anomaly. He might prefer to be part of a pack but his successful existence on Discovery Island is a testament to the resiliency and adaptability of wolves.

A wolf pack can range from 2 animals to 42, the largest recorded to date in North America, but most contain fewer than 10. Super packs of up to 400 wolves are occasionally reported in Russia. Will Graves, author of *Wolves in Russia: Anxiety Through the Ages*, speculates that figure may be a matter of impression rather than exaggeration.

"Wolves are known to cluster," he explains, "especially during wars, revolutions and extreme cold. So, super packs are probably large numbers of wolves clustering together and people seeing them report it as one pack."

The size of a pack's territory usually depends on the size of the wolves, the size of the pack, the abundance or lack of prey and the proximity of other wolf packs. Wolves in northern regions are often larger than those living close to the equator so they require more room to roam and hunt prey. From Takaya's story we know that given the right circumstances, a solitary wolf can get by on a very small piece of land. At the other extreme is the 10-member McKinley River pack in Alaska's Denali National Park, which once occupied 4,335 square kilometres (1,674 sq mi). And wolves following migrating caribou herds can inhabit areas as large as 63,000 square kilometres (2,432 sq mi). From July 2009 to April 2010, L. David Mech and H. Dean Cluff studied a pack of 20 wolves that inhabited a 6,640-square-kilometre (2,564 sq mi) range on Ellesmere Island in the High Arctic of Nunavut. Using straight-line distances, data from the

radio collar on the lead wolf revealed that he travelled more than 5,979 kilometres (3,715 mi), at one point covering up to 76 kilometres (47 mi) in a 12-hour period. Due to the high latitude, four months of the journey took place in total darkness. In addition to blackout conditions, the wolves, which primarily hunted muskoxen, endured temperatures as low as -53C (-63F). The nearly year-long study revealed no difference in the amount of territory covered at the opposite end of the spectrum when there were 24 hours of continuous daylight.

A pack's territory may be near or even overlap another pack's. Some packs will meet with no signs of aggression while others will vigorously defend their territory. One defence mechanism is howling. It doesn't require a lot of energy and, most of the time, a simple bout of robust howling makes it clear that "we're here, stay away," thus avoiding direct contact with rival packs and the potential for injury or death. Small packs make themselves sound larger by howling in different keys and not in unison. The sound can travel up to approximately ten kilometres (six miles) over open ground and six kilometres (four miles) in the forest. While he was working with the Association for Nature WOLF in the Tatra Mountains of Poland, wolf specialist Troy Bennett's howl surveys indicated that wolves can accurately pinpoint where another wolf is howling from even when heard from a distance.

To determine how the 40 packs in Superior National Forest in northeast Minnesota defended their territories, biologist Fred Harrington developed five distinct wolflike howls of his own and then recorded the responses from various packs. One of the first things he noticed was that wolves were more likely to reply if they belonged to a larger pack, if it was breeding season or if they were at a fresh kill or

When wolves eat an ungulate such as a deer, they consume nearly every part, including a lot of the bones. They do the same when they eat seals. These seal nails passed intact through the digestive tract of a wolf. Photo by Paula Wild rendezvous site. Wolves that howled back often stayed put, whereas those that remained silent usually moved away from the location of the human howls a third of the time. These may have been smaller packs seeking a buffer zone that would allow them to retreat if whoever was howling came closer.

Another non-confrontational method of territory defence is scent marking. Wolves tend to use the same routes, creating narrow wolf highways marked by urine and feces, each dribble and drop containing more messages than an average smartphone. These markers are often found in conspicuous spots such as trail junctions and can be more concentrated along a pack's boundaries, creating what Dave Mech refers to in *Wolves: Behavior, Ecology, and Conservation* as an "olfactory bowl." Like dogs, wolves can drink a lot of water and mete it out in little but significantly aromatic—at least to another canid's nose— sprinkles here and there. In the right climate and location, these scent markings can be detected by other wolves up to three weeks later. Since wolves hunt nearly every day, this is a highly efficient way to accomplish two important tasks at once.

Sometimes a confrontation can't be avoided. Wolves from one pack may invade another's territory in an effort to expand theirs or, less likely, members from different packs may inadvertently meet. The ensuing skirmishes can involve all the posturing, growling discourse and violence of the gang wars in the movie *Gangs of New York*. It makes sense that the larger pack would have the upper paw when it comes to wolf turf battles but the difference doesn't have to be much. Between 1995 and 2011, researchers documented 121 aggressive encounters between packs in Yellowstone National Park. They found that a pack with just one more member had a 140 per cent higher chance of winning. Seventy-one of the encounters became full-blown attacks with twelve resulting in the death of one or more wolves. And, to the researchers' surprise, in seven incidents, a wolf put its own life at risk to protect a packmate.

As well as the size of the pack, the age of its members is important. Adult males are larger and more aggressive than females, so having an extra adult male raised the odds of winning by 65 per cent. But a pack with a wolf aged six or older, no matter what the sex, had a 150 per cent better chance of being the victor. When it comes to wolf wars, experience seems to outweigh numbers.

The life of a wolf is hard and violent. They hunt large animals with sharp hooves and horns, disperse, defend their territory, care for young and struggle to maintain or improve their status in the pack. Pups have a mortality rate of close to 50 per cent and of those that survive two years, most will be dead by age five or six. There are a few verified accounts of wild wolves living until their early teens but that's unusual. It's estimated that intraspecies strife is the cause of 60 per cent of the deaths of wild wolves. The second highest cause of death is human-related, resulting from hunting, culls, being euthanized for livestock predation or being run over by motor vehicles or trains. In 2012, close to 50 per cent of the 15 wolves that died in Yellowstone National Park were killed by other wolves. Few die of old age.

When wolves let loose a mournful howl, it's all about affection and missing a particular wolf, whether they be mate, sibling or buddy. Researchers at Austria's Wolf Science Center noticed that their wolves always howled when a pack member was separated from the group. Since they are social animals, it was no surprise that the wolves reacted to being parted. But a scientific study testing the wolves' stress levels from swabs of saliva and recordings of howls produced startling results. The wolves howled when a socially dominant member of the pack was removed but they howled even more when a close friend—dominant or not—was taken from the compound.

Death is the ultimate separation. William Long once observed an injured wolf lying on a frozen lake emitting moaning howls like nothing he'd ever heard before. Nearby, several wolves ran in circles, howling continuously. When the wounded wolf became quiet, the others approached, sniffed him and then sat quietly watching. In *Among Wolves*, Gordon Haber describes how a male wolf remained near his mate when she was caught in a trap and a snare just outside Denali National Park. Evidence from the necropsy and the female wolf's GPS collar indicate that she struggled to escape for two weeks before the trapper found and shot her. From tracks and other evidence, it was obvious that her mate had stayed with her. After her body was removed, the male immediately travelled 22 kilometres (14 mi) to the den where he and the female had raised litters in previous years. The next day and for the following two months, even after he'd bred with another female, he regularly returned to the site where he'd last seen his former mate and howled.

CHAPTER 5

THE EATERS AND THE EATEN

The aim of life was meat ...
Life lived on life.
—JACK LONDON, *White Fang*

IMAGINE SIMPLY INHALING AND BEING ABLE TO TELL WHO HAS PASSED by and how long ago, what sex they are and what their general health is, where they've been, what they've eaten and what mood they're in. To a large degree, a wolf navigates the world through its sense of smell. The tip of its nose is a complex landscape of minute ridges and creases, which, when combined with the outer edges of nostrils, creates a print as distinct as that found on the end of a human finger. Each nostril can be moved independently, allowing wolves to determine which direction a particular smell is coming from. Inside the broad snout are approximately 280 million scent receptors, a princely amount when compared to a German shepherd's 225 million, a dachshund's 125 million and a human's scant five to six million. In "Understanding a Dog's Sense of Smell," Stanley Coren and Sarah Hodgson note that the spongy membrane that contains most scent cells in humans is about the size of a postage stamp while the comparable membrane, removed from a dog and ironed flat, is nearly as large as a letter-sized sheet of paper. For a wolf, the data input inhaled within a 24-hour period must be as much or more than the data received from Google searches made over the same amount of time.

A wolf's body is a near-perfect blend of the physical attributes necessary for its day-to-day life of hunting, travelling and discerning the nuances of pack behaviour. Cognitive ability comes into play too, most notably when hunting. And wolves' relationships with other animals—most often revolving around food—reveal the countless interactions that take place between wildlife. But it's their senses that really come to the fore in daily activity.

Humans generally depend on sight more than smell, but people can develop their olfactory abilities. Blind people often possess a heightened sense of smell and many stories about feral children indicate they primarily relied on scent rather than vision or hearing. In 1800, after approaching villagers, "Victor," also known as the Wild Boy of Aveyron, was eventually placed under the supervision of Dr. Jean Marc Gaspard Itard. Although estimated to be 12 years old, Victor was believed to have spent most of his life in the woods of southern France as he seemed totally unaware of the conventions of human life. He preferred to be naked even in the snow, chose to sleep on the floor instead of a bed and vigorously sniffed everything given to him. Once, after being lost for a few hours, he sniffed his caregiver's arms for some time before seeming to recognize her.

A wolf's nose alerts it to danger, the presence of pack members or enemies, female wolves in heat, and prey. Each wolf has distinctive scent glands on different parts of its body so it smells unique, at least to other canids. A possibly well-meaning but cruel study in the mid-1980s removed the scent receptors from adult captive wolves to see how they would respond. In a futile attempt to make sense of their environment, the poor beasts vainly sniffed objects for years.

Scientists know that wolves can smell prey 2.5 kilometres (1.6 mi) away. Gordon Haber, who spent most of his adult life researching wolves in Alaska, was convinced that wolves could smell a dead moose or caribou buried under three metres (ten feet) of snow, even if the wind was blowing the wrong way. Dave Mech's *Wolves on the Hunt* gives an account of a radio-collared female wolf with pups in Canada's central Arctic making a beeline for a caribou herd more than 100 kilometres (62 mi) distant. What surprised the researchers was the timing of the wolf's journey and the relatively straight line she made for the caribou. The week before her trek, the average daily distance between her den and the caribou was 242 kilometres (150 mi). The day she left, it had narrowed by more than half. If the wolf had veered to the northwest, she might have missed the herd entirely or not found them until later. There's no way to know if she smelled the ungulates from her den, picked up their scent partway through her journey or simply headed in the direction she'd found caribou before. But caribou are highly mobile so the wolf couldn't have depended on memory alone. The researchers speculated that if a human can smell smoke from a forest fire more than 100 kilometres (62 mi) away, why couldn't a wolf smell a caribou herd from the same distance?

Wolves are built to move. A deep, narrow chest provides plenty of lung power and a streamlined physique. Even a wolf's head is aerodynamic, with a sleek muzzle leading to triangular ears that are gently rounded on top. Each ear can be independently rotated, creating optimal antennae for picking up sounds. Experts say wolves can hear noises 10 to 16 kilometres (6–10 mi) away on open ground and frequencies possibly as high as 80 kilohertz compared to a human's upper range of 20 kilohertz. Long, slender legs end in wide paws that are equipped with the perfect padding and traction for manoeuvring through forests, as well as over rocky outcroppings and frozen lakes. The structural dynamic of inward-turning elbows and outward-turning paws results in a highly efficient gait that puts little or no stress on the shoulders. And webbed toes mean wolves are capable of fording rivers, lakes and even up to 13 kilometres (8 mi) of open ocean.

Wolves possess an innate sense of energy conservation and prefer to travel the path of least resistance, be it trail, beach, logging road or power line. On an off-leash walk in the woods, a dog will run all over the place the entire way. With no bowl of kibble or treat at the end of their journey, wolves tend to travel in more direct routes as they traverse their territory. But if a shortcut involves going through heavy brush, chances are they'll avoid it. These well-travelled runways sometimes connect to larger trail networks and may be used by generations of wolves for decades. When travelling through deep snow, wolves often follow each other single file, thus packing down a trail and preserving energy. And no matter what the terrain, padded paws mean they move across the landscape as silent as a cloud.

Wolves are long-distance runners that can maintain a trot of eight to ten kilometres (five to six miles) an hour without ever seeming to tire, a huge asset when it comes to travelling long distances and hunting. For obligate carnivores like wolves, meat is the sustenance of life. A successful hunt means survival. It's estimated that adult wolves spend 30 to 35 per cent of their time searching for prey. Even at rest they're a bundle of coiled energy ready for action at any time. Their territory varies and can include lakes, mountains or deserts or, for coastal wolves, it can be a conglomerate of several islands. But most important of all, a pack's territory must contain enough prey to feed the breeding pair, their offspring and any other pack members.

As predators, wolves are generalists that will eat anything, including hares, mice and fish as well as garbage or kills made by other animals. But they're particularly fond of ungulates. In North America, deer, elk, caribou and moose are staples of many grey wolves' diet. Small prey presents little risk but it takes a lot of mice to fill a wolf's belly and sometimes the effort is barely worth it. Although grey

Wolves have to work hard to catch hares. Both animals can reach speeds up to 60 kilometres (37 mi) an hour and the chase can cover a fair amount of ground. But a hare can make faster, sharper turns than a wolf and uses this to its advantage. This chase took place on Ellesmere Island, where wolves' only prey are hares and muskoxen. Photo by David Mech wolves can subsist on small prey when ungulates aren't available, it's usually more of a tide-me-over snack until a real meal is found. Arctic hares often lead the canids on a spirited chase. Going flat out, wolves and hares can reach about the same speed, 60 kilometres (37 mi) per hour for short distances. But the smaller hare can dart back and forth more quickly than a wolf and, when chased, tries to run uphill—meaning, if the hare's lucky, the heavier wolf is left behind. *Wolf Pack Hunts a Hare*, a BBC Earth video, shows one pack's strategy for outsmarting a hare: two wolves chase it from behind with two more riding the flanks to prevent any swift turns.

It's the larger prey that provides more of a reward. And more of a challenge. Wolves are crepuscular, meaning they're most active during the half-light at the beginning and end of day. It's no coincidence that elk, moose and deer are also usually on the move at these times. While studying wolves on northern Vancouver Island, Barbara M.V. Scott noticed that wolves in heavily treed areas seemed to hunt mostly by scent while those inhabiting higher, more open ground tended to rely on sight. It's believed that wolves can see at least as well as humans

and probably much better in the dark. Like cougars, their eyes are highly responsive to movement. Predators' eyes face forward and it's this binocular vision and the depth perception that comes with it that allow them to follow and chase prey. In contrast, most prey animals have eyes on either side of their heads, a big plus when it comes to detecting predators.

When pups are young, adults hunt in a radius around the den or rendezvous site. Later, when the pups have grown enough to travel, wolves tend to patrol their territory on a rotational basis, thus giving any prey they encounter a chance to relax and become less vigilant before the next visit. The entire pack is usually on the move by fall and this is when pups learn to hunt by participating, observing older members of the pack, and trial and error. Before his death in 2009, Gordon Haber had studied the Toklat pack in Alaska's Denali National Park for 40 years. Over that time he observed them attempting to hunt Dall sheep but being unable to pursue them quickly enough over the steep, rocky slopes. Eventually the wolves learned to cut off the sheep's escape route, sometimes lying in ambush for up to two days at a time to do so. This unique strategy allowed the Toklat pack to specialize in hunting Dall sheep and pass this knowledge down to succeeding generations. In 2005 the dominant male and female and two of their older offspring were caught in snares and killed. The remaining members of the pack, six juveniles, had no one to teach them how to ambush and hunt Dall sheep. The loss of this generations-long culture and tradition meant that, in order to survive, the young wolves were forced to hunt hares.

Although wolves are coursing (chasing) hunters, they'll often attempt to get as close as possible before the race begins. In addition to the Dall sheep, they've been observed hiding to ambush beavers and bison, which may be a way of maximizing their success. Sometimes wolves trot right by prey with neither paying much attention to the other. On the Prairies and Great Plains, wolves often wandered close to or even among bison without causing undue alarm, and deer have even been known to reside near wolf dens without the herd being decimated. In *How Animals Talk*, author and naturalist William Joseph Long describes watching two deer look up alertly and then go back to eating as a pack of wolves trotted by. The wolves, in turn, seemed to not even notice the deer. When Long followed the wolves' back trail, he found a recent kill where they'd been feeding. Long believed that animals project a field of energy that alerts others to their presence and intent.

Sixty years later, R.D. Lawrence, a naturalist and author of more than 30 books, delved further into this relationship between predators and prey. "The prey animals know when the hunter is hungry and when he is not," he writes in *Secret Go the Wolves*. "Hunger sparks aggression, which in turn puts tension in the body as the adrenaline flows; and there is scent, the exudation from the chemicals that the endocrine glands shoot into the bloodstream to prepare the organism for physical action. Wild senses are too keen to miss these things." Contemporary wolf experts confirm that wolves don't seem overly interested in prey they accidently run into. They speculate that wolves like to be the decision makers when it comes to the time and place of an attack to ensure the situation is to their advantage.

The size of the ungulate frequently predicts how it will react if confronted by hungry wolves. Smaller animals, such as white-tailed deer and caribou, often scatter and run; larger prey, like moose, musk-oxen and bison, are inclined to stand their ground or run a bit before facing off against their pursuers, while the medium-sized elk use both strategies. Wolves may approach prey directly or quietly watch it for a while. Then they lope toward a lone animal or herd and may even run behind or alongside them for a ways. As the animal or herd takes off, it's easy to single out prey that's limping, lagging behind or otherwise appears weak. Wolves constantly test prey in this way and, at times, seem to have an uncanny ability to spot vulnerable animals even before they run and to predict the trajectory of their escape. As opportunists, wolves do kill healthy animals but most of the time they go after the young, old, weak, injured or sick. It isn't always obvious to the human eye, however, that an ungulate is vulnerable. It wasn't until the 1990s that researchers discovered the grandmother effect. Even if a doe's diet has always been adequate, if her mother's wasn't, that nutritional deficiency can show up in the third generation, resulting in a weak deer.

Once a likely target has been selected, wolves shift into high gear. That's the beginning of a race between the eater and the eaten, one running as fast as it can for its life, the other for food to survive. The chase can be aborted in seconds and mere steps if the prey acts vigorous and healthy or it can take hours and cover a long distance. One chase cited in *Wolves on the Hunt* involved a wolf running after a caribou for eight kilometres (five miles). This may have been a young or desperate wolf, as the hunt was not successful and the amount of energy expended resulted in no reward. An even longer hunt involved a single wolf pursuing a deer for nearly 21 kilometres (13 mi), far enough that the researchers were unable to determine the outcome. Although a wolf might not be as fast as an ungulate, the wolf scores more points when it comes to stamina.

Prey employ various tactics to avoid attack. Bison and muskoxen form outward-facing circles to protect their young and some ungulates will turn and lash out with their hooves or antlers. While working as a helicopter pilot for an Alberta government wolf study in the 1990s, Gary Flath witnessed a savvy cow elk outsmart a pack of wolves. "She

Although an adult wolf is capable of taking down an ungulate as large as a moose, teamwork makes for an easier hunt. Here a pack goes after a bull elk in Yellowstone National Park. Wolves were reintroduced to the park in 1995 in an effort to curb the excessive elk population.
Photo by Doug Smith, US National Park Service

backed into a curve of river with a steep bank on either side of her," he says. "The wolves tried to put her in the water but she stood her ground. The wolves howled and barked and walked back and forth in front of the cow but she wouldn't move. The wolves finally gave up and went after a young bull elk." A similar incident occurred with a crippled bison in Yellowstone National Park. The bison backed into a rock crevice, creating a standoff until a few wolves distracted her long enough for a wily old-timer to sneak behind, bite her rump and flush her out. Sometimes prey rebels against being chased by wolves. A trail camera in Poland's Białowieża Forest shows some bison being chased by wolves but then turning around and putting the run on their pursuers. A herd of elk did the same in Yellowstone National Park.

Many ungulates seek sanctuary in water. The fall of 2017, Dan Nystedt was using a drone to film a moose standing in the shallows of a large lake in northern Ontario when a wolf charged out of the woods. The moose ran a few steps in the shallows then turned to strike out with its hooves. The duo performed this back-and-forth dance for a

minute or so until the wolf latched onto the back of the moose's left front leg. The water muddied as the moose frantically circled in an attempt to shake the wolf off. Finally the moose partially submerged, forcing the wolf to let go. Jumping through the water and sometimes swimming, the wolf followed the escaping moose but eventually gave up and swam to shore. There the drone tracked it and another wolf running down a railway track and coming out farther along the lakeshore. The parting shot shows the moose swimming toward the centre of the lake. As the moose looked tired and agitated from the beginning, the drama may have been going on for some time. It might have escaped by swimming out into deeper water, but that strategy doesn't always work. It's not unusual for a pack to laze around on shore taking turns chasing an ungulate as it tries to get to land. In situations like that, it's just a waiting game until the prey tires and the wolves move in.

Seasons and weather can give an edge to predator or prey. For a while after they're born, fawns are nearly scentless. This, coupled with their ability to lie totally still, makes them difficult to find. In hot, dry weather, prey scent evaporates quickly but in winter, deep snow can slow ungulates down. Their sharp hooves make frozen lakes slippery and may even break through thin layers of ice. At the other end of the spectrum, wolves' oversized paws serve as snowshoes on the ground and distribute the animals' weight evenly on ice.

Pack size can influence the type of prey wolves hunt. A study of four national parks in Canada and the US determined that packs targeting moose were significantly larger than those that went after white-tailed deer. Two to six wolves appears to be the optimum

Wolves in Ethiopia have forged an unusual relationship with gelada monkeys. The canids hunt rodents, which seem most active when the monkeys forage in grass. Although the wolves could easily kill a baby gelada, they rarely do. On the rare occasion when one does, the adult geladas chase it away and don't allow that wolf to come close to the monkey troop again. Photo by Jeffrey Kerby number for a pack hunting elk, while nine or more makes for a successful bison hunt. A larger wolf pack means more meat is needed but also provides more resources to care for pack members that may be injured during a hunt. "Influence of Group Size on the Success of Wolves Hunting Bison," a study published in the November 2014 issue of PLOS *Journal*, notes that, although there may be some freeloaders, there's probably a great deal of cooperation in large packs hunting prey such as bison.

At times, wolves' cooperative nature may even extend beyond hunting with their own kind. In east Africa, Ethiopian wolves appear to have formed an unusual alliance with monkeys. Researchers observed the wolves hunting for rodents—and having more success—when they were among a troop of gelada monkeys, a type of baboon. The wolves wandered through large groups of six to seven hundred geladas, with the primates showing no fear even when the predators were very close. And even though the wolves were perfectly capable of killing baby geladas, they rarely did. The wolves always mingled with the monkeys during midday when rodents in the area were most

active. Researchers speculated that the grazing monkeys disturbed the rodents, making it easier for wolves to hunt them, and that the wolves deliberately avoid harming the monkeys to take advantage of this opportunity.

While tracking wolves in southern Israel's Negev Desert, researchers from the University of Tennessee were surprised to discover a striped hyena hanging out with wolves. This was an unlikely alliance, as wolves live in packs and striped hyenas are typically solitary creatures unless crowded around a big kill or travelling with young. Striped hyenas are not known to associate with other carnivores and have a reputation for killing dogs, even large breeds. But the Negev Desert is one of the most inhospitable landscapes in the world, which led the researchers to believe survival may be what brought the two species together. Each possesses specific skills: the wolf is faster and highly accomplished at bringing down large prey, while the striped hyena is more of a scavenger and is particularly adept at sniffing out human garbage.

Ungulates and wolves both have long legs built for running, but operating as a pack gives wolves the advantage. Often the faster and smaller females and younger males will lead the chase, conserving the energy of the dominant male so he can take down the prey. Wolves may also run in relays with those in the back taking it a little easier until it's their turn to be the front runner. And it's not unusual for one or more wolves to distract prey so other wolves can stealthily approach from the rear. The prime age for hunting is around three to five years, when a wolf has reached its full weight and strength, has

The life of a wolf isn't easy, especially when it comes to obtaining food. The large prey they hunt, such as moose, elk and deer, frequently kick them and gore them with their antlers. When a wildlife veterinarian conducts a necropsy, it isn't unusual to find scars and evidence of broken bones and jaws. The fact that wolves can survive for years with these injuries is amazing. The damage to the top of this wolf's skull was probably caused by a kick from an ungulate. Photo by Helen Schwantje the experience to back up its physical capabilities and, if lucky, has not been injured or begun to experience signs of encroaching old age.

An adult ungulate is a formidable adversary whose sharp hooves and antlers are potentially lethal weapons. A kick from a hoof can shatter a jaw, break a leg or crush a skull, while antlers can puncture a lung or toss a wolf onto hard terrain. Wolves sometimes grip the rear or underside of their prey using their body weight to slow the animal down. It's not unusual for wolves to be kicked or dragged along the ground and even bashed against trees, rocks and shrubs. A full-grown bison or moose can weigh more than 10 times as much as a mature wolf but even smaller white-tailed deer have been known to stomp wolves to death. "Wolves have a very hard life," says Helen Schwantje, wildlife veterinarian for the BC government's Ministry of Forests, Lands, Natural Resource Operations and Rural Development. "Between intraspecies aggression and the size of the prey they kill, they get beat up a lot. Tooth, jaw or skull fractures are common, both fresh and healed, as well as scars suggesting healed skin trauma."

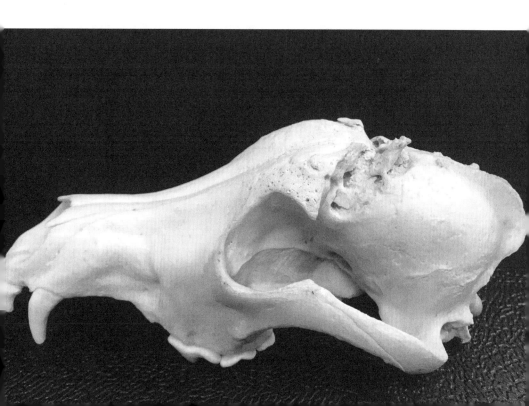

Each time a wolf attempts to take down large prey, there's a chance it will be maimed or killed. What's surprising is how often wolves get seriously injured and survive. There are many stories of researchers seeing wolves running with the pack only to later discover that one had a leg that had been broken sometime in the past and may have totally atrophied below the break. Yet, when watching from a distance, they had no idea they were observing a basically three-legged animal. These wolves must have been incapacitated for some time after the injury and perhaps never recovered sufficiently to participate in hunts. Yet the rest of the pack allowed them to feed on fresh kills and perhaps even brought them food while they were recovering. Working in pairs or larger groups allows wolves to take down big prey, and is also a way to hedge their bets, creating a sort of family insurance policy by spreading out the work and risk, as well as guaranteeing there's a backup plan when a member gets injured.

Once a pack chases down or wears out large prey, they must incapacitate it. Cougars usually hunt alone and stalk their prey silently, then make a sudden dash to deliver death by breaking their victim's neck, biting into cervical vertebrae or holding the prey's muzzle clamped shut until it suffocates. Since wolves don't have claws designed for gripping, they bite at their victim's rectum, rear legs and flanks to slow it down or disable it. This is when wolves sometimes go for wild rides at the end of a bison's tail using their formidable jaw and neck muscles to hold tight. Once the prey is no longer able to run, the wolves tear into it. Sometimes a wolf will bite the victim's throat or hold its snout closed to speed up death. Finding, chasing and killing prey is exhausting work so it's not unusual for wolves to rest before consuming it. But once they do, it's a free-for-all of tearing at hide and hair and ripping off chunks of meat, each wolf competing for whatever it can get. Sometimes the prey is literally torn apart. In his 1870 book, *Sheridan's Troopers on the Borders*, De B. Randolph Keim writes: "A wolf feast over the carcass of a buffalo is one of those sharp-toned entertainments, which could only be compared to an old-fashioned tea-party, composed of snappish octogenarians, paralytic, and generally debilitated characters of both sexes ... each one guzzling to his heart's content, and growling and finding fault with his neighbor."

Most of the time the ungulate dies relatively quickly due to shock and loss of blood but it's possible for one to live for some time, even with extensive injuries. While hunting grouse in November 2008, Michael Veine, writer and former editor of *Outdoor Life*, came across a wolf that had tackled a deer at the edge of a stream. He estimated the wolf ate slightly more than two kilograms (four pounds) of meat over several hours. Every time the deer attempted to escape, the wolf pulled her head down and went back to eating. Eventually, with a good portion of her hindquarters gone, the unlucky animal was unable to get away even when the wolf temporarily disappeared. Veine was tempted to put the doe out of her misery but knew the wolf was likely to return and was afraid any human scent might cause it to abandon its meal, thus making the deer's death meaningless.

Wolves have formidable tools for piercing tough hides and ripping apart big chunks of meat. On a mature wolf, the canine teeth, which it uses to grasp prey, are incredibly strong and can be a little over 3 centimetres (1.2 in) long on a good-sized male. The elongated jaw can exert up to 1,500 pounds of pressure per square inch (psi) and is capable of cracking skulls and crushing bones. In comparison, a German shepherd can maybe get up to 750 psi while the average human is capable of only about 120 psi. Wolves' teeth are designed for crushing, ripping, slicing and tearing. Old wolves, sometimes called "gummers," can have a hard time of it, as their teeth may be worn down to nubs. And if you've ever watched a dog eat, you'll notice that they gulp their food. Wolves are the same, swallowing large chunks of meat whole in an orgy of feeding. Some old-time hunters called the stupor wolves experience after gorging as being "meat drunk" and took advantage of this lethargy to easily dispatch them.

In one experiment, 10 captive wolves weighing an average of 41 kilograms (90 lbs) were starved for two days and then allowed to eat as much as they wanted. They each gained approximately 8 kilograms (18 lbs), nearly one-fifth their original weight. In another instance, a lone captive wolf gained just under 9 kilograms (20 lbs) after gorging on horse meat. Wild wolves also experience big variances in weight depending on how recently they've eaten. Odds are, the heavyweight wolves that sometimes make the news have just come off a big kill.

Finding and killing prey is a time-consuming, risky business fraught with danger for both hunter and hunted. In the majority of hunts, the wolf's success rate is estimated to be somewhere between 1 and 9 per cent. So it only makes sense that wolves aren't wasteful. Small prey like mice are gulped down whole and most of an ungulate is eaten, including much of the hair and bone. Depending on the size of the pack and kill, wolves can stay with a carcass for a couple of days, resting in between feeding sessions or, as Mark Elbroch and Kurt Rinehart noted in *Behavior of North American Mammals*, eight wolves can devour a yearling caribou in three hours. Most wolves lead a feast-or-famine existence and may easily go 14 days with little or nothing to eat. Chunks of meat will be taken back for a denning female and partially digested food regurgitated for young pups. If there are left-overs, wolves will cache pieces of meat or regurgitated matter for later consumption. In *Secret Go the Wolves*, R.D. Lawrence recounts an incident in which his first wife, Joan, received a lapful of warm, regurgitated beaver as a token of affection from one of the semi-wild, captive wolves they were raising.

On occasion, when prey is abundant and vulnerable, usually due to belly-deep snow, wolves will kill more than they can eat within a few days. The circumstances for this "surplus killing" rarely occur in the wild but unprotected livestock can present an opportunity for an easy hunt that is impossible for wolves to pass up. If the carcass is not consumed by scavengers or moved by humans and the wolves themselves are not destroyed or bothered by humans, the canids will return to finish their feast. "Wolves do not kill for fun or because they are bloodthirsty," explains Doug Smith, senior biologist at the Yellowstone Center for Resources. "They might not be able to eat everything immediately, but they will return and finish the carcass if they can."

A successful kill is an ever-changing blend of endurance, cunning, strength, experience, strategy, cooperation, luck and perhaps something more. There's a language among animals that often isn't understood by humans. Smells, sounds, sight, body language and vocalizations are part of it. But so is an intuitive sense that informs animals about what's going on around them. In the past, most scientists were skeptical that animals were capable of communicating in a voluntary, meaningful way, but people who have shared close company with a dog, cat, horse or other domestic animal often suspect that, as well as expressing themselves vocally and physically, at times they seem to be telepathic. It's common knowledge that dogs often appear to know when members of their human family are returning home or appear to offer comfort when a person is sick or grieving. While those incidents could be related to time of day, excellent hearing and body language, that isn't always the case. I can't count the times I've been working at my computer and thought, "I should take Bailey for a walk," and my dog has run over wagging his tail. It wasn't a regular walk time and, as far as I knew, I hadn't shifted my posture in any way. Often I was even still typing.

From his observations in Maine and Nova Scotia, William Long concluded that "wolves, more than any other brutes, receive silent warnings from one another" and that "wolf cunning is deeper than its five senses." In *How Animals Talk*, Long recalls being aware several times of a wounded wolf spending time on its own but always seeming to know just where its pack had made a fresh kill. The wolf would slowly make its way to the carcass, eat and then hide again. This could be attributed to a wolf's extraordinary sense of smell or a howled message, or perhaps something else.

The nuances of what helicopter pilot Gary Flath witnessed go deeper. The helicopter was above the treeline when Flath noticed some Rocky Mountain bighorn sheep grazing on a south-facing slope below the ridgeline of a mountainous area in Alberta. Not far from the bighorns, he saw six wolves making their way down a trench in the side of the valley wall where the sheep couldn't see them. Flath landed the helicopter to watch. "The wolves got below the sheep and hid in the snow just before the treeline," he says. "Two other wolves remained on the ridge. As soon as the six wolves were in place, the ones on the ridge charged the sheep. The sheep threw their heads up and bolted for the trees, the snow flying as they got into the deeper stuff. Just before the treeline the other wolves burst out of their hiding place and got two of them. The whole episode was totally silent and for much of it the two sets of wolves couldn't see each other. Yet the timing was perfect. It was like they were in radio contact. I was amazed at the wolves' silent, out of sight communication." Others, such as Gordon Haber, have seen similar incidents. In *Among Wolves*, he writes about tracking a pack with a small plane and watching how the members split up, going in separate directions out of sight of each other for great distances, then approaching their prey from different angles to launch their attack.

When wolves kill large prey they put on a banquet for a coyotes, foxes, bugs, birds and a multitude of other creatures. The only problem is, none of the guests are invited. Life for wildlife is all about survival, and getting enough to eat is a big part of that. Why bother obtaining your own food if someone else provides it? Scavenging is part of the wildlife dining infrastructure: as soon as something dies, and often before, a multitude of critters show up to take advantage of the situation. The death of a deer can bring the cycle of life full circle: a wolf kills the deer to eat, other animals consume the leftovers, the rotting carcass and scat from the wolf and scavengers enrich the soil and ungulates feed on the plants that grow, eventually becoming potential prey for wolves.

Depending on the location and weather, the species of party-crashers varies. But wolves' most constant companion at the feast of meat is the raven. Their association can be traced to ancient times. In Norse mythology, the god Odin was often depicted sitting at his throne with two ravens, Huginn and Muninn, and pet wolves, Geri and Freki. The ravens, whose names translate as "memory" and "thought," travelled far and wide, bringing news back to Odin, while the wolves, whose names both mean "the ravenous or greedy one," were docile creatures that Odin fed by hand.

Ravens are found throughout the northern hemisphere in most, if not all, traditional grey wolf territory. A small black bird and a large carnivore may seem like an unlikely pair but ravens and wolves actually have a lot in common. They both mate for life, make individually distinct sounds, eat meat and defend their territories. Like wolves, ravens play, hunt and scavenge food together and sometimes cache it. Young ravens disperse to form their own families but some may remain with their natal group to fill the role of babysitter, bring food to nesting females and feed young chicks. Although ravens don't live in flocks, they do on occasion sleep in communal roosts. And, like wolves, ravens are loyal and will care for an injured mate.

But the real magic of wolves and ravens is the way they interact. Ravens follow wolves, or their howls, seeming to know that at some point food will be available. An online video clip of wolves hunting bison in Yellowstone National Park tells the whole story: first up is a pack of wolves harassing five bison with a cloud of ravens overhead; later on, the pack is feeding on a bison carcass surrounded by a circle of ravens standing in the snow. But it isn't just wolves leading the birds to chow time. Wolves have been observed following ravens or their calls to downed, injured and even healthy prey. And because ravens follow migrating caribou herds in the Arctic, Inuit hunters often follow them to find prey, and ravens are said to sometimes follow the hunters. One story says that if a raven tips a wing at an Inuit hunter, they're assured of finding caribou. So meat eaters follow meat eaters hoping for a successful hunt.

Certain wolf packs and ravens even seem to form social bonds. Ravens appear to play with or tease wolves, but maybe that's just their way of saying, "Get off your duff and start hunting!" Many scientists believe that wolves and ravens evolved together and, over time, formed a unique symbiotic relationship in which each is rewarded by the presence of the other. Some are convinced that it's primarily the raven, with its ability to fly and see far distances, that does most of the leading to prey. Others speculate that while waiting for their share of the prize, ravens are more alert than gorging wolves and warn them of possible danger, such as approaching grizzly bears or humans. But the truth of the matter is, if they want to dine on ungulates, ravens

need wolves. Although ravens will kill and feed on newborn calves and fawns, they always go for the soft bits such as eyes and rectums, as their beaks and claws aren't capable of penetrating tough hides. They need wolves to kill large animals and rip them open so they can access the meat.

The equation of wolves, a dead ungulate and ravens is just about as reliable as *one plus two equals three*. In a study published in *Animal Behaviour*, Rolf Peterson notes that in his 27 years of observing wolves on Isle Royale in Lake Superior, ravens showed up every time wolves killed a moose, often within one minute of the takedown. University of Vermont zoologist Bernd Heinrich also established that ravens and wolves are close associates. His data, which he writes about in *Mind of the Raven: Investigations and Adventures with Wolf-Birds*, shows that ravens were found near wolf packs up to 99.7 per cent of the time in winter at Yellowstone National Park. On occasion wolves and ravens will feed together on a carcass but, more often than not, wolves want first dibs, so they expend time and energy chasing ravens off the kill.

Peterson, along with colleagues John Vucetich and Thomas Waite, decided to determine what effect scavenging ravens have on wolves on Isle Royale. Although they weren't able to measure the amount of meat pilfered, they estimated that wolves could lose up to 20 kilograms (44 lbs) of meat from a carcass each day to ravens and that the number of wolves present made a significant difference to this amount. Two wolves might lose as much as 37 per cent of the meat,

When wolves kill an ungulate or any large prey, they're not the only ones that benefit. Bugs, birds, coyotes and other creatures scavenge as much of the carcass as they can. Ravens and, to a lesser extent, magpies always seem to be present to join in the feast. They can steal a lot of food, so wolves often have to interrupt their feeding to chase the birds away. Photo by Jim Peaco, US National Park Service while a pack of six only lost 17 per cent. Those were conservative estimates and not unusual. Other studies estimate that a single raven can remove up to 2 kilograms (4.4 lbs) of meat a day from a large ungulate carcass, and researchers in the Yukon once watched ravens remove approximately half of a 300-kilogram (660 lb) moose carcass. While the average number of ravens at a wolf kill is 30, up to 135 have been counted at Yellowstone National Park. That's a lot of meat for wolves to lose.

Peterson and his colleagues speculate that ravens might be part of the reason wolves hunt in packs. Using data from previous studies at Isle Royale, they determined that two wolves hunting a moose would be the best balance of meat earned and energy expended obtaining it. They'd witnessed individual wolves killing moose 11 times so they knew a pair would be up to the challenge. But a half-ton of moose meat would be extremely difficult for two wolves to defend from ravens.

As large apex predators, adult wolves are rarely hunted by anything other than humans. But that doesn't mean they can drop their guard. Dogs chase cats, and that often happens with wolves and cougars. Unless cornered or defending young, a cougar confronted by a pack will quickly tree. While it might be urban myth, there are stories of wolves waiting until cougars are forced out of trees by cold, hunger or maybe frustration and then killing them. What is certainly true, however, is that packs of wolves can and do kill adult, as well as young, cougars. They also chase cougars off their kills. When wolves returned

While waiting to open the gate to the public at Thornton Creek Hatchery on the west coast of Vancouver Island, John Simmons watched a bear being followed by a wolf. They were both looking for salmon carrion and the bear seemed unaware of the wolf's presence. Then the wolf picked up a salmon tail, which must have crunched as he bit into it. The bear turned and moved closer to the wolf and they both sniffed each other for a few moments before going their own ways. Photo by John Simmons to western Wyoming, researchers with Panthera's Teton Cougar Project noticed that cougars, especially females with cubs, were being pushed into the fringes of prime hunting territory by increasing wolf populations.

But when it comes to one-on-one confrontations, cougars tend to be the winners. Cowichan Lake, BC, resident Rod Mizak was lucky enough to witness and film such an encounter from his vehicle early one morning in May 2015. He and a couple of friends were driving on a logging road when they came across a cougar and a wolf in a fatal embrace in the middle of the road. The battle was silent and still: the wolf on top holding the cougar to the ground by biting into the side of its face; the cougar on its back clasping the wolf as close as possible. Mizak estimates they watched for about 10 minutes, then one of them stepped out of the vehicle and, perhaps distracted or wanting to get a better grip, the wolf released its hold. The second it let go, the cougar lunged for the wolf's throat. Mizak says he'll never forget the crunching sound the wolf's neck bones made as the cougar bit down.

Bears are a different story, and one with a multiple-choice ending. Bears and wolves may walk by each other at fairly close quarters with

no fuss and numerous people have seen a lone wolf and bear eating off the same carcass. But altercations are common. Black bears have killed female wolves defending dens and wolves have dug up and killed the cubs of hibernating black bears. Wolves will also go after black, grizzly and polar bear cubs outside the den. This works best if there are at least two wolves: one to distract the female while the other attempts to isolate one of the cubs. Wolves also kill adult bears that are old, young or otherwise vulnerable.

Most confrontations occur when young or food are involved. With the advantage of size and strength, grizzly bears, even females with cubs, are not shy about challenging wolves for possession of a carcass. And wolves are the same. Being smaller than a bear means they're faster and more agile. Employing teamwork, wolves will feint, circle around and, on occasion, even bite a bear on the butt in an effort to keep it away from or get it off a kill. It's not unusual for a big grizzly to lie down on a carcass to protect as much meat as possible.

Once, from the helicopter he was piloting, Gary Flath witnessed two wolves harassing a grizzly on an elk carcass. "One wolf would try to grab a piece of meat and the grizzly would lunge at it—never leave the carcass, just lunge at the wolf, which always got away. While that was going on, the other wolf would sneak in and get a chunk of meat. The wolves took turns baiting the bear and stealing meat. It was like birds teasing a squirrel. That grizzly was mad!"

A lone wolf will usually avoid a bear but there's strength, safety and perhaps a bit of bravado when part of a pack. Rarely is a wolf or bear injured in skirmishes over a carcass but, always aware of how much energy is required for how much of a reward, wolves have been known to choose a third option when it comes to claiming a share. Even if they're the ones who made the kill, sometimes they'll simply wait nearby for the grizzly to eat its fill and move on.

Wolves are complex social animals that develop hunting techniques based on geography, prey habits, and pack experience that is passed down to succeeding generations. They spend a lot of time and energy finding and taking down prey, risking serious injury and death each time they do so. As pack animals, they communicate with each other in a variety of ways, including methods that elude scientific explanation. There's no doubt about it: wolves are smart, tough and sometimes exhibit behaviour beyond human comprehension.

CHAPTER 6

COYWOLVES AND WOLF-DOGS

It's wonderful to watch their progress after they've been here a while. It's like a lightness of being, a regaining of confidence.
—WENDY SPENCER

THE ELK CARCASS LAY ON THE SNOW COVERED BY A BLANKET OF ravens. When a narrow snout intruded, there was a rustling of black wings and an irritated series of high-pitched chirps from a bald eagle. Wily coyote had joined the feast. Not far away, a pack of wolves dozed with bulging bellies, but the eagle's call alerted them to the coyote's presence. Heads low, they approached the intruder and gave chase. The coyote was fast but not fast enough—soon tufts of fur filled the air.

Wolves have convoluted relationships with other members of the Canidae family, especially coyotes and dogs. They often attack and sometimes kill them, on occasion they ignore them and, given the right circumstances, they befriend or breed with them.

Normally, wolves and coyotes go together about as well as a leaking propane tank and a lit match. They'll occasionally kill each other's young but the main source of conflict is food. Coyotes are sly scavengers capable of stealing far more than a raven. Their small, sleek build means they're quick and nimble but each chunk of stolen meat is a gamble between life in the form of nourishment or death at the jaws of wolves.

But under certain conditions, an overwhelming urge to procreate and a scarcity of breeding partners can radically alter the antagonistic relationship and result in wolves breeding with coyotes. Different species breeding with each other is not unheard of. Most people know that a mule is the offspring of a male donkey and a female horse. Interspecies breeding occurs in the wild too. In Maine during the summer of 2003, DNA tests confirmed the hybridization of wild bobcats and lynx, resulting in litters of blynx, and in the Northwest Territories in 2006, the first recorded offspring of a wild polar bear and a grizzly was dubbed a "pizzly." When an animal's system receives a surge of hormones and there aren't many—or maybe any—of its own kind to mate with, everything can change. And it's possible that global warming, changing habitat and dwindling populations of some species will result in more genetic surprises in the future.

Wolves usually avoid mating with a full sibling or their offspring. Scientific research has shown, however, that they can breed with domestic dogs, Australian dingoes and coyotes, and that these couplings usually produce fertile offspring. In recent years, coywolves have been generating both media coverage and controversy. The term *coywolf* indicates a genetic stew of coyote and wolf with a bit of dog DNA thrown in. The controversy revolves around the name and the confusion over which animal—if any—it should belong to.

While the grey wolf evolved in Eurasia and eventually made its way back to North America, a smaller eastern wolf historically lived in the deciduous forests of southeast Canada and the eastern United States. "Unlike grey wolves, eastern wolves and coyotes evolved in the New World," explains Brad White, a professor of environment and life sciences at Trent University in Ontario. "They probably diverged as a species around 300,000 years ago and therefore share a lot of genetic material."

As settlers eradicated wolves from eastern North America, coyotes from the American southwest migrated east to fill the void. It's believed that the pressure of low population numbers and a strong instinct to breed persuaded some eastern wolves and possibly some red wolves to see western coyotes not as enemies but potential reproductive partners. The result of this interbreeding has long been called the *eastern coyote*. Although eastern coyotes are genetically different from western coyotes, there is not enough difference to consider them a separate species. Even so, some scientists believe eastern coyotes should more appropriately be called *coywolves*. Others disagree.

"The term *coywolf* is vague and means different things to different people," explains John Benson, assistant professor of vertebrate ecology at the University of Nebraska. "Some people use it to refer to eastern coyotes, which do have a past history of hybridization with wolves. The name is often applied to eastern coyotes in areas such as New York state and New England, where no wolves remain and hybridization no longer occurs. And in the Algonquin region, we now have contemporary hybridization between eastern coyotes and eastern wolves."

In a three-year study led by Benson, then a PhD student at Trent University, one-third of the canids the team captured in and adjacent to Algonquin Provincial Park were hybrids. It wasn't unusual to find packs composed of animals with various combinations of ancestry from eastern wolves, grey wolves and eastern coyotes. "The problem is, if we refer to eastern coyotes as *coywolves*, what do we call the contemporary hybrids between eastern wolves and eastern coyotes?" Benson asks. He, along with many scientists, prefers the term *eastern coyote* to describe coyotes in eastern North America with a past history of hybridization and *eastern wolf–eastern coyote* to refer to the hybridization currently taking place in parts of Ontario and Quebec.

To further complicate the issue of what to call certain wolf populations, in 2016 the Ontario government renamed the threatened eastern wolf the *Algonquin wolf* due to the canid's long history of hybridization with grey wolves and coyotes. Today, the animal is often referred to by either name. And some say that the eastern or Algonquin wolf might actually be a red wolf. "Red wolves are very similar genetically to eastern wolves," Brad White says. "Not everyone agrees, but it's possible that the red wolf is a remnant of the eastern wolf in the south and that the Algonquin wolf is a remnant in the north. Today, both the eastern and red wolf contain western coyote material from recent hybridizations."

Whichever name you choose, the eastern coyote or coywolf is an intriguing animal. To keep the animal's previous dual ancestry front and centre, I will refer to eastern coyotes as *coywolves*.

Wolves and coyotes generally don't get along, But when predator-control programs killed most of the eastern wolves in eastern North America, some began breeding with western coyotes. The result was the eastern coyote. Eastern coyotes, like the one shown here in her den, are somewhat different from western coyotes but still similar enough to be classed as the same species. Photo by Rory Eckenswiller

In what's been called a form of high-speed evolution and dispersal, coywolves are currently found in eastern Canada and range from Maine as far south as West Virginia in the United States. "This *Canis* soup is unique to the east," White says. "In the west, grey wolves and coyotes are distinct from each other. When wolves were reintroduced to Yellowstone National Park, they didn't breed with western coyotes, they killed them."

Both eastern wolves and coywolves are in between the size of a grey wolf and a coyote, with the former tending to be a bit larger. What's intriguing about coywolves are the physical characteristics and behavioural traits they tend to inherit from their ancestry. They have longer legs than coyotes, plus bigger paws and a broader skull, which provides space for bigger teeth and a stronger jaw. Like wolves, they sometimes hunt in packs and take down larger prey than coyotes normally do. Their habitat ranges from forested areas, which are preferred by most grey wolves, to more open spaces near human habitation, where coyotes are often found. Even though coywolves can be large—extreme estimates are as high as 36 kilograms (80 lbs)—they usually weigh around 17 kilograms (37 lbs) and are often mistaken for coyotes. Due to similarities in colour and markings and overlaps in size, it can be difficult to definitively tell eastern or red wolves from coywolves without genetic testing.

Coywolves may get their size and strength from wolves, but they tend to have the mindset of a coyote and are proving to be remarkably comfortable around humans. Some are conducting their everyday lives in densely populated areas like Toronto, Montreal, Boston, Chicago and New York. Most people never see them or have any idea they're present. That's largely due to the fact that urban coywolves are usually on the small side and are often totally nocturnal. Researchers were surprised to discover how this silent predator was finding its way into heavily populated areas. By tracking radio-collared coywolves, they discovered that the canids' most frequently used travel corridors are railway tracks. The animals seem to view wherever the tracks intersect with green spaces—such as parks or golf courses—as an open invitation to claim the spot as their territory.

Like western coyotes, the coywolf has a diet that can include everything from Canada goose eggs to deer and small livestock including sheep, goats and chickens, as well as berries and fruit. To round out the menu, cities and suburban areas usually have an abundance of other sources of food, including rats, rabbits and raccoons, that have also adapted to human habitat. Coywolves also eat garbage, pet food and occasionally pets. And sometimes people feed them.

Western coyotes have been aggressive toward people and so have coywolves. Staff at Nova Scotia's Cape Breton Highlands National Park have received reports of bold, fearless eastern coyotes, as they call them, since around 2000. As well as following people, sometimes closely, they have chased cyclists, biting the rear tires of bikes as if trying to take down prey. In October 2009, 19-year-old singer-songwriter Taylor Mitchell was mauled to death by coywolves while on the park's Skyline Trail. Incidents outside the park include coywolves attacking dogs, trailing people and, in at least two instances, attacking them. In one attack, a coywolf knocked a 14-year-old boy off his bike and attempted to bite him but was unsuccessful due to the heavy protective pants the teen was wearing. All coywolf attacks have been linked to habituation and possibly being fed.

Plausible sightings of coyote-wolf hybrids have been reported as far east as Michigan and Wisconsin in the US and a 2012 study in Manitoba indicated that nearly 10 per cent of the wolves tested showed signs of coyote-wolf hybridization. "Production of Hybrids between Western Gray Wolves and Western Coyotes," a paper published in PLOS ONE in February 2014, documents an attempt to artificially inseminate western coyotes with sperm from BC grey wolves. Out of nine coyotes, three became pregnant, with one successfully giving birth. The six pups that survived showed physical and behavioural traits similar to both parents. Although it's technically possible for western grey wolves and coyotes to mate, it's unlikely they'll do so in the wild unless circumstances change drastically.

"The situation in the west is different due to the presence of both western coyotes and grey wolves," notes Brad White. "I think coy-wolves will continue to expand west due to the evolutionary potential from their two species parents. They will also hybridize with western coyotes and generate new material for selection, especially in urban settings."

The relationship between wolves and dogs is even more complex. Dogs evolved from ancestral wolves, yet dogs have been bred to hunt wolves and the two often fight and sometimes kill each other. At times they put up with each other, or even enjoy one another's company. They also breed, with or without human intervention.

As soon as he heard barking, Dave Eyer knew something was up. He and his wife, Dodie, live on 65 hectares (160 ac) an hour's drive northwest of Clinton in BC's interior, so it could have been anything from a female grizzly with cubs to a mule deer wandering by. He stepped outside and saw Bailey, the short-legged golden retriever-dachshund cross they were looking after, standing uphill in some open pines. In the field below, a wolf had its rear end in the air, the typical dog pose for "I want to play!" The wolf sprang to the side, repeated the posture, then trotted downhill toward some thick bush. When the dog didn't follow, the wolf returned and went through its antics again. A rancher had told Eyer about a pair of coyotes using a similar strategy on his dog. When the dog followed, it was soon running for its life with the coyotes close behind. Convinced Bailey was in danger of being lured to his death, Eyer fired his shotgun over the wolf's head. It fled and Bailey came inside. When Eyer went out to read the story on the ground, he was surprised to find only one set of tracks, not the several he'd expected. He wondered if the wolf had really wanted to play with Bailey.

Interspecies friendships are most common among domestic animals or those in captivity. It's difficult to determine how often it might happen in the wild. Once I looked out my writing room window to see a wild rabbit grazing on the lawn among five deer. One of the deer licked the insides of the rabbit's ears, gradually working its way down to the cotton-ball tail. After a few minutes the rabbit shook itself and hopped away, only to have the deer follow and begin its attentions again. I wondered if the ungulate was using the bunny as a mobile salt lick or being affectionate. The rabbit's attitude seemed to be one of tolerance.

And tolerance may have been what was going on when Paul Paquet incorporated dogs into his early wolf research. Now senior scientist at both the Raincoast Conservation Foundation and Raincoast Conservation Science Lab at the University of Victoria, Paquet used huskies to track and identify scent markers of wolves and coyotes in Riding Mountain National Park in Manitoba during the 1980s. "The dogs and wolves were well aware of each other," he says. "They approached each other at times and two huskies were nose to nose with wolves on several occasions. They would react to each other's barking or howling but there was no real antipathy or aggression."

There are many stories about friendships between wild wolves and domestic dogs but the most famous has to be that of a black wolf that developed a crush on a yellow lab in Juneau, Alaska, in the winter of 2003. Nick Jans was startled when the wolf appeared and his dog broke loose and ran toward it. But instead of fighting, they began to play. Romeo, as the wolf came to be called, wasn't into a monogamous affair: he flirted, played and walked alongside many dogs at his favourite meet-and-greet spot near Mendenhall Glacier. After some initial hesitation, many people allowed Romeo to approach their dogs, sometimes left him toys and eventually weren't overly concerned when he came near them or their children. Romeo's reign as playboy of the park wasn't without controversy, however. Some wondered if the black wolf was responsible for the disappearance of a couple of small dogs, and once Romeo was seen carrying a pug some distance away before dropping it. Was Romeo looking for an extended play date or did he have something more menacing in mind?

Six years on, Romeo was a familiar—and popular—canid in Juneau. Then, late in September 2009, he disappeared. Two men were later arrested for taking big game (Romeo and bears) by unlawful methods. Romeo was mourned by many and the following winter locals held a memorial for the black wolf and placed a plaque commemorating him on a path he frequented. Many suspect Romeo was easy to shoot as he had no fear of humans.

On occasion, wolves and dogs do fraternize but most meetings have a more sinister tone. Altercations are possible whenever the two share the landscape, be it farm, wilderness setting or walking path just outside town. Wolves have hung around Prince Rupert, BC, for years; residents even created a Facebook page to let each other know where the predators have last been sighted. In 2010 a man saw a wolf pick up his neighbour's pug and, in true Canadian fashion, whacked the wolf with a hockey stick. The wolf glared at him and trotted off carrying the dog. The man rounded up the pug's owner and they gave chase with more neighbours, including a pregnant woman and some children, joining in. They cornered the wolf against a chain-link fence and pelted it with rocks until it dropped Bob, who was only slightly wounded. The general consensus was that the pug's pudginess had saved it from more serious injuries.

Not all dogs survive, of course. In 2016, Baby, a 39-kilogram (86 lb) German shepherd let herself out of a cabin near Labrador City in eastern Canada. Her owner found her head with large paw prints around it just down the beach from home. Wildlife officials confirmed Baby had been killed by wolves. A decade ago, a man I met in passing told me about the time he looked after a friend's two large dogs at Nuchatlitz Inlet off the northwest coast of Vancouver Island. "One morning the dogs were whining to get out," he said. He obliged, started to put the coffee on and heard a horrible commotion. "I opened the door and saw four wolves ripping the dogs into quarters and eating them." As a safeguard against wolves, some Scandinavians are equipping their dogs with Kevlar vests and collars that are spiked or give off electric shocks when clamped down on.

The carnage goes both ways. Hunting wolves with hounds is an age-old tradition in Eurasia and North America. Certain breeds, such as Irish and Russian wolfhounds, were specifically bred for the task. In *Hunting the Grisly and Other Sketches*, Theodore Roosevelt notes that not any dog would do. Even those that faced off regularly with bears or cougars were reluctant to chase wolves. "The immense agility and ferocity of the wild beast, the terrible snap of his long-toothed jaws, and the admirable training in which he [the wolf] always is, give him a great advantage," he writes. Roosevelt considered the best wolf-hunting dogs to be smooth- or rough-coated greyhounds and deer hounds. Even interbred with other breeds, these hounds averaged 76 centimetres (30 in) tall at the shoulder and weighed around 41 kilograms (90 lbs). They were fast, brave and ferocious. In fact, they were the only breeds Roosevelt witnessed chasing down and killing large adult wolves without any assistance from humans. Although six or more hounds were best, just two or three were enough to get the job done. "The feat can only be performed by big dogs of the highest courage, who will all act together, rush in at top speed and seize by the throat," Roosevelt explains.

Most domestic dogs are inadequately equipped, both physically and mentally, to defend themselves against a wolf. That's why Dave Eyer didn't take any chances when the wolf tried to entice Bailey into the woods. When asked about the incident, Valerius Geist, professor emeritus of environmental science at the University of Calgary, replied, "A wolf may spend years confronting dogs as enemies but they are highly social and can suffer greatly from loneliness. A pack of wolves would kill a dog immediately, a wolf after a cat would eat it and one trying to play with a dog was probably doing just that. This is how hybridization takes place."

Dogs were the first animals to be domesticated but how, when and where they parted from wolves in the evolutionary chain of events remains unclear. It's also not known how the canid became domesticated. Perhaps an early hunter-gatherer killed a female that had recently given birth and kept the pups, or someone raided a den and took pups back to the family cave. Or maybe the canids smelled meat cooking over an open fire and crept close, initially hoping for discarded scraps and eventually being fed deliberately. And contrary to popular opinion, domestication doesn't necessarily take a long time. A Siberian study in the late 1950s found that succeeding generations of wild foxes acted like domestic dogs and craved human companionship within 10 years.

Recent genetic research suggests that dogs diverged from their wolf ancestors in Europe, the Middle East and parts of Asia anywhere from 10,000 to 38,000 years ago. The latest theory is that as humans moved across Eurasia, they took their dogs with them and the animals bred with other dogs and also wolves at different times and places over thousands of years, creating a scattershot of DNA that intrigues and befuddles scientists to this day. It's believed that the first dogs in North America probably arrived with early hunter-gathers who crossed the Bering Sea in boats or walked across the Bering land bridge from what is now Siberia to Alaska. There the dogs mated with wolves, meaning that even North American wolves may possess some genetic material from dogs. Out of all the colourations, humans seem to love the black wolf the best. Ironically, that may be the dog coming out in the wolf, as black fur is thought to be the result of a genetic mutation that first occurred in dogs.

Archaeological studies in Siberia raise interesting questions about humans' early relationships with wolves and dogs. One discovered genetic links to Siberian huskies and Greenland sled dogs in a 35,000-year-old rib from a now extinct wolf. Several gravesites discovered in the Cis-Baikal region of Siberia contained dog teeth and bone implements, as well as one nearly intact dog skeleton, alongside human remains. Another revealed the complete skeleton of a male wolf, estimated to be nine years old, lying on its side, legs slightly curved to cradle the skull of a man.

In both cases, the humans and animals were buried at the same time. DNA indicates that the dog was eating the same food as the humans, so was likely domesticated, but the wolf was not. Although it's unknown what role dogs and wolves played in these people's lives, it's obvious they were held in high regard.

The difference between the life of a domestic dog and a wild wolf is vast. Wolves hunt for and kill their food, sometimes going for weeks with little or nothing to eat. There's no vet care for wounds or diseases and breeding is dictated by a female's hierarchy in the pack. Dogs, on the other hand, have been bred to develop specific looks and traits. Many live in houses, sleep in a dog bed or share their owner's bed, regularly visit veterinarians, are fed a selection of special food and sometimes have their toenails painted and wear sweaters and rain jackets. Today's dog has evolved galaxies away from its ancient wolf ancestors.

It's easy to understand the allure of a wolf-dog, a cross between a wolf and a domestic dog. To many, it seems the best of both worlds, a beautiful wild canid combined with a companion animal. What most people don't realize is that the degree of wolf can vary greatly. Wolf-dogs are usually categorized as high, medium or low content depending on the ancestry of the parents. A high-content wolf-dog's genes would be predominantly wolf, say 85 to 99 per cent, whereas a low-content wolf-dog would have 49 per cent or less wolf content.

Although wolves occasionally mate with domestic dogs on their own, most wolf-dog hybrids are human-engineered. Perhaps the earliest evidence of intentional breeding was found in 2004 when archaeologists discovered a wolf-dog jawbone in a warrior's burial chamber in a Teotihuacan pyramid. The ancient city is estimated to be more than 2,000 years old. More recent intentional crossbreeding has paired wolves with German shepherds, Alaskan malamutes and poodles, often in an attempt to create a better working dog or simply to study the effects of hybridization. The offspring of wild wolves and German shepherds were used to guard Czechoslovakian borders during the Cold War. Three decades later, the South African Defence Force attempted to use wolf-dogs to track down guerillas fighting the apartheid regime.

Today, most wolves are bred with dogs as pets for private ownership. And that's where the problems begin. With first generation high-content wolf-dogs starting at $3,000 US, some breeders are more interested in the money than screening buyers and informing them about caring for an animal that's part wolf. And unless you're willing to pay for genetic testing, there's no way to know for sure how much wolf DNA an animal has. The legality of owning a wolf or wolf-dog varies from region to region and most vets either don't know much about wolf-dogs or are unwilling to treat them. If a wolf-dog is found running at large or injures livestock, a pet or a human, it often gets caught up in the legal limbo of one organization deeming it wildlife and another a domestic animal, meaning no one is mandated to take responsibility. The animal is usually destroyed.

Xoe Stratford was nine years old when Gary Allan took his high-content wolf-dog, Tundra, to her school on Salt Spring Island for a talk on wolves. The way Tundra and Xoe are looking at each other speaks volumes about the relationships between humans and wolves. Photo by Anne Marie Davidson

When I started researching wolves, I wanted to observe them, which, of course, is easier said than done. None of the wild wolf encounters I've had lasted more than five minutes. Then a friend told me about Gary Allan. Allan had four wolf-dogs at the time and operates an education and advocacy program called Who Speaks for Wolf. With Tundra, a high-content wolf-dog, he's given presentations to more than 150 schools and many community groups. They've also visited Canuck Place Children's Hospice; Helping Spirit Lodge, which supports women and children who have experienced domestic violence; and numerous Indigenous groups. Allan told me how Tundra often sought out and spent time with students with disabilities on school visits, and about their 30-minute private audience with Jane Goodall when she was in BC. The most mystical experience he recounted, however, involved a beach trip with the Campbell River Laichwiltach Learning Program where, as two wolf-dogs ran free and staff and students were drumming, two eagles soared overhead.

A butterfly of excitement tickled my ribs as I drove up the east coast of Vancouver Island toward the ferry to Sointula on Malcolm Island, where Allan lived at the time. And truth be told, the butterfly was sharing space with a bit of nervousness. The only wolf I'd ever been within touching distance of had been dead. What would being with four near-wolves be like? Should I avoid eye contact and quick movements? Speak softly or not at all? "Don't be silly, Paula!" I told myself. "You grew up with three dogs in the house and have had dogs most of your adult life. These aren't wolves, they're wolf-*dogs*. Just treat them the way you would any strange dog." I was so wrong.

As I pulled into the driveway on Boogeyman's Hill, Allan came out to introduce me to the "pups" that were peeking into the front yard portion of their compound. Enticed by chunks of European wiener, Mahikan (the Cree word for *wolf*) approached Allan cautiously. Quick, nimble and jet black with greyish patches along her sides and chest, Mahikan grabbed her treat and disappeared. Nahanni, whose creamy white coat reflects his Arctic ancestors, hung back, not too sure about the stranger standing on the other side of the chain-link fence. Although they're from different litters, Mahikan and Nahanni were both four months old when I met them and Allan estimates their wolf content at around 95 per cent. Hinting at what would be his adult size, Nahanni weighed 23 kilograms (51 lbs) to Mahikan's 17 kilograms (37 lbs).

My reception in the house was a different story. Seven-year-old Tundra and twelve-year-old Meshach vigorously sniffed and fussed over me, eager for attention. Sleek and slender in her summertime coat, 39-kilogram (86 lb) Tundra looked every bit like the grey wolf she almost is. Meshach, the patriarch of the pack, had a thicker body, broader muzzle and coarse, bed-head hair. At 50 kilograms (110 lbs) he outweighed all the others, but was the lightweight when it came to wolf DNA, possessing only about 40 per cent. With one glance at the double-wide mattress tufted with fur in the middle of the living room floor and the mosaic of nose prints on the sliding glass door, I knew that Allan's pack had adapted to life with humans. Or so I thought until we went into the backyard.

That's when I discovered how un-doglike wolf-dogs can be. Ninety-nine per cent of four-month-old dogs would have run toward me and jumped up with tails wagging, fervently licking any bare skin they could find. Mahikan and Nahanni vanished. It turns out that even captive-born wolves and high-content wolf-dogs are often born with an innate fear of humans and must be socialized to humans at an extremely young age. Allan got Tundra when she was three weeks old and they bonded immediately. Mahikan and Nahanni were five weeks old. When he brought them home, they hid under the furniture trembling with fear. So Allan arranged mattresses in an empty trailer at the side of the house, sat with them for 15 hours each day and slept with them at night for the next three weeks until they became somewhat used to him. They'd been in the wolf run for a couple of months by the time I met them but refused to join the older wolf-dogs in the house and were still extremely wary around humans—even Allan and his wife, Sally, who spent a lot of time with them.

"Because the pups were so skittish, I decided that the back deck was shared territory and the grass was wolf territory," Allan explains. "Unless I'm cleaning up or need to do something, I stay on the deck and let the pups come to me." Over the course of the day, Allan and I moved back and forth from deck to house frequently. Often, Allan would lie down on the deck. At nearly 2 metres (6.6 ft) tall, he figured he looked like the equivalent of a grizzly bear to the pups. Eventually Mahikan and sometimes Nahanni would go to him for a treat or belly rub. Whenever Meshach wandered over to me, the pups happily followed—but as soon as they caught sight of me on the other side of him, they darted off. I tried to be as still as possible but even raising my hand in slow motion to brush a piece of hair out of my eyes was enough to cause a panicked stampede. I hoped I wouldn't sneeze.

When Meshach sprawled on the deck next to Allan, Mahikan and Nahanni eagerly crowded around but their focus was on the wolf-dog, not the human. They crouched down, backs rounded and ears pinned back—a classic submissive pose—and continually licked Meshach's muzzle. They did the same to Tundra all the time too. It seemed to annoy the older wolf-dogs and they'd growl and bare their teeth in a fearsome display but that only seemed to make the pups love them all the more. "The pups have the strongest bond to each other, then to the older wolf-dogs and then to humans," Allan says. "After Tundra and Meshach, they like Sally best, then me. They approach women more quickly than men; I think they sense their nurturing energy."

As my hosts prepared dinner, Allan suggested I sit on the deck and talk quietly to the pups. "They might come up to you then," he said. I hadn't expected to find myself alone with three near-wolves but as soon as I was the only human outside, Mahikan retreated to her

den under the deck, Tundra went to sleep and, to my surprise, I found myself in a stare-down with Nahanni, the shyest of the lot. In a soft voice I murmured, "Hey there, Nahanni, that's a good boy," and what I hoped were other friendly sounding words. Nahanni wasn't interested though and strolled away after about 10 minutes. But a few seconds later I had that "someone's looking at me" feeling and turned my head to see him coming up the deck's side steps. Before I'd even blinked, he disappeared. I'll always wonder what would have happened if I hadn't moved. Would Nahanni have stood silently behind me? Sniffed my neck? Perhaps dared to lick it? Since none of the wolf-dogs showed any interest in my presence, I went inside. A short time later I watched Nahanni poop where I'd been sitting. I wonder what that says about my nurturing energy?

At the time, I didn't know how lucky I was. Affable Meshach allowed me to experience being around a low-content wolf-dog while the two shy pups exhibited behaviour very close to that of wolves in the wild and Tundra provided insight into the world of a highly social-ized, high-content wolf-dog. Allan figures her wolf genes make up 85 to 90 per cent of her DNA. I think of her as a wolf with a wee drop of dog. And it goes beyond the long legs, narrow chest, colouration and other physical attributes that testify to her ancestry. Unlike most dogs I know, who make a heck of a racket racing through the bush, Tundra moves silently. She spontaneously regurgitated her food to feed the pups on a regular basis even though she was removed from her mother too young to have experienced that. On walks in the woods, she'd stop and stare in one direction intently. When I asked Allan if she smelled something, he replied, "She's probably cognitive mapping." Cognitive mapping involves making a mental map of an

Nahanni (on the left) and Mahikan are high-content wolf-dogs. Although they are not siblings, they have been raised together since they were five weeks old and share a close relationship. Photo by Gary Allan extended outdoor environment that allows wolves and other animals to plan their routes and take shortcuts. Even humans do it, but less so now that there are so many electronic gadgets to help us out. Tundra howls like a wolf, too. Once, on an early morning stroll at François Lake in north-central BC, Allan, Tundra and Meshach heard two packs howling back and forth across the water at each other. When they finished, Tundra lifted her head and gave two long howls. The wild wolves probably wondered "who the heck is that?" The biggest difference, however, between Tundra and a dog is attitude. Most dogs are eager to please but as much as Tundra loves Allan, I'm convinced she sees him as a companion, not a master. She does what she wants when she wants in her own time. And Allan is most patient.

On my first visit to Allan's, that summer of 2014, I learned that he spent $600 a month to feed the two adult wolf-dogs and two pups 20 kilograms (44 lbs) of chicken a week. They got some of it raw and slightly frozen with bones and the rest cooked without bones. Grain-free kibble—wolves are primarily carnivores so grains don't agree with their digestive systems—was available anytime. Like her wild ancestors, Tundra sometimes went without eating for several days at a time.

When I asked Allan about the 2.5-metre-high (8 ft) heavy duty chain-link fencing with an inward overhang, he explained that wolves and wolf-dogs are the Houdinis of the canid world. They can climb chain-link fences, chew through wooden ones, dig tunnels under both and jump a barrier 2 metres (6.6 ft) high. To prevent digging, Allan set his fence into cement with 1 metre (3 ft) of wire mesh running underground into the compound. I later read about a grey wolf at what was then called the Dartmoor Wildlife Park in southwest England that climbed a tree in 2005 and made his way over a faulty electric fence. Two years later, the same Canadian wolf made his getaway climbing another fence.

Although a burglar might change his mind if he peeked in a window and saw what looked like a wolf, captive wolves and high-content wolf-dogs generally aren't good guards. They rarely bark and are wary of new people and situations, so might retreat if a stranger appears. Wolves and many wolf-dogs also have a high prey drive, so putting them in close proximity to pets, livestock and small children can be dangerous. "Wolves hate dogs," notes Allan. "They see them as interlopers in their territory. That's why the off-leash walks that are so rewarding with dogs are risky and sometimes not possible at all with wolf-dogs."

But the biggest obstacle to owning a wolf or wolf-dog is their mental perspective. Over the centuries, dogs have been bred to fulfill the desires of humans, whether that be as companion, work animal or simply the trendy fashion accessory of the day. Studies show that a large proportion of people are attracted to dogs with floppy ears and shorter, rounded muzzles. These are juvenile characteristics that all dog and wolf puppies have. As wolf pups grow, however, their ears stand upright and their snouts lengthen, whereas many dogs' do not. These juvenile traits also carry over into dogs' mental outlook. Compared to wolves, dogs are like Peter Pan, the fictional young boy who never grew up. According to Mission: Wolf, a sanctuary for captive wolves and wolf-dog hybrids in Westcliffe, Colorado, "Wolves mature sexually and emotionally at age two or three and become independent thinkers that have no reason to please humans. This is when they often become a challenge for many private owners to deal with. Dogs act like a wolf puppy all of their life and have adapted to our desire for them to please us."

Wolves have larger brains than dogs and use them in different ways. A study conducted by Dr. Monique Udell of the Department of Animal and Rangeland Sciences at Oregon State University, Corvallis, compared the responses of 10 human-socialized wolves, 10 pet dogs and 10 shelter dogs when presented with a piece of summer sausage in a box that required them to remove the lid to get the treat. The tests were conducted in three ways: with the canines in the room alone, with a familiar human observer present but not saying or doing anything, and with the same person encouraging them to open the box. Out of the ten wolves, eight got the treat within two minutes. Out of the twenty dogs, only one was successful. Udell noted that the wolves were more persistent when it came to problem solving, while the dogs showed little initiative, looking to the humans for assistance instead. Similar tests at Eötvös Loránd University in Budapest and the Wolf Science Center in Austria using wolves and dogs that had been raised identically since birth had the same results. The data from these studies suggest that to a certain—perhaps large—degree, domestication has made dogs dependent on humans.

As well as being independent thinkers, wolves appear to have some level of insight and forethought. In *Wolves: Behavior, Ecology, and Conservation*, Jane M. Packard recalls how the dominant male in a wolf

pack distracted nearby pups with food several times to keep them out from under the hooves of a wandering muskox that happened to be near the den entrance. Alaska researcher Gordon Haber tells a story about a yearling wolf helping pups cross a fast-flowing stream. The first pup was swept downstream and struggled to climb the high bank. When the second pup entered the water, the yearling jumped in and swam next to the pup, bracing it against the current and helping it up the bank. After observing this, the third pup crossed farther upstream, reaching its destination with ease. Gary Allan witnessed a problem-solving incident with Mahikan and Nahanni when they were about a year old. Allan glanced outside and saw that Mahikan had an electric cable wrapped around her neck, body and a front leg. He could tell she was frightened and struggling and knew she would only become more agitated if he went out to help her. In the meantime, Nahanni walked over and gently lifted the cable off her back and from around her neck, laying it on the ground so she could free her leg.

Wolves are resourceful, independent and intelligent. Unfortunately, these traits have a downside when it comes to wolf-dog ownership. People familiar with wolf behaviour can frequently predict how a particular wolf will react under certain circumstances. But with a wolf-dog, you're never sure what will happen. The genetic ingredients can vary from litter to litter and even between pups within a litter. Wolf-dogs can form close bonds with their owners

The Wolf Science Center in Austria hand-raises wolves and dogs and then conducts tests involving cooperation and cognition in an effort to understand the differences and commonalities between the two species. One study involved having the animals see different images on a computer screen and touch the one that would provide a reward. Once they mastered that, they were given more difficult visual discrimination tests. Although the results are not available yet, one aspect of the tests was soon obvious. Similar to humans, all the animals spent hours at the computer screen.
Photo by Rooobert Bayer, Wolf Science Center, Austria

and some are model pets, getting along with humans, dogs, livestock and even cats. But that's often an exception. Wolves and wolf-dogs can be trained but generally only do what humans ask if they want to. Eagerness to please is something people love about dogs and it's this trait that's frequently lacking or totally unpredictable in wolves and wolf-dogs.

A few people, however, are incredibly successful when it comes to training wolves and high-content wolf-dogs, but it involves a formidable amount of time, patience and knowledge. In the late 1980s, Andrew Simpson travelled to Australia and got a job working with the dingo trainer for the film *A Cry in the Dark*. When he moved to Vancouver, his first task on a film set was to get an unruly wolf-dog to behave. Within a week it was walking beside him off-leash. A few years later, Simpson and his wife, animal trainer Sally Jo Sousa, started Instinct Animals for Film. They specialize in wolves but work with everything from bears to wild birds and barnyard chickens.

Simpson believes you have to raise wolves before you can train them—and that includes sleeping with wriggling pups that aren't house-trained. Yet he readily admits that even a strong emotional bond and trust won't guarantee a wolf will do what you want it to when you want it to.

Among its numerous credits, Instinct Animals has worked on *Game of Thrones*, *Wolf Totem* and *Wolves Unleashed*. One of their most ambitious projects was transporting 13 wolves from their 65-hectare (160 ac) ranch north of Calgary to film in one of the coldest parts of Siberia. Simpson's commitment to the wolves is so great that he travelled in the hold of the plane to reassure the animals during the flight. On site, one challenge was to teach the wolves to be around a herd of 200 reindeer, their natural prey, without harming them. The biggest test, however, was getting the lead wolf, Digger, to fall through the ice into freezing water. Simpson was afraid that would destroy the wolf's trust in him, especially when the scene had to be filmed twice. But reassuring words, cuddles and a night in Simpson's bed put everything to rights.

Gary Allan, who, along with Sally and the pack, moved to Cedar on Vancouver Island in 2017, uses the same approach with his wolf-dogs. "You raise these animals with love," he says. "They are highly intelligent and need constant love and affection. Anyone who wants a wolf-dog should be retired or work at home with total flexibility to spend lots of time with them."

Owning a wolf or wolf-dog can be physically, emotionally and financially high maintenance. The time commitment is at times similar to that of a full-time job. It's difficult or impossible to find a babysitter and it can be a challenge to find a kennel when you go on vacation. And, as highly mobile, athletic animals, they need room to move. On her website, Sandi Ault, bestselling author of the *Wild* series, admits getting a wolf-dog was a romantic, not practical, idea. Mountain was an escape artist who figured out how to disconnect insulators so he could jump electric fences, trashed their belongings when left alone and needed an incredible amount of exercise. When they ran out of options to make it work, Ault, her husband and Mountain left suburban Kansas City to live in the Rocky Mountains of Colorado. They were willing to change their lives for a wolf-dog, but most people can't or wouldn't be inclined to. That's why so many wolves and wolf-dogs end up at sanctuaries like Wolf Haven International.

It was the day before Halloween and a steady drizzle pushed the morning from cool toward unpleasant. But the weather didn't dampen the enthusiasm of the 20 or so people standing by a sturdy gate. We'd just been treated to a 55-canid howl fest. As each animal answered and harmonized—or not—with the others at different times and pitches, the mingling and range of deep wolf tones and higher coyote yips created a symphony none of us will forget. Wolf Haven International is a globally accredited sanctuary for captive-born and displaced wolves, a little over an hour's drive south of Seattle. The facility also participates in captive breeding programs for endangered red wolves and Mexican grey wolves, as well as caring for some high-content wolf-dogs and coyotes.

At the time of my visit in 2016, the 33-hectare (82 ac) sanctuary set amid bigleaf maples and Garry oaks was home to 24 grey wolves, 14 Mexican grey wolves, 10 high-content wolf-dogs, 6 red wolves and 2 coyotes. Animals are typically paired with members of the opposite sex and live in outdoor enclosures with vegetation and trees. Wild wolves are successful in their hunts around one in ten times and Wolf Haven attempts to replicate this feeding schedule. Their animals are fed main meals two to three times a week and receive smaller food items, like a turkey neck, daily. Wolf Haven is a hands-off sanctuary, meaning staff minimize interactions with the animals, allowing them to live as natural a life as possible. When one dies, it's buried in the Wolf Haven cemetery.

Our reservation-only visit featured eight animals, a mix of grey and Mexican grey wolves, wolf-dogs and coyotes. The animals we saw were more at ease with limited human contact; the others are secluded for their own comfort. Wolf Haven is a true sanctuary in that it caters to the wolves in their care, not to visitors.

Without knowing, we'd picked the best time to visit: bone day. As soon as animal care specialist Erik Wilber drove the pickup through the gate, all the animals moved close to the fence, eager for the big blobs of gristle and bone (cow femurs) that would be tossed to them. We watched the canids gnaw on their treats and laughed as a raven struggled to steal a heavy piece of gristle. But as our guide told us a bit about each animal's personality and background, we were reminded of the reason for Wolf Haven. It, like other sanctuaries across North

America and Europe, provides a final home for captive wolves and wolf-dogs that have been abandoned or abused, or whose owners can no longer handle or control them.

"We get calls for placements from all over the world including South America, Iran, France, Japan and North America," says Wendy Spencer, the sanctuary's executive director. "Most are from private owners. We have four animals from a roadside attraction in Alaska that lived all their life—one was eleven when he came to us—on the end of an eight-foot drag chain. Another was kept in an apartment the first year of its life and abused. And we've recently taken in a wolf and a wolf-dog from a local breeder. He was having a life crisis and the animals were paying the penalty. If we hadn't taken them, he would have shot them." In her 20 years at Wolf Haven, Spencer's seen choke chains embedded in animals' necks and filthy kennels because owners were no longer able to safely get near the animal. "People get wolves or wolf-dogs as pups and everything's fine until the animal is around eighteen to twenty months old. The owners are lulled into a false sense of security but that can change as the animal matures and their natural behaviour comes to the fore. The needs of a wolf or wolf-dog are very different than those of a dog."

For some animals and owners it's tragic on both sides. "I've met owners who love their animals and have the best intentions but are misguided," says Spencer. "A mother and daughter bought Juno, a wolf-dog, from a breeder in Texas. They got her when she was ten days old and did all they could to reinforce the human-animal bond, such as bottle feeding her, letting her sleep in their beds, neutering her and taking her everywhere with them. But when Juno matured, she started testing and challenging them. The mom was just over five feet tall and petite. When she tried to put the leash on, Juno would snap and growl. The owner became fearful and Juno picked up on that and her behaviour escalated. When they approached us, their only other alternative was to euthanize Juno. Luckily, we had room. If Juno had remained with the woman and her daughter, I believe something bad would have happened. Juno was getting very aggressive. Selling wolves and wolf-dogs is very lucrative. These animals are bred for looks—the more wolflike the better—not temperament."

Although some people successfully keep wolf-dogs, the animals can be a dangerous, unpredictable mix of genetics. In 2006, a 56-year-old woman was mauled to death in the pen of her nine wolf-dogs behind her home in Salem, Pennsylvania. And in 2017, a three-year-old boy in Washington state reached into a pen to pet or feed two wolf-dogs and sustained injures so severe that his arm had to be amputated.

Spencer believes mid-content wolf-dogs have the most potential for aggression toward humans. "You're getting an unpredictable mix of an animal that has a strong prey drive and no fear of humans," she says. "Wolf Haven is unique in that we accept aggressive animals over well-socialized ones. Many facilities have wolf ambassador programs and let the public interact with an animal on-leash. They're not interested in a challenging animal."

The problem is, a lot of captive wolves and wolf-dogs need someplace to go and there aren't enough sanctuaries to take them all in. Wolf Haven doesn't take dogs or low-content wolf-dogs as they generally do okay with people experienced in handling northern breeds such as huskies and malamutes. "By the fourth or fifth generation the wolf genes are pretty diluted," Spencer explains. "Most animals sold as wolf-dogs have little or no wolf content and, when they're puppies, it's impossible for most people to tell without genetic testing. Most of the calls we get are requests to take wolf-dogs. We just don't have the resources to take them all and it's tragic because if we say no, that usually means a death sentence for the animal."

Most animals come to Wolf Haven when they're around four to five years old. They're mature, intractable and the owner can't handle them. Wolves in captivity can live a long time—one at Wolf Haven died shortly before she turned 20. "It's very difficult for older animals to adjust," says Spencer. "Wolves are wary about new situations. Captive wolves are caught between two worlds, the wolf world and world we force them to fit into. Some never settle; in those situations, it would be kinder to humanely euthanize them."

Since its inception in 1982, Wolf Haven has taken in only two wild wolves and those were exceptional circumstances: lone young animals that were habituated to humans and, although not causing problems, were in conflict with human activities such as ranching. "We don't believe in taking wild animals and making them captives," says Spencer. "Wolves are designed to travel hundreds of miles and live in cooperative family groups. Rather than save a life, we look at the quality of life. Again, in some instances, it's kinder to humanely euthanize the animal."

After I interviewed Spencer I got to watch videos of several animals that weren't on the public visitor route. Wolf Haven uses remote cameras to monitor certain residents without intruding on their lives. First up was a litter of red wolf pups learning to howl and scattering in fright the first time they glimpsed the white wolf in a nearby enclosure. The next video was a sharp reminder of why animals end up at sanctuaries. A DNA test conducted by the University of California, Davis, indicated that the animal was pure wolf or a high-content wolf-dog. The two- to three-year-old male had been at Wolf Haven for three weeks. The SPCA had removed him from a small kennel in a Texas feed store where he was the star attraction of the owner's menagerie. Houston had never been outside. It was heartbreaking to watch him cower when a raven flew overhead. Even the rain and falling leaves scared him. He'd been paired with another recent arrival, a six-month-old high-content wolf-dog, and was still getting used to his new life.

"The beauty of the sanctuary is that it takes these animals in and gives them a forever home," says Spencer. "Most of the animals at Wolf Haven have been abused, neglected and exploited by humans. You can tell they've just checked out, they aren't really there. You can see it in their eyes. It's wonderful to watch their progress after they're been here a while. It's like a lightness of being, a regaining of confidence. We consider it a success when even the ones that have been super socialized don't need humans anymore. They see workers go through the sanctuary but it's not a big deal. They can just be themselves."

The animals at Wolf Haven touched me in ways I hadn't expected. Even though they have a place to live, a companion and enough to eat, I don't know if that can ever make up for the loneliness and abuse many of them experienced in their early years. Studying the breeding

relationships between wolves and coyotes and wolves and dogs was enlightening. The first, born out of desperation, seems successful, while the second, often created by human greed, is fraught with unpredictable and often unfortunate results. Even though dogs and wolves share a common ancestor and many characteristics, the difference between them remains astronomical.

Houston was about two or three years old when he was rescued and taken to Wolf Haven International. He had not been outside or seen other wolves for most of his life. He now shares a a pen with a female wolf-dog named Zoe. Photo courtesy of Wolf Haven International

CHAPTER 7

WOLF WARS

A wolf makes his living by his teeth.
—LOUISE LIEBENBERG

ON A WALK IN THE WOODS AFTER A HUGE STORM, A LIME-GREEN COAT of moss glowed on the maple trees, translucent raindrops were cold on my cheeks and the cappuccino-coloured froth of Millard Creek battered its banks. And on tree branches at the beginning and end of the trail were shiny, silver Christmas ornaments. The compulsion for humans to mark and manage the land and all that's on it seems innate. We claim our territory with fences, buildings, lawns or crops and destroy what we fear or find inconvenient. Some alterations are beneficial, benign or beautiful; others create environmental havoc that may impact future generations indefinitely.

Writing about wolves means writing about death. Humans kill wolves for sport, for financial gain and because of the carnivores' predation on pets, livestock and wild ungulates, as well as their occasional transgressions against people. Wolves hunt to survive and feed their young and also kill other wolves to defend their territory. When wolves attack livestock they compete with ranchers, when they kill ungulates they compete with hunters and when they injure or kill humans, they generate a tsunami of emotions including fear and disbelief. If humans kill wolves, some people cheer while others get out their protest signs and berate politicians. There's no getting around it, the word *wolf* is synonymous with conflict.

People who raise livestock often hate wolves with a passion, and for good reason. Domestic animals can be killed, maimed so badly that they need to be euthanized, or stressed to the point that they don't gain weight, become pregnant or bear live offspring. While the battle with wolves continues in countries like Romania and Russia, where they were never eradicated, there are regions in western Europe that are experiencing the predator for the first time in 50 or even 200 years. Protected by European Union (EU) sanctions, the wolf has travelled fast and far. A 2017 estimate for the number of wolves in Europe, excluding Russia, ranges from 12,000 to 20,000, a definite increase from what it was 100 years ago.

In 1990, wolves were basically unheard of in France. Then in the summer of 1998 something spooked or chased 280 sheep over a cliff. They'd been grazing on the open grasslands of the Massif des Monges in the French Alps. It was a bloody, heartbreaking mess of dead animals and bloated carrion birds punctuated by the bleating of injured or dying sheep. It took weeks to round up the animals that had escaped the massacre. A few months later it was officially declared: wolves had returned to Massif des Monges.

Late one evening Troy Bennett, a member of the livestock cooperative that suffered the loss of so many sheep, was carrying a paralyzed lamb over his shoulders when he glanced into a treed area and saw a wolf watching him. "Our eyes met and were locked, I was drawn into them. People talk about the wolf's stare, how it holds you, how it holds its prey," he says. "When a wild wolf looks into your eyes it looks deep and you cannot look away. Something holds you there. Whether it is hypnotism or fear or something else I'm not sure. I didn't feel fear, but I was held. In that look I felt something change in me."

When Bennett locked eyes with the wolf, he saw a beautiful, mystical creature. When he thought about the sheep, he knew that creature was also a ruthless predator. The 29-year-old was used to seeing wildlife when he was on the mountain with the flock but after he saw the wolf, he began to look at the landscape with a predator's eyes. Was that a good spot to surprise prey? Was this the place to chase them toward a cliff? His encounter with the wolf changed everything. Bennett went to Romania to study wolves in the Carpathian Mountains with the Large Carnivore Project as well as local shepherds. He also obtained a diploma in wolf studies and conservation from Compass Education and Training, an online education facility based in Scotland. By the time he returned home, he knew why his family was losing fewer sheep than the neighbours: his family put the sheep in a barn at night and had a livestock guardian dog that considered the flock his pack. Eventually Bennett became a consultant for others wanting to learn how to prevent wolf livestock predation, as well as a guide for nature treks in southeast France.

A December 2017 email from Valerius Geist informed me that the wolf situation in Europe was "boiling." It was no surprise—few people respond to wolves in the same manner as Bennett and the tension had been building for some time. In 2016 Spanish protesters hung six decapitated wolf heads from roadside signs, an entire wolf carcass from a street light and placed other carcasses in city office buildings and grocery store parking lots. The next spring wolf cadavers were found on the side of the road and inside a park employee's vehicle. Wolves in Greece have been found with their ears cut off or skinned alive and the brotherhood of shoot, shovel and shut up is vigorously practised in remote villages. A display of dead livestock with a life-sized plastic wolf behind them in the central square in Hanover, Germany, shocked Christmas shoppers in December 2016.

The French are no less irate. Farmers have taken their sheep to city streets, blocking traffic at various locations, including the Eiffel

Tower in Paris. In the fall of 2015, the president of Vanoise National Park in the French Alps, his deputy, and a park ranger were held hostage overnight by 50 shepherds who demanded that they be allowed to kill park wolves to protect their flocks. Shepherds from the Roquefort-sur-Soulzon region say wolves are threatening the future of France's renowned roquefort cheese. Governed by strict rules, tradition demands that the milk used to make the tangy blue cheese must come only from ewes allowed to graze freely every day except in extreme weather. But now the sheep are finding wolves on their grazing grounds. Ironically, the image on one brand of France's "king of cheese" is Little Red Riding Hood gazing up at a Big Bad Wolf. Instead of cake for grandma, her basket contains a block of roquefort cheese.

While farmers attempt to protect their sheep from wolves, the majority of the French public—80 per cent in one survey—lobbies to save wolves from farmers. In 2016, thousands attended a pro-wolf rally in downtown Madrid after the display of beheaded wolves. And that's a big part of the problem. City-dwelling conservationists want wolves left alone and to even increase numbers if possible, while ranchers struggle to maintain their pastoral way of life. As Europeans vacate rural areas for a more urban lifestyle, the number of people raising livestock has dwindled. Agricultural land is left untended or is not even designated as such anymore. This provides more space for wolves, which, due to the shift toward environmentalism, are now protected in most of Europe by the Berne Convention on the Conservation of European Wildlife and Natural Habitats, signed by the Council of Europe in 1979, and, more recently, the EU Habitats Directive. It's now illegal to kill wolves in Europe except under special circumstances and permission is only granted after all other efforts to protect livestock have failed. Some countries, like Sweden, have authorized wolf hunts anyway and received warning letters from the EU.

The sentiments of livestock producers in the US are equally strong. The protection of grey wolves as an endangered or big game species, and their natural dispersal and reintroduction into Yellowstone National Park and Idaho in the mid-1990s, allowed wolf populations to rebound and, as they dispersed, move into areas where humans had not experienced wolves for close to a century. As they returned, the war between humans and wolves over land, life and livelihood flamed bright again. Many believe the US government is responsible for the presence of the predators but the reality is, they've been trotting south from Canada since the 1980s, if not before. Animals pay no heed to the arbitrary borders of humans.

Ranchers' lives are subject to many circumstances, such as weather and disease, over which they have no control. It's not uncommon for one or more members of a family to work at outside jobs in an effort to even out or top up the annual income. Depending on the size of an operation, losing 30 animals, half a dozen or even 1 can severely affect the profit margin. Finding injured or dead animals takes an emotional toll, too. Adding losses from predators to the mix of issues ranchers face on a daily basis can be the tipping point to financial disaster and a tornado of fury. When wolves showed up on nearby ranches after the Yellowstone reintroduction, bumper stickers proclaiming, "Wolves are government sponsored terrorists" and "SSS" (shoot, shovel and shut up) were prominently plastered on numerous pickups.

In the early 2000s, after an absence of more than 70 years, wolves wandered into Washington state. It's estimated that between 2008 and 2016, the population grew by more than 30 per cent annually. That's at least partially due to the state's progressive management plan, which requires the presence of 15 breeding pairs before wolves can be removed from the state's endangered species list. There was only one wolf pack in Washington when a 2008 survey showed that 75 per cent of residents welcomed wolves. Six years later, only 64 per cent felt the same way. More packs meant more trouble for livestock producers, and most of the wolf packs are clustered around the northeast corner of the state in ranch country. The majority of pro-wolfers live a more urban lifestyle in big cities like Seattle and Tacoma in the western portion of the state. As of 2017, only one wolf had been spotted on the liberal side of that cultural division.

Like Europe, North America has experienced a huge shift in demographics. In 1800, city dwellers were a scant 3 per cent of the population, a century later it was 14 per cent and, as of 2017, more than 80 per cent of people residing in Canada and the US live in cities. As well as the difference in location, attitudes have changed too. Conservationists are appalled at the whole-hearted destruction of wolves in the past and now understand the important role wolves play in ecosystems. Many feel that ranchers are doing too little or nothing at all to prevent wolf predation and are also concerned about livestock being grazed on public land where, all too often, little in the way of protection is provided. In a twist of fate, those who live far from wolves are the ones who want them around. Today, they are in the majority and their voices are loud and clear.

In 2013, the Washington Department of Fish and Wildlife invited a broad range of livestock producers, hunters and others to work together to recommend strategies for reducing conflict with wolves. The Wolf Advisory Group has done much to smooth the rough edges of divided opinions. Unfortunately, all the collaboration, assistance and education did not prevent some ugly situations. In 2014, a Washington state rancher tried a few strategies to deter wolves from killing his sheep but was unsuccessful. Officials from the Washington Department of Fish and Wildlife eventually shot one wolf. The rancher says he lost 300 sheep worth about $100,000, but that wasn't the end of his problems. He started getting a lot of crank phone calls, there was an attempt at identity theft, and social media postings announced a three-day party at his ranch complete with free food, drinks, music and camping. He suspects most of the problems were caused by people angry over the wolf being shot. Other ranchers feel intimidated about signing up for or letting it be known they're participating in a coexisting-with-wolves program. After Fish and Wildlife officials, ranchers and others received death threats, a new state law was passed in May 2017, exempting personal information, such as names and locations, from being publicly disclosed regarding people who report or respond to wolf attacks. This includes anyone reporting wolf predation on their livestock, participating in a state program to prevent attacks, and killing problem wolves.

Livestock producers in Canada have the same problems and frustrations as those in the US and Europe but true to the country's reputation as a "polite nation," so far there haven't been any displays of decapitated wolves or publicly known death threats to ranchers and government officials. There are, however, a surprising number of ranchers who are reluctant to say they're involved in or even interested in programs related to coexisting with wolves. And accessible, up-to-date statistics on livestock predation by wolves in Canada are pretty well impossible to find. Part of the problem is proof. Each province has its own rules for filing a predation claim, including the type of livestock, predators that are covered under the program and the rate of compensation. What they all share is the need for a dead animal whose death can be attributed to a wolf or wolves. Sometimes livestock just disappears; other times scavengers destroy the evidence before a claim investigator arrives. Training has been implemented to show ranchers how to document and verify wolf kills but the death of an animal is often only part of the cost. There's also the reduced sale value of other animals due to stress-related weight loss, the time spent treating injured animals, cows that don't conceive or abort due to stress, and so on.

United States Department of Agriculture stats for 2010 documenting cattle deaths listed the following causes: respiratory problems at 26 per cent, digestive problems at 13 per cent, calving problems at 12 per cent and weather at 12 per cent. Deaths caused by animals were: coyotes at 3 per cent, domestic dogs at 0.6 per cent, cougars and other large cats at 0.5 per cent, vultures at 0.3 per cent, wolves at 0.2 per cent and bears at 0.1 per cent. A 2015 study on wildlife predation in Alberta prepared by the Miistakis Institute states that 74 per cent of beef producers experienced impacts from carnivores. Specifically, 65 per cent of all producers had problems with coyotes, followed by wolves at 31 per cent, cougars at 21 per cent, black bears at 19 per cent and grizzlies at 14 per cent. The difference in numbers for wolf predation reflects the low population of wolves in the US and the greater numbers of them in Canada.

The Alberta study also noted that 62 per cent of Alberta beef producers didn't report losses to the Wildlife Predator Compensation Program. For a lot of ranchers, submitting a claim for compensation isn't worth the time and effort. Also, it's hard to get a hate on for a disease and they can't do anything about the weather but they can kill a predator. The only problem is, killing wolves doesn't always work. Killing one or both of the breeding pair of a pack can splinter the social order, which may result in more animals breeding and lead to more wolves, not fewer. Eliminating the entire pack simply opens up the territory for a new one to move in. Some ranchers don't want the wolves near their place shot because the pack doesn't bother livestock and they don't want to risk a sheep- or cow-killing pack showing up.

A seven-year study initiated by Defenders of Wildlife and published in the February 2017 issue of the *Journal of Mammalogy* states that the use of non-lethal deterrents on one ranch resulted in 3.5 times fewer losses than in adjacent areas not using them. The tools were noisemakers, lights, shepherds and dogs. Other ranchers have experienced some level of success with fladry (brightly coloured ribbon hung on fencing; many say red is best), guard animals such as donkeys or llamas and even cow bells. Agencies promoting non-lethal predation control urge all ranchers to eliminate boneyards, the places where they dump dead animals, as they're a magnet for scavengers. In some US states, Fish and Wildlife officials have put radio collars on a wolf or two in a pack to monitor their activity. When the predators get near free-range livestock, ranchers are alerted so they can increase their deterrents. Some radio collars trigger a noise-making device when the wolf approaches a herd, which scares the predators off. The presence of humans seems to make a difference, too. Some ranchers hire people to ride the range the way cowboys did in the nineteenth century, before livestock producers successfully lobbied to have most wolves killed. Cattle that are aggressive toward predators fare better than those that run away. One rancher watched wolves creep inside an electric fence only to have all 200 cows charge at once, successfully chasing the carnivores off.

Liesl and Cody Lockhart of Candll Lamb & Cattle Co., along with their three young daughters, raise livestock near Debden, Saskatchewan, where the agricultural prairie of the south joins the

forest land of the north. They live in wolf country, not far from Prince Albert National Park, where the predators are protected. In the fall of 2017 they had about 450 sheep and 2,500 cattle. "We got sheep before we got livestock guardian dogs [LGDs] and found out quickly that wasn't working," says Liesl Lockhart. "There was mass panic as we tried to buy any LGD we could find."

Six years later they have eleven LGDs, a mix of five breeds including Great Pyrenees, Kangals and Anatolian shepherds. Each plays a role in the protection of the livestock and complements the others. "If a predator's close, one dog will sound the alarm in the pasture," Lockhart explains. "The white dogs [Great Pyrenees] will gather the flock together in a tight group. They'll stay with the sheep and bark. Then there's a staggered line of dogs moving away from the sheep to create a buffer zone. The Kangals are the ones that go out the furthest and chase the predators. We rarely deal with wolves anymore. Our neighbours do, though, and have lost stock." Preliminary results from a recently completed four-year LGD study in the US indicate that, as the Lockharts found out, a mix of LGDs works best. A bonus is that LGDs will stay with and protect injured or dead livestock until the owner arrives to either care for the animal or document that it was killed by a predator.

In the fall of 2017, wolves were killing 180-kilogram (400 lb) steers the Lockharts were running on leased land about two hours away from the ranch. Even though they mark their dogs with animal-safe orange paint so people know they're LGDs, using LGDs that far from home is risky as they've lost dogs in the past to trappers and

Livestock guardian dogs are proving to be a valuable resource when it comes to preventing livestock predation by wolves. This Anatolian shepherd is wearing a spiked collar. The collar protects the dog's throat if it gets into an altercation with a predator and also lessens aggressive behaviour between livestock guardian dogs. Photo by Liesl Lockhart hunters who thought the dogs were feral. So the Lockharts called in a predation specialist who used lethal control to remove two specific wolves they'd seen multiple times near the cattle. Even with the risk of disrupting pack dynamics, sometimes there's no other choice. In this case, the predation stopped immediately.

The Lockharts have lost a few dogs to predators over the years, especially in the beginning when they didn't have as many as they needed. Anatolian shepherds are big dogs, usually about 81 centimetres (32 in) tall, with mature males weighing 50 to 66 kilograms (110–145 lbs). When a predator killed one, the Lockharts started using spike collars. "Spike collars save the lives of sheep, dogs and wolves," Lockhart points out. "They reduce any aggression between the dogs and protect them if they engage with predators." They also invested in Kangals, LGDs that are about 5 centimetres (2 in) taller than Anatolian shepherds and can weigh up to 82 kilograms (181 lbs) when fully grown. Kangals are fast, strong and agile and have been known to chase predators for up to 23 kilometres (14 mi). Having a pack of LGDs is expensive but it works for the Lockharts and they consider it part of the cost of raising livestock.

Some people have concerns about LGDs being aggressive toward humans, and they can be. The Lockharts had two children, age three and under, when they got their first one. "I wouldn't trust any dog with really young children no matter what the breed," Lockhart says. "But I probably trust my dogs more than most people do. The girls do all the socializing and leash training. Some people can't touch their LGDs but we knew that wouldn't work here, this is a family farm. It is possible to have well-socialized LGDs and for them to be really strong working dogs."

Louise Liebenberg, an Alberta livestock producer and co-owner of Grazerie, Canada's first predator- and wildlife-friendly ranch, gives presentations throughout North America and Europe on raising LGDs and co-existing with wolves. "I run into the same livestock predation problems, anger and arguments about wolves worldwide," she says. "It's a very touchy subject. Sometimes when I'm talking to a bunch of ranchers, the resistance is so high I feel like I'm going to get lynched. But it's no use arguing about wolves, they're here to stay unless we kill them all. I'm more interested in looking at ways to keep my livestock safe."

Along with her husband, Eric Verstappen, Liebenberg raises sheep, cattle and horses on the high prairies of northern Alberta. The couple believes in sustainable, respectful use of the land, which involves protecting it and coexisting with the wildlife that lives there. The many strategies they employ to coexist with predators include composting dead livestock, removing sick and weak animals from the flock, and lambing indoors during the winter when predator pressure is low. They also use flexible electric sheep netting when grazing and are prepared to quickly remove livestock from pastures if necessary.

Liebenberg told me that most of the farmers she talks to do very little to prevent predation, in part due to a culture of expecting the government to solve the problem and not really having the tools, money or time to implement other strategies. Few ranchers trust the research on conflict mitigation, believing that it all comes from anti-ranching lobbies. And some fear reprisals from other ranchers if they express an interest in non-lethal control. "The research is confusing and sometimes slanted," Liebenberg admits. "But people aren't making the translation of practical research to practical applications on the farm. A big problem is the really big grazing reserves with something like two cowboys looking after 3,500 cow and calf pairs."

The ranch has lost one ewe and one calf to wolves over the last 10 years, mostly due to a human management error. Liebenberg usually understands why an incident occurred and alters their management plan to prevent it from happening again. "You can't just use one management system all the time due to habituation; you need to combine various methods." In 2017, a wolf gave birth to seven pups in the middle of the farm. "It was very stressful and we had to be super vigilant until the fall when the pack moved on. Now I have to change my strategy to make sure that doesn't happen again."

Liebenberg counts herself lucky: she has connections in the US and Canada who are willing to help, with some even offering to camp by her livestock to keep watch. She says a lot of Canadian farmers are overwhelmed and scared about what could go wrong and don't feel like they have anyone to turn to for support. Many feel that the traditional method—shooting wolves—is the only solution. After a spike in wolf predation on cattle in 2008, ranchers demanded a bounty be put in place to help reduce wolf numbers and the Alberta government agreed. "The stats on predation have gone back to what they were before but the bounty remains in place," Liebenberg says. "In Switzerland they have an emergency program to help farmers experiencing problems. A team of people show up with electric fencing and LGDs and support the farmer until the wolves move on. They also teach the farmer different ways of doing things. I'd like to see all the money spent on dead wolves funnelled into a program like that."

The old way of thinking was that wolves needed remote areas to live in but as populations rebound, it's becoming apparent that, with enough prey and protection from humans, they can live anywhere. Ranches that abut forested land will have more problems and small operations will take a harder hit. As long as there are wolves, some predation will occur. For many, it's a new era in ranching, and it will take time and money to work out the kinks. There's no one solution that fits all; each ranch needs an individual predation program and must be prepared to modify it over time.

Last year a sheep farmer with a small operation told Liebenberg that he was losing a sheep a day and would be out of business in a month. She lent him one of her LGDs and the problem stopped the day the dog arrived. "I like talking to individual farmers as they're more open to change," she says. "I try to move the conversation away from 'is the wolf good or bad?' A wolf makes its living by its teeth. It's up to us to let him know if he's welcome on our farm or not."

Although much of the twenty-first-century crusade against wolves has been about livestock predation, there is a tandem battle taking place. Wild ungulates are wolves' traditional prey. At times and for various reasons, governments decide wolves have killed too many. Some claim pressure is exerted by hunters or the manufacturers of firearms and ammunition and there's no denying that ungulate populations can reach alarming lows. This can be due to disease, hard winters, lack of forage, predators and human actions. But when it comes to predators, wolves are the ones that most often end up on the wanted list.

The culling of wolves to save caribou is highly controversial, especially in BC and Alberta. Although some biologists, wildlife organizations and Indigenous people support the culls, a firestorm of opposition has pitted biologist against biologist, prompted environmental organizations to launch lawsuits against government agencies and raised international ire with the public condemnation of the cull by pop star Miley Cyrus, actress Pamela Anderson and wildlife crusader Paul Watson, who organized a successful campaign against the aerial slaughter of wolves in northern BC in 1984.

Caribou and reindeer are the same species (*Rangifer tarandus*) but called by different names in North America and Europe. Both have experienced population declines, primarily as a result of changes to their habitat. The bigger and stockier caribou inhabit most territories and provinces in Canada, as well as some northern US states. There are three types of caribou in Canada: the Peary, found only on islands in the Arctic; the barren-ground, which live on the tundra; and the woodland, which inhabit forested areas. Depending on location, the BC government refers to specific herds of woodland caribou as southern mountain, central mountain, northern mountain, and boreal. Smaller than moose but larger than deer, caribou are recognizable by their long, flat antlers, which may be up to one metre (three feet) long and can be found on both sexes. They have large, scoop-like hooves that distribute their weight over snow, allowing them to run on it without breaking through the top layer as other ungulates often do. Their unique hoof shape also provides an effective tool for scraping away snow to uncover forage.

Like most wildlife, caribou lead a precarious existence. Finding food, birthing and caring for young, enduring extreme weather conditions and evading predators and disease are all part of life. Their populations can fluctuate dramatically under natural conditions. In more recent times, woodland caribou have experienced the added stress of dramatic alterations to the landscape due to climate change, logging, mining and the oil and gas industry, plus recreational development and activities. Their habitat is crisscrossed with roads, as well as seismic and power lines; the stillness is shattered by snowmobiles, trucks and equipment. In some areas these changes have made caribou habitat more welcoming to moose, and wolves have followed.

A creation story of the Inuit describes how the first people feasted on caribou but because they killed only large, strong animals, the herds became vulnerable. So the wolf was created to feed on the weak and old. But now the ratio of wolves to caribou in some places is greater than it was in the past, adding another challenge to the ungulates' survival.

Globally, caribou are listed as vulnerable by the International Union for Conservation of Nature (IUCN), with populations decreasing. Caribou in BC and Alberta are currently classed as endangered by the Committee on the Status of Endangered Wildlife in Canada (COSEWIC). That means provinces are mandated to improve the situation by the federal government. Dwindling caribou herds have been a problem in Canada since the 1940s. In recent years, BC and Alberta have tried a variety of initiatives to reverse the decline. Moratoriums have been placed on new tenures and development for commercial winter recreation and resource industries. Some habitat has been protected—in April 2018, the BC government pledged $2 million to fund caribou

This photo of a wolf carrying the hindquarters of a caribou was taken in Alaska's Denali National Park and Preserve. Caribou and reindeer populations worldwide are declining due to climate change and human-caused fragmentation of their habitat. Photo courtesy of the US National Park Service habitat restoration—and some areas have been closed to snowmobile use. Six years ago, BC spent about $10,000 per animal to transplant 20 caribou from northern BC to the Kootenays in the southeast in an effort to bolster the 14-member Purcell herd. One of the caribou died and, due to weather, the rest were dropped some distance from the herd they were supposed to join, with most ending up in Montana or Washington state. Trial or "passive adaptive management" experiments have involved sterilizing wolves, increased hunting to reduce moose populations, supplemental feeding of caribou, and maternal denning pens, where cow caribou and their newborn calves are protected and fed for a period of time.

In BC, a five-year test wolf cull was launched province-wide in the winter of 2014–15. At that time, the South Selkirk caribou herd in southeastern BC had plummeted to 14. By 2018, at least 24 wolves had been culled from the area and it was believed that only 3 caribou remained. Within the same time span, more than 300 wolves had been culled in the South Peace region of northern BC. The cull and experimental measures are ongoing, and correspondence from the BC government states that a combination of supplemental feeding, maternal penning and wolf culls has improved caribou numbers in some areas.

Since 2005, the Alberta government has culled more than 1,000 wolves by shooting them from helicopters, poisoning them with strychnine and trapping them with neck snares. An early 2018 posting on the government's website noted that most caribou herds in the province were declining with some at risk of expiration. Around that time, the province announced it was suspending portions of its draft plan to protect caribou, as measures to date had already had a negative economic impact on the province. It also requested federal funding to assist with caribou recovery.

No one wants to see caribou disappear, not even one herd. But is it right to kill one animal to save another? It's more common than most people think. A few examples include a test badger cull in Britain in the fall of 2013 to prevent the spread of tuberculosis to cattle, the killing of lake trout in Yellowstone Lake to boost cutthroat trout numbers and, in the late 1990s, the culling of Pacific harbour seals in the Courtenay River on Vancouver Island in an effort to rejuvenate runs of chinook salmon and steelhead trout. It was eventually discovered that part of the seal problem was due to lighting on two bridges that showed hungry seals exactly where the migrating juvenile fish were.

Most people accept the fact that the human footprint on the environment is responsible for many, if not all, wildlife issues, and support the "we caused the problem, we need to fix it" plan of action. Statistics show that people—albeit uneasily at times—will generally condone killing one animal to save another if it's a short-term endeavour, but balk if the plan continues for a lengthy period of time. It's also easier for a government to sell a cull of fish than of a mammal.

Back in 2008, William Lynn, a research scientist at the George Perkins Marsh Institute at Clark University in Massachusetts, suggested that ethics should be part of wildlife management. Ten years later, that concept still hadn't caught on in some jurisdictions. The debate over playing god with wildlife came to the fore in the early 2000s when the cutting of old-growth forests brought the larger, more aggressive barred owl into spotted owl habitat, which traditionally ranged from BC to California. In 2013 it was believed there were only 10 spotted owls left in BC. Despite protests, BC has removed more than 150 barred owls and the US Fish and Wildlife Service has culled around 1,145. Spotted owl populations have increased where barred owls were removed and have continued to decline where they were not.

Science is big on fact and scant on feelings. In fact, people often say wildlife decisions should be based on science, not emotion. That might be true for humans but what about the animals? Authors Carl Safina and Marc Bekoff explore the inner lives of animals in their respective books *Beyond Words* and *The Emotional Lives of Animals*.

Safina describes Twenty-one, a wolf in Yellowstone National Park, showing kindness toward a younger, sickly sibling—which the others ignored—by spending time with him. Safina felt so strongly about the emotional capacity of wolves that he elevated them to a "who," a pronoun usually reserved for humans, rather than an "it," which is routinely used for animals. Bekoff points out that wolves are able to read and express their feelings to others. And that, as well as being more social than coyotes or dogs, they have more varied facial expressions and tail positions that they use to communicate. In *Among Wolves*, biologist and long-time wolf researcher Gordon Haber wrote about the deep bonds between wolves, as well as their empathy, family traditions and culture. He was so moved by what he witnessed that he stopped using the word *pack*, replacing it with *family group*.

Discussing the subject, writer Susan Ketchen says, "I think this is all a shift happening in our culture. We need to dump the pejorative 'anthropomorphic' and recognize that animals are capable of complex cognition and emotions. If we have to kill them for food or culls, so be it, but let's not pretend that it's insignificant, that we're just cutting down weeds." In May 2015, the New Zealand government echoed this sentiment by formally recognizing animals as sentient beings that can experience "positive and negative emotions, including pain and distress." They backed the announcement up with legislation to ensure that animals are treated with care and compassion.

Ethics is basically a discussion about whether something is morally right or wrong. How that something is done is part of the equation. BC and Alberta have culled wolves with poison, snares and aerial sharpshooters in low-flying aircraft. The chase, noise and injuries of some animals before being shot to death from the air must cause physical and emotional distress. Strychnine does not provide a swift, pain-free death and frequently affects unintended animals, either directly or from scavenging the remains of the targeted animal. Snares are banned in much of Europe and the Canadian Federation of Humane Societies says they cause an "agonizing and prolonged death." In a 2014 *National Geographic* article, Mary Pearl, a conservationist with the City University of New York, pointed out that the majority of animal ethicists believe that avoiding suffering is more important than avoiding death.

The British badger cull of 2013 was halted as it was determined the animals suffered for five minutes which, under national guidelines for the humane treatment of animals, was deemed too long. In the fall of 2016, a report prepared by members of the BC Provincial Mountain Caribou Recovery Science Team recommended adding a portion of the Revelstoke-Shuswap region to the aerial shooting of wolves program. The report also states, "There are no humane methods to directly reduce wolf numbers, but aerial removal is the only method of killing enough wolves (and entire packs) to reduce wolf densities with no risk of by-catch."

So, how effective are wolf culls? Culling wolves may assist at-risk caribou herds in the short term but it's a lot like bailing the ocean, and would need to continue until herds have increased significantly. Correspondence in late 2017 from the BC Ministry of Forests, Lands, Natural Resource Operations and Rural Development stated the overall caribou population within the wolf control areas had increased from 166 to 192 caribou over the past year. Some herds have stabilized but not experienced any gains. Government officials estimate that Alberta caribou herds are shrinking by about 8 per cent annually, with some declining by twice that much. For the cull to be effective, biologists estimate that 80 per cent of wolves in caribou habitat would have to be killed every year indefinitely.

Both the BC and Alberta governments acknowledge that the primary cause of caribou decline is the human-caused degrading, destruction and fragmentation of caribou habitat. In October 2017, the federal government released a plan calling for a minimum of 65 per cent of caribou habitat to be left undisturbed. In Alberta, more than 80—some say as high as 96—per cent of some caribou habitat has been damaged or fragmented by commercial development and activities. Even if Alberta was willing and able to shut down commercial industry in critical caribou habitat, some scientists believe it could take 20 to 30 years for the habitat to regenerate enough to sustain caribou. Stan Boutin, a professor in the biological sciences department at the University of Alberta, estimates it could take up to 50.

In addition to habitat destruction, climate change is affecting the undisturbed lichen-rich environments caribou depend on, as well as birthing times and the appearance of springtime plants. Studies predict that if greenhouse gas emissions remain the same, North American caribou could lose close to 90 per cent of suitable habitat by 2080. If the scientific crystal ball gazing into the future is correct, caribou habitat may be restored in 30 to 50 years but 10 to 20 years after that, climate change could wipe the ungulates out. In the meantime, thousands of wolves could be killed for naught.

"Caribou in the north are already being affected by climate change," says Paul Paquet, an internationally recognized authority on carnivores, especially wolves. "The science has been very clear for some time that killing wolves is not effective and would only provide a little window of time for caribou. It appears that caribou are on a long-term slide to extinction; not because of what wolves and other predators are doing but because of what humans have already done."

Humans have a long tradition of killing wolves, usually in inhumane ways. We banish them for interfering with livestock and use them as scapegoats for errors in land management. But we now know that wolves have a place on the earth and that they are a valuable component in the checks and balances of wildlife. Mistakes are easily made but, once recognized, need to be rectified. Better ways of dealing with livestock predation and habitat disturbance and fragmentation must be implemented and governments need to step up to the plate to ensure people have the knowledge and resources to make that happen.

CHAPTER 8

WOLF WATCHERS

Nothing in life is to be feared,
it is only to be understood.
—MARIE CURIE

SUDDENLY PAUL PAQUET WAS SURROUNDED BY AGITATED WOLVES. HE wasn't sure what was going on, then realized pups were present and left immediately. The biologist had recently canoed into Manitoba's Riding Mountain National Park to study wolves and hadn't known the den was there. That night the wolves visited his camp three kilometres (two miles) away. Paquet sat in his tent while one wolf peed on it and another pressed its face into the thin fabric, providing a close-up outline of its head. "They were there about fifteen minutes," Paquet says. "At first I wondered if they were more unhappy about my unexpected visit to the den than I'd thought, but they were just checking things out. I didn't know their den was so close and they didn't know my tent was nearby. Their tolerance of my intrusion was a surprise."

With 45 years of research and more than 100 peer-reviewed articles to his credit, Paquet has an abundance of wolf stories, but two are especially memorable for him. The first took place in a remote village in the Italian Apennines when he was six. "My dad stopped at a gas station and I wandered around back. I've always had an affinity for dogs and was transfixed by the big one watching me. As I moved toward it, the gas station attendant ran out and grabbed me by the shoulder, yelling in Italian: 'Not a dog! Not a dog!' That was the first time I saw a wild wolf."

The second event occurred when he was studying the social behaviour of some orphaned wolves being raised in captivity in Portland, Oregon. Fourteen-year-old Susan Bragdon asked Paquet if she could work with him and, by doing so, turned wolf research on its head. Her job was to observe and record social behaviour related to positions within the pack, but Paquet noticed she was recording different behaviour than what he'd seen over the last couple of years. One day he discreetly watched her and was shocked to discover that she was noticing behaviour he'd missed. "She identified an adult female as the dominant wolf of the pack," he says. "That was unheard of in the 1970s; everyone believed that a male was always dominant. That was an important insight for me. I'd gone into the study with preconceived ideas but she was uncontaminated by the prevailing view of the times so saw what was really going on." Bragdon, now an international lawyer and US patent attorney, later presented the new information at a global wolf symposium.

Humans have studied wolves ever since they first trod the same path. In the early days, it was a matter of survival to determine if the canid posed a threat or if the human should kill the wolf to obtain its warm fur pelt. Later there was an exploration of body parts to be used as medicine or ceremonial regalia. Eventually trappers, hunters and ranchers studied wolves in order to eliminate them more effectively. It was only about 100 years ago that biologists began a more formal investigation of the beast. A lot of early research involved examining wolf carcasses and while that provided information on size and body condition, it did little to enlighten people about wolf behaviour. Because wolves are so elusive, research of live animals often took place in zoos and private menageries. It's been said that more wolves have been studied in captivity than any wild animal except primates. Observing captive animals is where the terms *alpha*, *beta* and *omega* came into use regarding wolf social structure and hierarchy. In the past, many captive wolves kept together were not from the same family group so exhibited different behaviour than wolves in the wild. It's now known that wild wolf packs are family groups and that the alpha male and female are the animal equivalent of human parents.

Although research on captive wolves provides valuable insights into wolf behaviour, it wasn't until Adolph Murie was sent to evaluate the relationship between wolves and Dall sheep in Mount McKinley National Park (now Denali National Park) in the southern interior of Alaska that science got a glimpse of the real wild wolf. Based at Sanctuary Field Cabin No. 31, the 40-year-old biologist meticulously recorded everything he observed about wolves from 1939 until 1941 and continued to study wolves and other wildlife throughout his National Park Service career. His book *The Wolves of Mount McKinley* is regarded as a classic, and his *Ecology of the Coyote in the Yellowstone*, published in 1940, is the first book to speak out against the killing of predators in national parks. Another first was Murie's discovery that wolves eat mice.

Writers, as well as scientists, have a long history of being attracted to wolves. Tall tale or not, Farley Mowat's 1963 *Never Cry Wolf* placed the canid in the public's eye in a way that had never been done before. Mowat's book describes the wolves he studied when he was an employee of the Dominion Wildlife Service in Canada's Arctic along the border of Manitoba and what is now Nunavut in the late 1950s. His job was to investigate the "carnage being wreaked upon the deer [caribou] population by hordes of wolves." His book, however, portrayed the canids as benign, even likable creatures, and he received a lot of flak over some of the details. One of the more controversial was his comment that the mainstay of the wolves' diet was mice, not caribou. Some say Mowat relied on Murie's research as much as his own observations.

Despite, or perhaps because of, the blend of fact and fiction, *Never Cry Wolf* shifted people's perception of wolves from "beasts of waste and desolation," as Theodore Roosevelt once called them, to ones worthy of protection. When *Never Cry Wolf* was translated into Russian it even influenced the treatment of wolves in that largely die-hard wolf-hating country. Mowat probably had no idea how timeless his book would be. Sixty years ago he was criticizing the Canadian government for conducting wolf culls to save caribou and, if still alive, he would probably be protesting the wolf culls taking place in BC and Alberta today. One thing has changed, though. My 1963 copy of *Never Cry Wolf* calls it a "charming and engrossing scientific study" while the 1992 McClelland & Stewart version bills it as juvenile fiction.

Mowat blended fancy and fact in *Never Cry Wolf*, presenting himself as a young biologist who closely observed wolves in their natural habitat—even going so far as to mark his territory the same way they did. Ludwig "Lu" Carbyn is the wildlife biologist who turned Mowat's fantasy into reality. In the early 1970s, as an employee of the Canadian Wildlife Service, Carbyn was sent to Jasper National Park to determine why wolves weren't keeping the elk population in check. Although Carbyn may not have intentionally urinated on any territorial boundaries, he found a wolf rendezvous site and inserted himself into the landscape. Basing his strategy on that of Jane Goodall's 1960 study of chimpanzees in Tanzania, Carbyn approached the rendezvous site every day, sitting in the same place and slowly increasing the amount of time he spent there. Eventually the wolves became habituated to his presence and paid him no mind. And so a new era of scientific wolf watching began. The upshot of Carbyn's investigation? Wolves in that part of the park had been decimated by a predator control program, leaving too few to curb the elk population.

While Carbyn was observing wolves and elk in Jasper National Park, a unique study focusing on wolves and moose was taking place on Isle Royale in the US. The long, skinny island is tucked in the northwest corner of Lake Superior in Michigan, not far from Thunder Bay, Ontario. The nearest land is 24 kilometres (15 mi) away; frigid water, high winds and wicked winter storms can make access difficult if not impossible. In recent times, the island's wolf and moose populations have been measured by births and deaths as the arrival of newcomers and dispersals away from the island have been impossible. This portion of Isle Royale National Park is also the site of the longest continuous study of any predator-prey system in the world. As of 2018, wildlife biologists have been documenting the relationship between wolves, moose and the ecosystem for 60 years.

When moose came to the island in the early twentieth century, via either an ice bridge from Canada or swimming across from nearby Minnesota, they found a remote, isolated strip of land of about 544 square kilometres (210 sq mi) covered in boreal forest, small lakes and bogs. Adolph Murie began the first study of the moose during the winter of 1929–30. There were no predators so death occurred due to old age, hard winters or lack of forage. Everything changed when wolves crossed an ice bridge from Canada in the mid-1940s. The Wolf-Moose Project was launched in 1958 under the direction of Durward Allen, a wildlife ecologist at Purdue University in Indiana. Wolves had been hunted to extinction in nearly all the contiguous United States, making Isle Royale one of the few places where they were present.

Accessible only by private boat, seasonal ferry or seaplane, the island is unique in that most visitors—from early Indigenous people to modern-day tourists—typically spend time there only in the summer. There are no roads or full-time residents and development is limited. The area became a national park in 1940 and is closed to the public from November to mid-April each year. It's as close to a lab setting as you can get and still be wild.

Most ecological studies are considered long-running if they last five years but Allen opted to continue beyond that time span. For seven weeks each winter, a research team observes moose and wolves, charting their numbers and recording data, getting around mostly in a small ski-plane. Wildlife ecologist Rolf Peterson, then a professor at Michigan Technological University, became project lead in 1975. When I talked to him in 2017, he'd been studying wolf-moose dynamics on Isle Royale for 42 years. He's currently co-investigator, working with John Vucetich, who has headed the project since 2006.

Unknown to Allen at the time, the decision to continue the study beyond five years was a pivotal moment in wolf research. In the beginning, the predator-prey balance seemed to vary little. But a decade in, the moose population had doubled, only to be reduced by half at the end of the next 10 years. In the meantime, the number of wolves had expanded to 50 in three packs, leading researchers to wonder if the abundance of wolves meant the moose would be wiped out. But within two years, canine parvovirus, a new mutant virus from the mainland, had cut the number of wolves to 14. Now the scientists wondered if the wolves would disappear. They survived, although even when the disease had run its course and prey was abundant, wolf numbers never rose above the low teens. Researchers suspected the cause was extensive inbreeding as the wolves were thought to have descended from just a couple of founders. With few predators, the moose lived longer and more calves survived. By 1996 the population had mushroomed to 2,400 but a hard winter, lack of forage and tick infestation killed all but 500. Researchers wondered if the resulting low availability of prey might further threaten the survival of the wolf population. Then the Old Gray Guy showed up.

Old Gray, so named for the amount of white in his coat as he aged, travelled to the island from Ontario in 1997 on an ice bridge, one of five that have formed in the last 20 years, each existing for only a few weeks. He was a welcome addition to the current population, which was sadly lacking in genetic diversity. Old Gray immediately became a very successful breeder in a pack that increased to 10, making it the largest on the island in 20 years. His offspring became breeders in all the resident wolf packs within three years. This genetic rescue allowed the wolves to survive even when the prey base was low. The only problem was that in 2007 the last wolf that wasn't a direct descendant of Old Gray died, leaving a population consisting only of very close relatives. The reproduction necessary to maintain the wolf population faltered and finally ceased altogether.

By 2017 the only two wolves left on the island were a nine-year-old male and his seven-year-old daughter, which also happened to be his half-sister since they shared the same mother. Over the last few years, the male has attempted to breed with the female when she came into heat but she aggressively refused his advances. They were so interbred, it's unlikely any pups would be fertile or even survive. "The decline in the wolf population is due to the lack of new genetic material coming to the island," says Peterson. "In the 1960s there were good ice bridges in eight out of ten years, now there's only about one in ten years. This has become more common with climate change."

With only two wolves on the island, the moose population keeps increasing and there are already signs of reduced forage. December 2016 saw a shift from the traditional hands-off management policy of the US National Park Service when they announced the possibility of reintroducing 20 to 30 wolves to Isle Royale within three to five years. Although the 60-year-old genetic lineage of the original wolves will probably be lost, new wolves will preserve the integrity of the island's ecosystem.

"It would have been good if the introduction happened five years ago when there were still native wolves on the island," says Peterson. "If they reintroduce wolves now, it will be starting a whole new population. But without predators, moose will destroy the balsam fir and most other tree species. The forest canopy is already disappearing in parts of the island that have been over-browsed. If that continues forest degradation will be dramatic and all species on the island will be affected."

There have been many surprises on Isle Royale but two significant events stand out for Peterson. "The first was the canine parvovirus that almost killed off the wolves and allowed a huge increase in moose and over-browsing. The second was the arrival of Old Gray, which meant the revival of the wolf population. That clearly revealed the importance of genetic diversity. Those were the biggest unanticipated events that transformed the dynamics."

Perhaps the most astonishing revelation of the Wolf-Moose Project is that, when nature is left to its own devices, balance doesn't seem to be present. Instead, widely fluctuating extremes dependent on many factors, including climate, disease, fire, prey and predator numbers, and genetic diversity, or a lack thereof, seem to be the norm. This raises interesting questions about how humans have related to nature in the past, how we are currently doing so and what might be best for the future. The real lesson of Isle Royale is that nature is unpredictable. As John Vucetich notes on the project's website: "Every five-year period in the Isle Royale history has been different from every other five-year period—even after 50 years of close observation. The first 25 years of the chronology were fundamentally different from the second 25 years. And the next five decades will almost certainly be different from the first five decades."

The knowledge from 60 years of observation on Isle Royale has come from analyzing the past, not predicting the future. And if humans can't predict what will happen in the relatively closed ecosystem of Isle Royale, how can they do so in more complex ecosystems where the human footprint is larger and the dynamics of wildlife and vegetation are constantly changing? Even so, it seems to be human nature to want to manage the land and all that's on it. And sometimes we're successful.

Reintroducing wolves to areas where they were once populous is not new. The US federal government has been attempting to reintroduce captive-born red wolves and Mexican grey wolves to the wild since 1987 and 1998 respectively, with limited success. And in 1995 and 1996, 35 Canadian grey wolves were relocated to the wilderness of central Idaho. The wolves weren't warmly welcomed. In his memoir, *Wolfer*, Carter Niemeyer mentions a handmade sign in an Idaho store window that summed up the general feeling: "Kill all the God damn wolves and the people who put them here." But when 14 grey wolves from the Hinton, Alberta, area arrived in Yellowstone National Park in 1995, joined by 17 wolves from Pink Mountain near Fort St. John, BC, in 1996, the results amazed everyone. What was unusual was the number of wolves relocated and that researchers were able to document the changes to the ecosystem.

As the world's second-oldest national park, Yellowstone is a grand expanse of rivers, forests, grasslands and canyons, as well as hot springs and geysers. It also includes part of the Rocky Mountains. Most of the nearly 9,000 square kilometres (3,475 sq mi) of parkland is located in the northwest corner of Wyoming, with small portions spilling over into Montana and Idaho. More than four million people visit the park each year to enjoy the scenery, hike and view wildlife. Parks weren't sanctuaries for wildlife when Yellowstone was created in 1872. On the contrary, park officials in North America and other parts of the world often eradicated predators to create havens for ungulates. It's estimated that Yellowstone's last wolf pack was exterminated in 1926. Of course, the lack of predators meant the elk population exploded and over-browsing became a concern. From the 1930s until 1968, park officials culled elk in an attempt to deal with the problem. By the late 1960s, however, early environmental movements were advocating for change. The creation of the US Endangered Species Act in 1973 required the government to take meaningful steps to restore species in danger of becoming extinct. All wolf populations in the lower 48 states were classified as endangered in 1974.

The first eight Canadian wolves arrived in Yellowstone on January 12, 1995, with six following a week later. Still in their shipping crates, the wolves were transported by bobsled to temporary wolf-proof holding pens a little less than half a hectare (one acre) in size. Each family group, with wolves ranging in age from about nine months to five years old, was given its own pen, which was guarded from a distance to make sure no unauthorized people wandered into the area. Twice a week the wolves were fed ungulates that had died in or near the park and all human contact was kept to a minimum. Several of the animals rebelled against captivity. One managed to wriggle its way over the overhang of a three-metre (ten-foot) fence to freedom. He then tunnelled his way into the pen to release the others. This wolf and two others had already worn their teeth down by gnawing on the pen in an effort to escape.

Finally, with great anticipation the doors to the other acclimatization pens opened on March 21. Biologists and a few reporters

waited ... and waited ... but the wolves didn't seem interested in leaving. It wasn't until Dave Mech, a senior research scientist with the United States Geological Survey, suggested the wolves might associate the doors with their human captors that holes were cut in the rear of the pens. Each wolf had been radio-collared and, after the "back doors" were created, signals indicated they spent some time going in and out before loping off into the vastness of Yellowstone. For the first time in nearly 70 years, the snow was dimpled with wolf tracks.

The reintroduction was considered a non-essential experiment and, of course, controversy was rampant. Nearby ranchers didn't want wolves at all; some people felt that nature shouldn't be tinkered with and others claimed that by using Canadian wolves, a non-native species was being brought into the park. Doug Smith, senior biologist at the Yellowstone Center for Resources and head of the Yellowstone Wolf Project, has laid the non-native species rumour to rest numerous times. The original wolves and the newcomers were all grey wolves and when older skulls at the Park museum were compared with skulls of of Canadian wolves that died in Yellowstone, there was only a slight variation in size, meaning any difference was insignificant. Politics and the courts have been involved in the Yellowstone Wolf Project almost from day one, with the status of the wolves ping-ponging back and forth from endangered to not, and overall management of wolves shifting from federal to state government and back again.

Fortunately, the conflict has done nothing to alter the overwhelming success of what Smith calls one of the most important

In 1995 and 1996, wolves from Canada were relocated to Yellowstone National Park. The last wolf pack in the park had been killed in 1926. This wolf is being released from its shipping container into a temporary pen at Rose Creek. Photo by Jim Peaco, US National Park Service acts of wildlife conservation in the past century. The wolves not only survived, they thrived. Park records show three packs with a total of 21 wolves in 1995 (some wolves bred in the pens and had litters that year), steadily increasing to a high of 13 or 14 packs with 174 members in 2003. Some wolves stayed in the park, others dispersed to nearby states or even farther. The original plan called for additional wolves to be reintroduced but that proved unnecessary. Ranchers still aren't thrilled but a growing stream of tourists flow into the park to watch wolves and the economic benefit ripples out into nearby communities. As of May 2017, the National Park Service estimated that people visiting Yellowstone to see wolves brought $35 million to the area annually.

The presence of wolves also rippled out through the landscape. Among other prey, they killed cattle, coyotes and elk. The cattle predation was less than expected, the killing of coyotes didn't prove critical, and fewer elk was good news as there had been too many. The presence of wolves makes elk more cautious. They don't linger near rivers and streams to eat willow and aspen and, when they do browse on these delicacies, they're on the lookout for predators. This is what's known as the "landscape of ecology" or "landscape of fear," where just the possibility of a predator being nearby is enough to alter behaviour. Although some biologists consider the premise overrated, it's probably at least partially responsible for prompting Yellowstone elk to move around enough to allow the willows and aspen—which, in many cases, had been nibbled to stubs—to flourish again.

Willow grows well in the elevated water tables that occur near beaver dams, and beavers like munching on willow, so when beavers reappeared in Yellowstone after a long absence, it was a win-win situation. A bonus was that the marshlands the beavers created attracted songbirds that had been missing from the region for decades. It seemed to be what scientists call a trophic cascade: a situation where one predator (wolves) kills or alters the behaviour of their prey (elk), allowing that animal's prey or food source (willows) to expand, ultimately affecting the entire ecosystem. There's a lovely short video titled *How Wolves Change Rivers* that celebrates wolves and the trophic cascade they created in Yellowstone.

But is that really what happened? There's no denying that wolves contributed to change in Yellowstone's ecosystem and that they were given the credit when elk populations dropped, but other factors were at work as well. For some time hunters had been allowed to kill elk that roamed outside park boundaries. In 1995, the year the first wolves arrived, hunting doe elk was also permitted. Climate change was having an effect on the landscape, cougars returned to the park and were preying on elk and, sometime in the early 1990s, lake trout were illegally introduced into Yellowstone Lake. The new fish began displacing the smaller cutthroat trout native to the area. Cutthroat trout spawn in shallow water and were a regular part of grizzly bears' diet. As cutthroat populations decreased, grizzlies found it difficult to scoop up lake trout spawning in deeper water and began to prey on elk calves. So many changes were happening in the park at or around the same time, making it impossible to credit one animal as the cause of it all.

As the elk population declined so did the wolves, most likely affected by having less prey as well as outbreaks of canine distemper and mange. As of December 2016, at least 108 wolves in 11 packs more or less lived full-time in the park. The population averaged 83 to 108 wolves from 2009 through 2016. Doug Smith, who was involved with the reintroduction from the start, admits that wolf numbers never got as high as they expected based on the prey base, leading him to speculate that once wolf populations reach a certain density, social regulation of their numbers occurs naturally.

Nonetheless, more than 20 years after wolves were reintroduced, Yellowstone remains a mecca for studies on how wolves affect an ecosystem, the benefits of an intact ecosystem and, most of all, how everything that happens to one aspect of nature splashes over onto another. Now, hundreds of thousands of people go to Yellowstone every year for what's been called the best wolf watching in the world. The wide terrain of the Lamar Valley means it's possible at times to see more than one pack at once and the throngs of people lined up at the roadside with their zoom lens cameras and spotting scopes can't get enough of it. At least one local resident goes wolf-watching every day and it's not unusual for people living farther away to make multiple visits per year. The descendants of the Canadian wolves now enjoy status as media darlings.

The biggest thrill for all researchers is to learn something new about their subject and that's just what happened when the Raincoast Conservation Foundation started studying wolves on BC's central coast. Most people know that wolves primarily prey on ungulates and also eat smaller animals like mice and hares. Not everyone knows that some wolves also eat a lot of fish. There are numerous accounts of wolves stealing fish from Indigenous weirs and low tide traps, as well as video clips of wolves and grizzly bears fishing nearly shoulder to shoulder along Alaskan rivers. Look up Brook Falls, Alaska, and you'll find more bear-watching websites than you can shake a salmon at. That's because every summer, many of the Katmai National Park and Preserve's brown bears make their way to the river to feast on sockeye that are swimming and jumping up the high falls on their way upstream to spawn. In July 2007, folks gawking at the large grizzlies saw another creature just as intent on the food-laden water. A grey wolf found a spot among the bears, watched the water, then jumped in to snag a fish. The female, which appeared to be nursing, carried the salmon into the trees only to reappear

Some wolves catch and eat a lot of fish. Many wade into shallow streams to catch fish as they're swimming upstream to spawn. Others, like this female, jump into fast-flowing and deep water to grab their meal. Photo by Paul Stinsa within minutes and repeat the process. Within an hour she'd caught 15 fish, which viewers suspect she was taking to a den or passing on to another wolf to do so.

Wolves that eat fish aren't that unusual. Research indicates that the now extinct Ezo wolf of Hokkaido in northern Japan ate marine mammals, as well as salmon. In times gone by, wolves were seen pulling salmon from the Columbia River in Oregon. Wolves in Yellowstone National Park eat trout while those in northwest Denali National Park take advantage of chum and coho (silver) salmon runs. As far removed from each other as these fish-eating wolves are, they all have one thing in common. They're typically using these resources to supplement the primary mainstay of their diet: ungulates. But there are wolves that rely on fish, marine-oriented mammals such as seal, mink and river otter, as well as clams and other seafood for the bulk of their food. These wolves once inhabited the temperate rainforests that rimmed the Pacific coast from southern Alaska to northern Mexico. Now those rainforests are only found in southeast Alaska and BC north of Howe Sound.

BC's central coast is where these unique seafood-eating wolves have been studied most extensively. The area isn't for everyone. In fact, the majority who see it do so from a plane or boat. Not many people actually put foot to ground. If you don't know what you're doing, the ragged collection of islands and far-reaching inlets makes it easy to get turned around and the open Pacific Ocean can push in rain, wind, fog and big swells any time of year. Inland, rugged mountains boast snow-capped peaks and heavily scarred rock faces, while along the coast, the temperate rainforest can be dense and dark. Tucked away in sheltered bays are Indigenous villages: ancient sites buried under a tangle of salal, as well as currently inhabited communities.

Ian McAllister first visited the central coast in 1990. The landscape and the lack of a large-scale conservation plan for it made an impression on him. Twenty-seven years later, he's left his mark on the land. In 1996, McAllister and his wife, Karen, along with current executive director Chris Genovali, wild salmon program coordinator Misty MacDuffee, senior scientist Paul Paquet and others created the Raincoast Conservation Foundation (RCF). The organization bases its studies on rigorous, science-based primary research and has been integral to the research and protection of the land and waters of the area.

Initially, RCF chose bears and salmon as the focus of its studies. "Bears only took us so far in our understanding of the coast," says McAllister, now the executive director of Pacific Wild. "Grizzlies weren't represented on the large island system at that time and hibernate for part of the year. But everywhere we went, we bumped into wolves. They're the uncontested apex predator of the rainforest." What surprised him the most were the social bonds and structure of the wolf packs he saw, as well as their habitual nature. Before he understood how regular they were in their seasonal cycles of travel and life, he wandered around looking for them. "Eventually, I began to let the wolves' habits direct my movement," he explains. "It was very challenging at first, but I learned that wolf rhythms, like human rhythms, repeat based on previous success."

Part of 2000 and 2001 was dedicated to the study of wolves from Cape Caution north to the Portland and Observatory canals, which border southeast Alaska. For Chris Darimont, then an RCF scientist and PhD student at the University of Victoria, these were the most adventuresome years of his life. "I was in my mid-twenties, working in an incredible land- and marine-scape," he says. "We covered thousands of kilometres of coastline by sailboat and speedboat and I worked with a very knowledgeable Indigenous man, Chester Starr. He was a tracker, hunter and fisher from the Heiltsuk Nation. He'd spent a lot of time by himself outdoors when he was young so his VHF radio call sign was 'Lone Wolf.' I learned a lot from Chester about wolves and his people's presence on the land and water, as it is now and was in the past."

As the crew made their way up the coast, they stopped on sandy beaches and tidal flats to look for wolf sign. Scat was observed visually, then packaged up for lab analysis later. In the spring, when wolves shed their winter coat, fur was collected from their beds. All of the work was conducted in a non-invasive manner, which meant the wolves weren't captured in live traps, sedated or radio-collared. What startled Darimont, now a science director at RCF, as well as Raincoast Chair in Conservation Science at the University of Victoria, was how connected the wolves were to the ocean. "Everyone thinks of wolves as a terrestrial predator," he says. "Their behaviour and ecology is linked to ungulates. One of the first things Chester asked was, 'Are we looking for wolves that eat deer or wolves that eat fish?' So the Heiltsuk knew all along." Tongue-in-cheek, Darimont refers to BC coastal wolves as "Canada's newest marine animals."

Another revelation was the size of some of the wolves' territory. "In very similar habitat in southeast Alaska, wolves normally have around two hundred square kilometres of habitat but on an offshore island group southwest of Bella Bella, they were surviving on twenty-two square kilometres of land," Darimont explained. "There were no deer left so they were almost completely subsidized by the ocean." It's possible that some wolves living on outer islands may seldom, if ever, see a deer.

It was soon evident that the shore was the wolves' highway, with the ebb and flow of tides providing the green or red lights for easy travel. The ocean, rivers and land along the coast served as a smorgasbord, offering fish, barnacles, clams, herring eggs, seals, river otter, mink, geese and sometimes whale carcasses. There are two types of coastal wolves: those that live on the mainland and nearby islands and those that inhabit the outer islands. The mainland and inner island wolves eat more deer, while the wolves on the outer islands can have a diet that is as high as 90 per cent marine-oriented. The difference in diet means that wolves found on the inner and outer islands of the central coast are about 20 per cent smaller than wolves that live in the interior of BC.

Coastal wolves are also known for the red and brown tinge to their coats, similar to the colour of intertidal algae in the area. RCF's nine years of observation and sampling of scat and wolf fur shows genetic, ecological and behavioural differences between coastal wolves and those that live in the interior. A 2009 study on central coast wolves conducted by Darimont, Paquet and others noted that where wolves live and what they eat can affect their behaviour and physical characteristics. It appears that the saying "you are what you eat" applies to wolves as well as humans.

The RCF researchers studied wolves in an unobtrusive, some would say old-fashioned way. Today, advanced technology, such as trail cameras and drones, is making it easier to track and observe wolves without stressing them or influencing their behaviour due to the presence of humans. Wolves are among the most researched mammals in the world, yet after countless studies they continue to amaze both scientist and layperson. We study them, watch them and write about them in an effort to understand. As observers of nature, we long to have answers—but the more we know, the more the mystery surrounds us.

CHAPTER 9

A MYTH AS BIG AS A MOUNTAIN

There's a lot of variability in individual wolf behaviour. Some are quite tolerant of people and others are very wary and skittish.
—JESSE WHITTINGTON

MY LEGS WERE TIRED. WE'D BEEN HIKING ON QUADRA ISLAND FOR three days and I didn't have Rick's thigh and calf muscles, a legacy from his 25 years of tree planting. "I'm heading back," I said, confident that Rick, my partner for 30 years, would catch up with me before I got to the car. The Surge Narrows Trail had been a lovely, peaceful hike with no one else around. Sure enough, just before I reached the parking area, Rick jogged up behind me. We hopped in the Toyota and I took a bite of apple as Rick drove around the corner and stopped for a deer in the middle of the road. It took a couple of seconds for our brains to register that the long-legged animal was actually a wolf. We watched it watch us, then *poof!* it disappeared.

Rick pulled up to the spot where the wolf had been. "It's no use," I said. "It's long gone." Rick pointed and there, just inside the trees, the wolf was staring at us. We stared back, admiring the thick ruff of fur around its neck. Rick asked for the camera and, determined not to lose sight of the wolf again, I searched my day pack by feel. Hoodie, hiking guide and a package of moleskin foam were tossed on the floor and I felt the apple roll off my lap to join them. At last I handed the camera to Rick but as soon as he aimed it at the wolf, the animal was gone. "How does it do that?" I asked, swearing that I hadn't even blinked. I was convinced the show was over but once more Rick pointed and, at the top of a rock the height of a two-storey house, the wolf stood silhouetted against the sky, looking down at us. We experienced heavy-duty eye contact for long, silent minutes. I didn't move, perhaps didn't breathe. Time was fluid, at once stretching into infinity and contracting into a single heartbeat. There was no air, sun or rain. Only steady, yellow eyes. And then it was over.

This time the wolf's vanishing act was for real, or maybe we just couldn't see it in the shadows beneath the trees. As we drove off, I wondered why the camera had spooked it. Had someone shot at the wolf in the past? Or was it just uneasy about anything out of the ordinary? I also wondered how I would have felt if I'd met the wolf in the woods as I hiked out alone. This was years before I ever dreamt of writing about the canids and I knew little about their behaviour. I'd read about packs and was curious why the majority of wolves I'd seen had been on their own, and travelling during the day, when I thought they were usually active at night. But most of all I wanted to know how a relatively large carnivore could be in full view one minute and nowhere to be seen the next.

Another thing I wanted to figure out was why wolves killed people in Europe and Asia but were considered timid and harmless in North America. Analyzing my research, I wondered if land mass had something to do with it. Less land and a denser population in many Eurasian regions means humans and wolves are often in closer proximity to each other than in North America. Also, unlike Eurasia, most early settlers in the New World were armed and able to defend themselves. If people were injured or killed by wolves, others would often hunt the canids down and kill them. And in the early days of settlement, wolves' natural prey was still readily available. Later, as settlement progressed, changes to the landscape and the introduction of livestock in North America precipitated a war on wolves that was faster and far more widespread than any eradication program in Eurasia, resulting in far fewer wolves.

In the spring 2011 issue of *Human–Wildlife Interactions*, researchers Dave Mattson, Kenneth Logan and Linda Sweanor point out that man-eating carnivores are often specific individuals, prides or packs that attack people in a particular location. They also note that this activity is learned and can continue for decades. In North America, these animals were probably among the first destroyed. The wolves that remained had either learned to fear humans and avoid them or lived in wilderness areas where people were seldom seen. Few wolves near human habitation meant there were rarely any problems. When researchers reviewed records regarding wolf attacks on humans, the only ones found for the past 100 years or more were attacks by rabid animals. So for many years, people believed a myth as big as a mountain: that healthy wolves in North America pose no danger to humans.

True, most wild wolves in North America are wary of people. They see us but we rarely see them. Nonetheless, there are documented accounts of aggressive behaviour, attacks and even deaths. In fact, two in-depth reports, "A Case History of Wolf-Human Encounters in Alaska and Canada" by Mark E. McNay and "The Fear of Wolves: A Review of Wolf Attacks on Humans" by John D. Linnell et al., reveal that, although wolf attacks are extremely rare, there has been an increase in aggressive wolf-human encounters in North America since the 1970s. That two large, independent reports, one published by the Alaska Department of Fish and Game and the other by the Norwegian Institute for Nature Research, were published in 2002 is significant.

There have always been wolves around Ein Gedi, a small, isolated kibbutz in Israel near the Dead Sea. But when a camping area was built nearby, wolves got used to eating scraps and food garbage. Eventually they started going into the kibbutz to forage for garbage and eat cats. After numerous attacks, the situation became dangerous for kibbutz residents and campers, so Israel Nature and Parks Authority hazed the wolves with paintballs. They also launched an education program about secure methods of handling garbage and the hazards of leaving pets and pet food outside. Photo by Avishag Ayalon

Each publication involved scores of biologists, law enforcement officers and human-wildlife conflict specialists. They were curious and concerned about changes in wolf behaviour, the reasons why it was occurring and the possibility of increasing conflict with humans.

All wild animals are potentially dangerous. Attacks on humans by grizzly and polar bears, as well as cougars, are well documented. Elk injure more people in Canada's Banff National Park than any other animal, while across the border in Yellowstone National Park, bison hold the same honour. When it comes to North American carnivores though, wolves rank substantially lower on the attack scale than all species of bears, as well as cougars and coyotes.

That isn't always the case in Eurasia. Predatory wolf attacks in certain parts of India are alarmingly frequent. More than 200 children were killed and more injured in the Hazaribagh, Bihar and Koderma regions of India between 1980 and 1995. All were under the age of 16 and alone; most lived in poor, rural areas where agricultural land had replaced forests and the prey base had been depleted. Due to the time span, several packs and generations of packs were likely involved and

exhibiting learned behaviour. In 2012, a 56-year-old Russian woman used an axe to kill a wolf that was attacking her sheep and turned on her. Four years later, after being bitten by a rabid wolf, a Russian man beat it with a stick before strangling it to death with his hands. The summer of 2017, 10 young children were attacked by wolves in Israel's Ein Gedi Nature Reserve. That fall, a coroner stated that a British woman hiking in northern Greece had probably been killed by wolves. Officials in Israel and Greece consider the attacks predatory.

Protected by the European Union and the Berne Convention, wolves are repopulating their ancestral territories in Western Europe. They've been spotted on the outskirts of Brandenburg, Germany, have left scat and tracks in the Forest of Rambouillet, an hour's drive west of Paris, and in 2017, trod Danish soil for the first time in 200 years. Under cover of darkness, they're crossing busy highways and bridges and passing through villages. Some are scavenging garbage instead of hunting traditional prey. Paw prints are found in yards, livestock has been killed and dogs that are used to hunt moose—almost a national pastime in Sweden—have been injured. Some rural communities in Finland provide expensive taxis to take children to school in wolf country. A popular belief in North America is that wolves require vast tracts of wilderness in order to survive. "Wolves Living in Proximity to Humans," a December 2016 paper published by the Swiss-based organization KORA Carnivore Ecology and Wildlife Management, indicates that isn't necessarily so. Out of 31 European countries surveyed, 28 reported that some pack territories included human settlements, and all pack territories in Portugal did. Some featured den sites that have been used for decades and are less than three kilometres (under two miles) from villages.

Although wolves were targeted as vermin in Canada and Alaska, fewer people and large expanses of wilderness meant wolf populations weren't as severely decimated. So more wolves survived in the northern portion of the continent—and that's where more recent attacks against humans have taken place. "A Case History of Wolf-Human Encounters in Alaska and Canada" includes attacks and incidents from Ellesmere Island in the High Arctic south to northern Minnesota, and from Labrador in the east to the Alaska Peninsula in the west. Still, the myth that no healthy wolf would harm a person remains deeply entrenched in North American culture.

Based on data obtained from "The Fear of Wolves" and "A Case History of Wolf-Human Encounters in Alaska and Canada," along with verifiable accounts that took place after the two reports were published, a casual tally I conducted for 1917 to 2017 totalled 4 deaths and at least 58 attacks and 75 incidents involving wild wolves and humans in North America. An attack was defined as physical contact, either directly or by the person fending off a wolf with a tripod, backpack or other item, while an incident involved no physical contact but the wolf came close to the person and showed no fear, or it appeared that the wolf was going to attack but was killed before making contact. The breakdown into 50-year increments was startling. From 1917 to 1967, I found 2 deaths, 13 attacks and 6 incidents. From 1968 to 2017 there were 2 deaths, 45 attacks and 69 incidents. The two deaths between 1917 and 1967 were caused by rabid wolves. Investigators said the two deaths in the latter 50-year period, one occurring in 2005 and the other in 2010, were likely predatory.

There are various explanations for the jump in attacks and incidents. Low wolf populations meant that some regions didn't have any wolves for close to 100 years or more. Where wolves were present, sometimes there were so few that the animals were rarely seen, plus they had learned to avoid people. Some wolf populations were protected, either because of sparse numbers or because they were classed as big game animals with regulated hunting seasons. This protection and the ending of bounties allowed wolf populations to slowly recover and start to expand their range in the 1970s. The human population has grown, too. And as more people moved into urban areas, the popularity of outdoor activities increased, especially after the introduction of mountain bikes, lightweight camping gear and kayaks, which made semi-wild or wilderness areas more accessible to a broader range of people. So over time, people began spending more time in wolf habitat, just as some wolves are now spending more time in human habitat.

Although some wolves in North America may be dispersing or approaching rural areas by chance, others are including human-use areas as part of their territory. Wolves have ventured into the communities of Banff and Tofino at night and "downtown" Ucluelet in the middle of the day, and have been spotted on the outskirts of Missoula, Montana, and in urban areas of Manitoba. Newspaper articles have mentioned that some women in north-central Idaho carry handguns when going for walks and are reluctant to let their children wait for the school bus alone. In 2017, a one- to two-year-old healthy male wolf was discovered in Cloquet, Minnesota, population 12,000, after attacking a dog in a residential street. John Hart, the US government wildlife biologist who investigated the report, was surprised to find wolf scat filled with eggshells, chicken bones and pet hair within the city limits. In an article posted on the International Wolf Center website, Hart noted that he only had to walk a few minutes in any direction from wolf tracks or sign such as scat or fur to find a busy interstate highway, homes and businesses. The sign he discovered indicated that the wolf was not a transient passing through but had been living very close to people for several weeks or more.

In many instances, the small towns are adjacent to wolf habitat and heavily logged areas. Deer and other ungulates have moved near and even into communities to take advantage of garden browsing and as a safeguard against predators. The predators follow their prey, discover new sources of food in household pets or small livestock and are occasionally fed. Due to the rise of human-wolf interactions, some people speculate that certain populations of wolves may be losing their fear of humans, perhaps because they're no longer shot at on sight. All of these scenarios create the potential for more interactions between wolves and people.

The only place a person is guaranteed to see a wolf is a zoo, a sanctuary or maybe Yellowstone National Park. Even people who live, work or spend a lot of time enjoying nature in or near wolf habitat rarely see wolves. Jennifer Patey and Michelle Sexton weren't thinking about wolves when they took their children snowmobiling in a wooded area between Wabush and Labrador City in southwestern Labrador in January 2015. They were shocked when a wolf suddenly appeared and charged the snowmobiles with teeth bared. It bit at the vehicle skis and then stood up on its hind legs, lunging at the three children. The women managed to outrun the wolf, eventually coming across wildlife officers who happened to be in the park checking passes that day. The officers took off after the wolf on their own snowmobiles. They were unarmed so one of them ran over the animal, which died a few minutes later. Tests confirmed the wolf was rabid. Patey and Sexton shudder to think how the encounter might have ended if the wildlife officials hadn't been close by.

It's not unusual for wolves to chase and attack moving vehicles during the furious phase of rabies. On a stretch of highway not far from where Patey and Sexton had their run-in, a rabid wolf wreaked havoc on three vehicles in June 2001, ripping off bumpers and leaving a trail of claw and bite marks behind before being hit by another vehicle. In January of the same year, a rabid wolf punctured a tire and inflicted other damage on an Ontario Provincial Police car in Ramore, Ontario.

Without laboratory tests, it's not always possible to determine if an animal is rabid or not. In "A Case History of Human-Wolf Encounters," McNay notes that people in Alaska often suspect disease when they see a wolf near or in a rural village and choose to shoot it. By checking lab and incident reports, he discovered that most of the wolves showed no sign of rabies and did not appear to be habituated to humans or food-conditioned. Whereas habituated animals are not afraid of humans, a food-conditioned animal has learned to associate a positive reward with people. They become driven to hang out at high-use human areas such as campgrounds to obtain this reward. If they're not habituated, they'll sneak into camps or yards at night. An animal can be food-conditioned but not habituated, and vice versa. McNay believes the Alaskan wolves were simply unfamiliar with people and hadn't learned to fear and avoid them.

William "Mac" Hollan was prepared for flat tires, bugs and bears when he set out on a 4,426-kilometre (2,750 mi) bike ride in 2013 with two buddies from Sandpoint, Idaho, to Prudhoe Bay, Alaska, to raise money for a school charity. On a July afternoon, his companions, Jordan Achilli and Gabe Dawson, stopped for some minor bike repairs. When Hollan heard panting behind him 30 minutes later, he thought they'd caught up to him. He glanced back and his first thought was "Big dog!" but as the animal lunged for his foot, narrowly missing the bike pedal, Hollan changed that to "Wolf!" The 35-year-old student teacher kicked into survival mode. He shifted his bike into high gear, pedalled harder than he ever had before and grabbed the bear spray in his handlebar bag. The wolf got a jolt of pepper spray in the face and dropped back about 6 metres (20 ft). But a few seconds later, it was ripping open the panniers on the back of the bike, leaving a trail of tent poles behind. Hollan blasted the wolf with spray again, with the same result.

He was about 97 kilometres (60 mi) west of Watson Lake on the Alaska Highway with nowhere to go. Relief flooded him when a big rig came around a corner, but despite Hollan's frantic waving, it drove by. Three more vehicles did the same. So far, high speed pedalling and intermittent shots of pepper spray were keeping him out of reach of the wolf but Hollan wasn't sure how much longer the spray or his legs would hold out.

Tom Littlejohns witnessed a common scene while taking photos of wolves feeding on a carcass at a private reserve in the Crazy Mountains near Bozeman, Montana. A grizzly appeared and the fight was on. Although there was lots of growling and snapping, the wolves didn't appear to take any undue risks and managed to evade the bear's long claws. Littlejohns was lying in the snow about 20 metres (22 yds) away but the bear and wolves didn't seem to notice him. As usual, the bear won. Photo by Tom Littlejohns

OPPOSITE, TOP: Although wolves hunt and feed together, they also have strict social hierarchies, with some wolves being more dominant than others. Feeding on a carcass can be a companionable affair but it isn't unusual for one wolf to put another in its place. Photo by Tom Littlejohns

OPPOSITE, BOTTOM: When most people think of wolves' prey, they think of ungulates such as deer, moose and elk. But wolves along the coast of southern Alaska and BC also eat fish, clams and seals. Wolves will feed on dead seals that they discover on shore and will also kill pups and even adult seals that are resting on land. Photo by Cheryl Alexander

ABOVE: These four-month-old Arctic pups are enjoying the sun from the entrance to their den on Ellesmere Island in Nunavut. Tests on some of the well-chewed bones littered around the area indicate the den may have been used for 700 years or more. Photo by Dave Mech

David Smith was camping on Kinnaird Lake in northern Alberta when he saw a buck jump into the water, followed by another splash that turned out to be a wolf. Although the wolf did its best to bite the buck's rump, it soon gave up. The wolf may have been young and inexperienced, as it would be very difficult for a lone wolf to take down a healthy buck in deep water. Photo by David B. Smith

These red wolf pups are probably only a few days old. Like many wild mammals, wolves are blind and deaf for their first few weeks of life and spend most of their time sleeping and being nursed by their mother.
Photo by Ryan Nordsven, US Fish and Wildlife Service

ABOVE: Three wolves run and chase each other through deep snow after feeding on a moose kill in Kluane National Park and Reserve in the Yukon. The other nine members of the pack were too full to move. Photo by John Hyde

OPPOSITE, BOTTOM: Wolves' bodies are built for snow. Long guard hairs and a thick undercoat keep them warm, and wide paws provide excellent traction on snow, ice or rocky terrain. Photo by Doug Smith, US National Park Service

Wolves are often on the move. They trot tirelessly to search for prey, to patrol their territory or to get from one place to another. They put on special bursts of speed when chasing prey. And sometimes they run for fun or when playing with each other. When a wolf is running, it's not unusual to see only one paw on the ground. Photo by iStock/Tomas Maracek

Wolves howl to keep in touch with other pack members, to keep other packs away from their territory and as a way to socialize. They also howl when they're lonely, in pain or grieving. Photo by Cheryl Alexander

ABOVE: Wolves are very active. They have been known to trot 76 kilometres (47 mi) in a 12-hour period and swim up to 13 kilometres (8 mi) of open ocean. This wolf is leaping into Brooks River, in Alaska, to catch sockeye salmon. She caught 15 in a single hour. Photo by Paul Stinsa

OPPOSITE, TOP: Wolves that live along the BC and southern Alaska coast often have reddish and black markings in their fur. No matter where a wolf lives, its fur is usually a colour that helps it blend in with its surroundings. Photo by Grayson Pettigrew

OPPOSITE, BOTTOM: Wolves are curious. They also come close to or into human-use areas far more than most people realize. And despite their name, grey wolves' fur can be any colour from black to creamy white. Photo by Una Ledrew

OPPOSITE, TOP: Eastern wolves are only found in North America. They were once populous in southeastern Canada and the eastern United States, but as European settlers eradicated wolves from the landscape, their numbers dwindled. Eastern wolves are now primarily found in and near Algonquin Provincial Park and are classed as endangered by the Ontario government. Photo by Michael Runtz

OPPOSITE, BOTTOM: Eastern coyotes evolved from interbreeding between eastern wolves and western coyotes. They have a unique genetic background, which can average around 60 to 65 per cent coyote, 25 to 30 per cent wolf and 10 per cent dog DNA. Due to the wolf genes appearing in these coyotes, some people also call them *coywolves*. These hybrids are predominantly found in northeastern North America. Photo by Jonathan G. Way

ABOVE: Coyotes are found in much of Canada and the United States. Some live in the wild and some feel quite comfortable in big cities. Photo courtesy of the US National Park Service

ABOVE: Red wolves were extinct in the wild by 1980. Captive breeding programs have kept the species alive and some wolves have been reintroduced back into the wild in North Carolina. It's estimated there are only about 30 red wolves in the wild today. Photo courtesy of the US Fish and Wildlife Service

OPPOSITE, TOP: The grey wolf is the largest member of the wolf family and the only wolf found in both North America and Eurasia. As seen here, wolves sometimes place their rear feet into the track left by the front paws. Photo by Cheryl Alexander

OPPOSITE, BOTTOM: This female Mexican grey wolf is the dominant female in the Iron Creek pack in New Mexico. Mexican grey wolves were trapped and poisoned into near extinction by 1973. Five were caught and kept in a captive breeding program and some animals have been released in New Mexico. It's estimated that around 114 now live in the wild. Photo courtesy of the US Fish and Wildlife Service, Mexican Wolf Interagency Field Team

Wolves have close family bonds and the entire pack helps look after young ones. When very small, pups get milk from their mother. Later, older pack members regurgitate partially digested meat from kills to provide "baby" food for the pups. Young wolves often lick and nudge the snouts of older wolves hoping to trigger this regurgitation. Photo by iStock/mirceax

Then he saw a steep incline coming up ahead and knew that would be the end of the race. He remembered all the videos he'd watched of wolves running down prey and was filled with terror. He prepared to use his bike and remaining pepper spray to his best advantage when, just before the hill, he spotted an RV coming up behind him. Hollan wheeled his bike into the middle of the road and waved his arms, screaming, "Help me! Help me!" As the RV stopped in front of him, Hollan, still yelling, bolted over the handlebars, bear spray in hand. He ran to the rear door of the motorhome but it was locked so he started climbing in the passenger window. As Hollan sat in the RV shaking and swearing, the wolf attacked his bike, standing over it like it was prey. Another vehicle pulled up and Melanie Klassen got out and started yelling at the wolf, eventually throwing her metal water bottle and hitting it in the head. A few more vehicles stopped and the occupants threw rocks at the wolf. When one hit it on the head, it took off. Around this time Hollan's friends arrived with his tent poles and after Hollan calmed down a bit, the shaken trio continued their journey.

No one really knows why the wolf chased Hollan and attacked his bike. It acted like it had rabies but it's unlikely a rabid wolf would give up. In most incidents, rabid wolves attack whoever is trying to help the victim. Hollan felt like the wolf was trying to run him into exhaustion as if he were prey. The quickly moving bike could have excited the wolf's chase instinct, similar to a running ungulate, and the wolf did bite at the rear of the bike as it would go after prey. Although it's possible, Hollan doesn't think the food in his panniers prompted the chase. And since it ran off, there was no way to determine if the wolf was sick or starving. A biologist Hollan talked to later suggested the wolf may have been protecting its territory. Three wildlife conflict and safety specialists mentioned other possible reasons for the attack. One thought the wolf was acting predatory, while another suspected food conditioning. The third suspected food conditioning was involved but, if that was the case, was surprised that several direct hits of bear spray didn't deter the animal, and wondered about rabies.

Dog trainers believe dogs chase cars and bikes as a predatory response to something moving away from them. This may involve an instinct to attack, an effort to protect their territory or an attempt to chase and play with the moving object. Each of those motives involves the animal's natural prey drive to some degree. The only thing that's certain is that if Hollan didn't have bear spray, had packed it away or had fallen off his bike while using it and someone hadn't stopped to help, the story would probably have a different ending. Ironically, the slogan for the Idaho elementary school where Hollan worked then and now is "Home of the Wolves."

Like Hollan, Hilary Petrus also felt like a wolf may have been sizing him up and trying to wear him out. He was on an afternoon bike ride in July 2015 when he saw something come out on the road toward him. Petrus estimates he was doing about 40 kilometres (25 mi) an hour down a hill on Highway 17 about 140 kilometres (87 mi) east of Thunder Bay, Ontario, when it ran at him and passed close behind the bike. Petrus had worked in the bush for years and seen wolves so he was confident that's what it was. He was surprised by the encounter but not alarmed. But on the way home he spotted the wolf behind a guardrail in the same area. It ran at him again, then loped along about 6 metres (20 ft) behind. This time Petrus felt different about the situation. Partly because he was going uphill and doing only about 6 kilometres (4 mi) an hour and also because the wolf was following him, not just running by. A short while later, a truck came along and stopped to see if Petrus was okay and the wolf took off. Petrus said it looked a bit skinny but seemed otherwise healthy. Because this wolf remained in a certain area, wildlife officials speculate that it was food-conditioned and was spending time near the road as it had obtained food there before.

Not all cyclists manage to avoid contact when a wolf pursues them. In August 2013 a wolf knocked Mario Lagacé off his bike while he was cycling along Route 175 in the Laurentides Wildlife Reserve in southern Quebec. The wolf pinned Lagacé to the ground but did not growl, bite or snarl at him. At the sound of an approaching vehicle, the wolf retreated to the side of the road and Lagacé picked up his bike and started walking away. He flagged down help and, before driving off, he and the driver observed the wolf watching them for at least five minutes. Lagacé later found out that a cyclist had been chased on that section of road the previous month. This wolf may have been sick or hungry and the movement of the bike excited its chase instinct. But once the wolf took its "prey" down, it didn't act aggressive. It's difficult to say what would have happened if a vehicle hadn't come along. Chances are this wolf was also food-conditioned and was not looking to kill but to obtain a reward.

Wolves are built to run, chase and kill, as well as scout out any prey that looks vulnerable. A person hunched over the handlebars of a bike might resemble some sort of ungulate but it's the motion of something moving away quickly that excites the chase instinct. How a person should respond depends on the circumstances. In the case of a rabid wolf, the only choice is to kill it without being bitten or escape—even if it's up a tree—as fast as possible. The canister of accessible pepper spray gave Hollan the edge to stay ahead of the wolf until someone stopped to help. Pepper spray has been successfully used on a variety of animals including domestic dogs, wild elephants and polar bears. Lagacé did the right thing by getting up and walking away. He kept his bike with him, which could be used as a shield or even a weapon against the wolf, and by walking away he reduced the chance of arousing the wolf's predatory drive. Would the wolf have left sooner if Lagacé had faced it, raised his bike over his head and yelled, or used pepper spray? Possibly.

"If something is working, keep doing it; if not, try something else," advises Dave Eyer, wildlife educator and consultant. "Hollan was able to keep the wolf away so that was probably the right choice in that situation. He might have been able to outrun a different wolf. He thought ahead and came up with a strategy of what to do before he reached the incline. But for a different cyclist without his speed and stamina, the 'outrun it' strategy might have failed with tragic results. In general it's not a good plan to try to outrun a wolf on a bike. If the cyclist stops, it removes the chase stimulus and if the wolf is suddenly faced with a screaming, angry human armed with bear spray, it may decide to leave."

Sometimes what seems like an imminent attack is really a mistake. Valerius Geist, professor emeritus of environmental science at the University of Calgary, told me about a December evening in 1965 when he was dragging the skinned carcass of a mountain sheep he'd killed across a frozen lake. Suddenly he saw three wolves, one running straight at him, two hesitantly beginning to circle behind him. Geist kept his rifle trained on the running wolf. When it was about 15 paces away, it veered to the side, picked up his scent and did a backwards somersault attempting to stop. It and the other wolves ran off in separate directions. "I think they may have mistaken me for a crippled caribou bull," Geist explains. "I was carrying my long tripod and spotting scope over my shoulders, which may have simulated antlers of a sort."

The big question is how to determine a wolf's intent in order to make the correct response. When a predator is running toward someone, instinct and emotion tend to take over. And the wrong choice can lead to injury or loss of life—to human or wolf. There are many accounts of wolves running up to people who use moose or other calls while hunting. Most shoot the wolf in self-defence. But Geist told me another story about a man who didn't. He was surprised when the running wolf got close and then lay down and began to whine. A second wolf appeared and both watched the hunter closely before running off. Did the man make a conscious decision not to fire, or did he freeze at the unexpected sight of a wolf running toward him? Either way, there's no guarantee all wolves will react the same way. When a wolf ran toward a hunting guide at Joshua Green River, Alaska, he yelled and waved his arms but the wolf remained at a full run, staring directly at the man's face. The wolf showed no signs of stopping and was just a stride away from the end of the guide's rifle when he fired.

Wolves tend to respond to certain situations in fairly predictable ways. While three biologists were in the field near Churchill, Manitoba, they were startled when a wolf bounded toward one of them, ears up, tail straight out and eyes locked on him. Yelling and stomping toward the wolf turned it away. When another wolf approached, an air horn was used, but the arrival of a third prompted the men to climb trees. One wolf paced, barked and howled at the edge of the clearing and howling was heard in the distance. The wolves disappeared but came back whenever the men called to each other. After four hours, they climbed down, formed a defensive triangle and walked from tree to tree until they reached their vehicle three kilometres (two miles) away. On their retreat they spotted a den, which may have been the cause of the ruckus. According to Ken Laudon, then wolf management specialist for Montana Fish, Wildlife and Parks, the behaviour the wolves exhibited is typical when they are surprised at or near a den, rendezvous site or recent kill. The noise and bravado is an attempt to scare humans away. Once the wolves have assessed the threat, they usually back off but may follow or "escort" people out of the area.

Defensive wolves can be aggressive, though. Biologists darted a female wolf from a helicopter in Fortymile River, Alaska, in 1994 but were unable to approach her due to aggressive charges by a male wolf. Eventually they had to also dart the male, who they assumed was her mate. Four years later another biologist was attempting to dart a female wolf from a helicopter near Goodpaster River, Alaska.

The wolf turned, focused on the man and ran toward the open door of the aircraft. As the pilot manoeuvred upwards, the wolf sprang into the air, grabbing the landing gear with her teeth next to the biologist's boot. The wolf held on until her teeth slid down against a crosspiece, causing her to lose her grip and fall about two metres (seven feet) to the ground.

Problems with wolves don't happen just to biologists in remote areas or lone cyclists and hunters. Many occur in wilderness parks that are easily accessible to those who may not know or understand the consequences of human interactions with wildlife. Nowhere is this more evident than in Banff National Park in southwest Alberta about 110 kilometres (68 miles) west of Calgary. The park's more than 6,600 square kilometres (2,500 sq mi) contain a breathtaking array of rugged mountains, glaciers, forests and alpine meadows. Even more importantly, it connects with numerous other national and provincial parks, which together create a vast area that is designated the Canadian Rocky Mountain Parks UNESCO World Heritage Site. The two most well-known communities within the park are the resort town of Banff and the village of Lake Louise. Both are situated along the Bow River, which for much of the nearly 60 kilometres (37 mi) between the two is bracketed by the Trans-Canada Highway and the Bow Valley Parkway. The mountainous terrain makes the Bow Valley the primary travel corridor for humans and wildlife. While the year-round population of the Banff townsite is under eight thousand, the park receives close to four million visitors each year.

It's not unusual to see elk, bears or wolves alongside roadways; the park even has wildlife viewing tips and rules. But Christopher

Wolves are smart. When this pack in Banff National Park chased—or perhaps herded—an elk onto an overpass, some got in front while others stayed to the rear, effectively blocking the elk's escape.
Photo by Christopher Martin Photography

Martin saw more than he expected while driving just outside of Banff toward Lake Minnewanka one morning in February 2016. It was a female elk stumbling a few steps back and forth on a railway overpass. Curious, the professional photographer parked, grabbed his camera and hiked up the hill. Four wolves were preventing the ungulate from leaving the overpass, and biting at it from the front and rear. No one knows how the participants in this life-and-death struggle ended up on the structure but it was obvious that the wolves were incorporating the overpass into their attack strategy. By the time the wolves pulled the elk down, the audience had grown and included Parks Canada staff. After watching the wolves eat for a while, they moved the carcass so the predators wouldn't get hit by oncoming trains. In May the same year, motorists witnessed a wolf chasing a herd of bighorn sheep down Highway 40 about 20 minutes outside the park boundary, eventually taking down a young straggler.

Due to development and roads, these front-country wolves have to be somewhat habituated to people in order to survive, yet generally

don't pay much attention to them. However, a new breeding pair in the Bow Valley had four pups in the spring of 2016, and began visiting the townsite that fall. "We think they got into garbage and possibly people were feeding them," says Jesse Whittington, a wildlife ecologist at Banff National Park. "A lot of people visit Banff and we try to make it easy for animals to go about their lives with as little disturbance as possible. Elk live in a halo around town. Every morning we push them out in order to avoid conflicts. We've developed wildlife corridors where wolves can travel around the outside of town to naturally regulate the elk population." Additional efforts by Parks Canada to reduce the human impact on wildlife include fencing with a series of wildlife under- and overpasses along the Trans-Canada Highway, wildlife corridors that limit human access, prescribed burns and seasonal closures of certain areas, such as active den sites. Parks Canada also monitors the Bow Valley Parkway, closing it from dusk to dawn during key times of the year, allowing animals to roam freely without increasing their chance of habituation.

But that's not always enough. The spring of 2017, members of the Bow Valley pack were seen eating garbage at a construction site outside of town, and a wolf followed a cyclist on the Bow Valley Parkway, refusing to leave even when a motorist blasted their horn right behind it. The wolves also ventured into campgrounds, undeterred by barking dogs and people yelling, throwing rocks and honking vehicle horns. "Instead of going hunting, these wolves were looking for food at campsites," says Whittington. "Wolves kill deer, elk and moose, which is no easy feat and involves a very real risk of

Wolves can very easily become habituated to people and associate them with food. It isn't unusual for wolves and other wildlife to pass through campsites in national and provincial parks in the off-season, but once people arrive, normal behaviour is for wolves to stay away.
Photo by Simon Ham, Resource Management (Wildlife) Banff National Park

injury. Once they get a taste of human food they can become food-conditioned very quickly."

At the end of May the breeding female and a yearling flipped the lid off a cooler and stole a loaf of bread, despite the presence of shouting people. "We recommend people stay a minimum of 100 metres away from carnivores but this wolf was coming within 2 metres," Whittington says. "When I visited the campsite and saw all the children running around, I knew the situation was serious. There's a lot of variability in individual wolf behaviour. Some are quite tolerant of people and others are very wary and skittish. The other two wolf packs in the valley weren't causing any trouble. Attacks are really rare and usually involve wolves that are tolerant of people and food-conditioned. Some will directly attack or sometimes a person runs or falls and that can trigger a predator response."

Parks Canada collared several wolves so they could track their movements and haze them if necessary. "We monitor the collars 24 hours a day and whenever an animal goes where we don't want it to be we rush in and give it a negative stimulus, which can range from clapping our hands to shooting them with chalk balls or, in

extreme cases, rubber bullets," Whittington explains. "It takes a lot of effort, is not sustainable and doesn't always work." A good example of that is when Parks Canada had to haze two problem wolves in 2001. Unfortunately, the wolves only learned to avoid park staff. Once, the yearling female ran just fast enough to stay just ahead of the park employees chasing her. In the end, the wolves had to be euthanized before they passed their bad behaviour on to other pack members.

The summer of 2016, Parks Canada cracked down on messy and illegal campsites. No tent camping was allowed in some high-risk areas and no-stopping zones were designated on certain parts of the parkway. The following year they beefed up education in town about proper garbage disposal and erected billboards stating, "Human food kills wildlife." Staff visited campgrounds reminding people that dog dishes, as well as the residue of food left on barbecues, in fire pits or even in dirty dishwater, could attract wildlife. People were fined—the Canada National Parks Act allows fines of up to $25,000 for failing to store or dispose of food properly—and campers were encouraged to report those with messy camps by phoning a 24- hour tip line. "The key to the solution is to prevent wolves from becoming food-conditioned, not react to the situation after the fact," explains Whittington.

To compound the problem, some international tourists, familiar with game farms or safari parks where people are allowed and even encouraged to feed animals, were doing so in Banff National Park. "We're working with interpreters and local businesses to spread the message and looking at other ways we can reach visitors who speak a different language and have different cultures," Whittington says. Another problem is that Bow Valley wolves are the most photographed in the park due to their proximity to human-use areas. Since the wolves are usually on the move, visitors sometimes toss food out of cars to get them to linger long enough for a photo. Once a cooked turkey was found at the side of the road and there were troubling rumours that professional photographers were building blinds and putting food out for wolves. Parks Canada restricted the use of VHS radios by staff so people couldn't listen in and find out where the canids were.

In mid-2017, the Bow Valley pack was a nine-member family unit consisting of the breeding pair, three yearlings and four pups. By the end of the year, the two bold wolves had been euthanized, the pups had been run over by trains and a two-year-old male that had taken a walkabout outside the park was killed by a hunter. All that remained was the dominant male, who was limping, and one of his daughters. The Bow Valley pack's story is a sad saga highlighting just how precarious it can be when human and wolf habitats overlap.

No park employee enjoys euthanizing wildlife and Banff National Park staff were especially reluctant to kill the female in 2017 due to the young age of her pups at the time. But because of different yet similar events that had occurred in other locations, they knew what the consequences could be if the inappropriate behaviour continued. Algonquin Provincial Park is a mosaic of rivers and lakes set among coniferous and deciduous forests in southeastern Ontario. The park's proximity to the large metropolitan cities of Toronto and Ottawa adds to its popularity. Since 1963 the park has held periodic public wolf howls for visitors, who are thrilled if wolves howl back. On the flip side of that feel-good experience, from 1987 to 1998 the park was a hotspot for aggressive wolf behaviour, with more attacks taking place there than in any other location in North America within the last 100 years.

It began during the summer of 1987 when a 16-year-old girl shone a flashlight into a wolf's face at close range in the Whitefish Group campground. Perhaps startled or annoyed, the wolf bit her lightly on the arm. Park officials likened the response to a disciplinary action one wolf would give another. Nonetheless, the wolf had been close to people and exhibited fearless behaviour. It was killed and tested negative for rabies. Seven years later, in August 1994, a nine-year-old boy returning from an evening trip to the outhouse at the Big

Crow-Opeongo campsite ran when he saw a wolf. The wolf gave chase and bit him in the side. When the boy's father showed up the wolf backed off a scant two metres (six feet) and continued to stare at the boy until the father and other campers scared it off. A month later, a wolf bit a woman lightly on the back of the leg, then ripped up camping gear when she retreated to her tent. Throughout the summer, park officials received numerous complaints about a fearless wolf growling at people and destroying camping gear but showing no interest in food. This wolf was also killed and appeared healthy, with no sign of rabies or other disease.

So far, no serious injuries had occurred—but that changed in August 1996 when a family of two adults and three children aged three, seven and twelve slept under the stars at Tom Thomson Lake. A wolf grabbed the oldest child by the face and dragged him in his sleeping bag a short distance before the father could drive the wolf away. The

boy had a broken nose, was missing a piece of an ear and had puncture wounds to his gums, a tear duct and a cheekbone. Eighty stitches and reconstructive surgery were required. Park staff learned that in the past two weeks the wolf had interacted with other campers, some reporting the wolf's antics as playful, while others were concerned. The wolf ignored readily available food but tore up camping gear and chewed on clothes and shoes and once pulled a pack being used as a pillow out from under a sleeping man's head. Officials killed the 26-kilogram (57 lb) male wolf, which was deemed healthy. The necropsy revealed vegetables, string and clothing labels, indicating it had been into the garbage.

The fifth attack took place in 1998. Park officials estimate that, throughout the summer, thousands of people saw a friendly, curious wolf that came close to humans on an almost daily basis. Many people interacted with it in a playful way, including a group of wildlife students who spent 40 minutes doing so. The wolf would mimic people's behaviour, approach closely, then jump away—only to start the game all over again. The public was thrilled to see a wolf, especially one that seemed to seek out their company. But in September the wolf became fixated on a four-year-old girl walking with her parents. Pepper spray did little to deter it and the wolf only left after the woman and child went into a trailer. Two days later the wolf picked up a 19-month-old sitting on the ground a short distance from his father and tossed him about a metre (three feet) away. Grabbing the boy and his older sister, the mother jumped up on the picnic table while the

Paul Sokoloff woke up at one in the morning and saw a white blob in the opening of his tent. He jerked back, hoping it wasn't a polar bear. The botanist was on a field trip on Ellesmere Island in Canada's Arctic. When he realized it was a wolf, he grabbed his camera and took a quick photo before yelling to scare it away. The wolf left, then returned for a short time and ripped part of his tent vestibule. Sokoloff did not have any food in his tent and thinks the wolf was merely curious. Photo by Paul Sokoloff, © Canadian Museum of Nature father and other campers harassed the wolf. The wolf circled the picnic table several times before leaving. Park officials killed the 30-kilogram (66 lb) wolf later that day. It also tested negative for any diseases and appeared healthy.

Algonquin Park began keeping records about fearless wolves back in 1963, after one broke into a tent and ate some hot dogs, ignoring the baby napping nearby. Up until 1988, approximately 25 wolves were labelled fearless. The wolf involved in the 1963 incident was shot, as were 4 wolves between 1987 and 1996. But the other 20 wolves never caused any trouble and were not. So the series of five bites from four wolves in 11 years was a shock. Especially since park staff regularly told visitors, "There has never been a case of a healthy wolf harming a person in North America." They were also shaken because the attack on the 19-month-old appeared to be predatory.

All the wolves were healthy and looked like Algonquin/eastern wolves, which are smaller than grey wolves. DNA tests confirmed that they were not wolf-dog crosses or wolf-coyote hybrids. And because they looked so much like the distinctive small population of Algonquin wolves, Dan Strickland, chief park naturalist at the time, strongly doubted they were captive animals that had been released in the park. All the wolves that bit people had spent a great deal of time around humans, sometimes taking or chewing up their belongings. They were clearly habituated to humans but most did not appear to be food-conditioned.

Wolves seek prey that's vulnerable so it's no surprise that children and small adults are their primary human targets. "Human behaviour can trigger large carnivore attacks in developed countries," says a study compiled by an international team of researchers and published in the February 2016 edition of *Scientific Reports*, pointing out that an increase in large carnivores and people spending time in wild areas is not the only reason for a rise in attacks. Close to 50 per cent of the time, attacks are the result of people's risky behaviour. The most risky behaviour listed in the report is having your dog unleashed; the second is leaving young children unattended outdoors. Some Scandinavian elementary schools teach their students to not run but to stand tall, put their hands over their heads and clap loudly while yelling if they see a wolf.

The Alaska Department of Fish and Game publication "A Case History of Human-Wolf Encounters in Alaska and Canada" was inspired by a wolf attack on a young boy near Icy Bay, Alaska, in April 2000. The six-year-old was playing with a slightly older boy behind the logging camp school when a wolf came out of the nearby woods. The boys ran and when the younger one, who was wearing oversized boots, fell, the wolf jumped on him and bit him repeatedly on the back and buttocks. When people came to the rescue yelling and throwing rocks, the wolf picked the boy up and half-dragged, half-carried him toward the trees. As the wolf released the boy to get a better hold, a Labrador retriever got between the two and the wolf ran into the woods. A few minutes later a man followed it, blew on a predator call and shot the wolf when it appeared.

The wolf had been seen around the camp for about a year and had been fed at least once. Initially it retreated when approached by humans but, shortly before the attack, it had begun walking boldly through the camp. The wolf tested negative for rabies and distemper and, although it was small, the necropsy indicated it was in good health and had a normal amount of body fat. Alaskan wildlife officials were shocked that a non-rabid wolf had attacked a person and began to question the commonly held perception that a healthy wolf would never do so. When McNay's "Case History" report noted that non-aggressive habituated behaviour could rapidly escalate to strong aggression, some officials wondered if a healthy North American wolf would someday kill someone.

The most controversial attack in recent decades—and the most rigorously investigated to date—took place near Points North Landing, a mining exploration camp in northeast Saskatchewan. Twenty-two-year-old Kenton Carnegie, a geological engineering student at Waterloo University, was conducting aerial survey work for Sander Geophysics as work experience toward his degree. Around 3:30 p.m. on November 8, 2005, Carnegie left camp for a walk. When he hadn't returned by 7 p.m. two men, later joined by a third, went looking for him. They found Carnegie's footprints heading toward nearby Wollaston Lake. Although no one knows exactly what happened, one version, based on interpretation of the tracks and disturbances in the snow, suggests that one wolf followed Carnegie to the lake while two others angled toward him from opposite sides. Carnegie's tracks indicated that, as he perhaps became aware of the wolves, he turned back toward camp. Scuffle marks in the snow suggest that he attempted to fight off the wolves and was pulled down. There was a lot of blood on the snow and it didn't take the three men long to find Carnegie's body, which bore bite marks on his legs and head.

There were many controversial elements surrounding Carnegie's death. Altogether, nine experts—including carnivore specialists, forensic anthropologists, wildlife biologists, an animal behaviourist and bear experts—investigated the case in varying capacities. The National Geographic Society conducted their own independent investigation and, dissatisfied with the official inquiry, the Carnegie family paid for three independent investigations. The debate over which animal(s) killed Carnegie revolved around whether some of the tracks were made by wolves or a bear, whether some injuries were made by teeth or claws, the way the animal(s) fed on the body and the fact that the body was moved some distance from the kill site. Reading the investigative reports, it's clear that each investigator adamantly believed their theory was correct and, although nothing was said outright, there's a sense of acrimony between the different experts. One even hinted that the testimony of local Indigenous officials who assisted in the body recovery was not taken seriously. Although the official cause of death was eventually attributed to wolves, controversy over Carnegie's death and North American wolves attacking humans continues to this day.

What *is* known is that in the months leading up to his death, wolves and bears had been scavenging at the camp dump. The wolves brazenly ran up at the sound of the front-end loader and ripped into the bags as soon as they hit the ground. Four days before Carnegie's death, Todd Svarckopf and Chris Van Galder, employees at the camp, had an encounter with two wolves. As they entered a wooded section on a walk, a large wolf appeared. They were less than a kilometre (half-mile) from camp so they started to return but the wolf walked right up to Svarckopf. The men yelled and the wolf backed away but as soon as they started for camp again it followed. A second, lighter-coloured wolf appeared and focused on Svarckopf while the darker one zeroed in on Van Galder. Agreeing not to run, the two men used long spruce limbs to keep the wolves at bay as they slowly backed out of the forest. The wolves appeared to be trying to separate them and prevent them from leaving the woods. For 10 to 15 minutes, the wolves followed the men closely, snapping their jaws and snarling.

Back at camp, the men reported the incident but there are questions as to how seriously their story was taken. Two days after Carnegie died, two wolves from the local pack were killed. According to the necropsy report the wolves were "fat, well-muscled and in excellent nutritional condition." There was no sign of rabies or that the animals were wolf-dogs, and no evidence of human remains in their digestive tracts.

The 2005 Points North Landing tragedy wasn't the first or last time there's been trouble with wolves in northern Saskatchewan.

During the winter of 1980–81 wolves were rummaging through garbage at the dump near the tiny hamlet of Stony Rapids. When they started eating village dogs, trappers were hired to kill them. Three years later, a wolf grabbed a Key Lake mine employee's sleeve as it tried to snatch the lunch bag out of his hand. In December 2004, the year before Carnegie died, Fred Desjarlais was jogging back to his room from work at another mine site when a wolf leapt out of the ditch and bit his arm, leg, back and groin before he managed to subdue it and others came to his assistance. Just after midnight, one night in August 2016, a security guard at Cigar Lake mine heard a commotion and drove her quad over to investigate. About 50 metres (55 yd) from the main campsite the headlights picked up a wolf attacking a 26-year-old kitchen worker. The guard managed to scare the animal off with her vehicle and administered first aid until help arrived. According to Facebook posts from Cigar Lake, it wasn't unusual to see wolves, have them follow or watch people, or for them to enter job sites at night.

The three mine sites and Stony Rapids are within 200 kilometres (125 mi) of each other. Open landfills had been attracting scavenging wolves since at least the 1980s. At least two of the mines put electric fences around their dumps after men were attacked and one or more provided wolf safety information to employees and hazed problem wolves. But in 2015, one company was reprimanded by the provincial government for failing to maintain the electric fencing around its dump, which wolves and bears were again foraging in. Installing well-maintained electric fences, incinerating garbage, hazing wolves that come near people and human-use areas and providing employees with pepper spray and air horns would go a long way to preventing this problem.

The second human death caused by wolves in recent times also occurred in the north. By far the largest US state, Alaska is bordered by the Arctic Ocean to the north and Canada's Yukon Territory and BC coast to the east and is just shy of 90 kilometres (56 mi) from Russia at the closest points of land to the west. About a third of the square-ish state lies within the Arctic Circle, while to the southwest it tapers to a thin peninsula ending in a string of tiny islands separating the Pacific Ocean and the Bering Sea. Although Alaska has the smallest human population of any state, it's had the largest population of wolves in the US for the last century or more. The current estimate is seven to ten thousand. Wolf populations have never been considered threatened or endangered and are actively hunted and, at times, culled.

Within the last 100 years, the state has recorded three human deaths by wolves. A boy and an adult male survived attacks in 1942 and 1943 respectively but were infected with rabies and died from the disease. Another fatality occurred in 2010 near Chignik Lake, located on the Alaska Peninsula. Thirty-two-year-old Candice Berner had arrived to join the community's population of about 100 the week before to work with disabled children. On March 8, the 150-centimetre (nearly five-foot) woman went for a run. Her body was discovered a few hours later. There had been recent problems with local wolves but, as a newcomer, Berner might not have been aware of that. Eight wolves were killed near the village with six later being directly linked to Berner's body by DNA. Necropsies on the animals revealed no signs of rabies or other disease and no evidence that the animals were wolf-dogs. The state veterinarian's report noted that the wolves appeared to be in good health and one had "very large fat reserves." The biologist investigating the case found no indications that the wolves were defending a kill or had been fed by humans.

In the last century, a total of four people have been killed by wolves in North America. All were in remote, isolated areas, three were alone, three were small or slight, and evidence suggests that at least three of them were running or ran at some point. One person was armed with a rifle but none of the others had any defensive weapons or pepper spray. Two deaths were caused by rabid animals while the ones in 2005 and 2010 were caused by healthy, some say predatory, wolves. In both cases, there had been prior wolf problems; in one instance they were clearly habituated and food-conditioned. Four deaths in 100 years is like a raindrop falling into a pond, so small an amount as to almost be insignificant. But the two deaths caused by healthy wolves and the disquieting and dramatic increase in attacks and incidents is enough, I think, to lay to rest the myth that no healthy wolf in North America would harm a human.

CHAPTER 10

A PERFECT STORM

Wildlife management is comparatively easy; human management is difficult.
—ALDO LEOPOLD, *Game Management*

SLEET AND SNOW MADE THE JOURNEY OVER "THE HUMP" TO PORT Alberni in south-central Vancouver Island a slippery one. It was a few days before Christmas and most folks were buying last-minute gifts but my mind was on wolves. As we reached the outskirts of Port Alberni and turned northwest, I thought, "Yes, wolves could live here." We were on our way to visit Valerius Geist, a specialist in the biology, behaviour and social dynamics of large mammals in North America. Since 1995 he's lived on 8 hectares (20 acres) in a rural, semi-agricultural area bordered by Crown and private forest lands a short distance from the Beaufort Range. A robust 77-year-old in 2015, Geist met us at the door with a firm handshake and two warnings: he'd woken up with laryngitis and had noticed a peculiar smell in the house, perhaps a dead mouse, but he'd had no luck finding the source. I was far too interested in wolves to worry about snow, smells or germs.

By the time I visited Geist I'd learned a lot about how humans and wolves relate to one another. It was obvious that, aside from rabid wolves, most altercations had a backstory. But how long were they? How many encounters did it take to make a wary wolf a bold one? Were some wolves naturally more aggressive than others? I also wondered how actions that many consider innocuous or of a spiritual

189

nature were affecting the trend of increasing negative encounters. I'd heard some disquieting stories and, looking at a map, realized they all took place on the west coast of Vancouver Island and a 90-minute drive inland. I was curious if something unique had happened in this area, some combination of circumstances that created a perfect storm for negative interactions between humans and wolves. Geist was my first step in exploring this possibility.

"I saw my first wild wolf early one morning in May 1959, on Pyramid Mountain in Wells Gray Provincial Park," he told me. "It was watching me from a quarter mile away with an attentive look on its face. Its red tongue stuck out and the light was golden on its fur. I could see it clearly in my spotting scope." Two years later, while studying Stone's sheep in northern BC, Geist had many opportunities to observe wolves. "Timberlines were low," he recalled, "and the wolves spent much time in the open, plainly visible. I watched them for hours on end. These were large, painfully shy, cautious wolves that, on occasion, even panicked over my scent." When he moved to Port Alberni in the mid-1990s, Geist subscribed to the idea that wolves killed people in Europe and Asia but were timid and harmless in North America. That's what all the experts said and that's what he'd experienced in the north. Like everyone else, Geist considered the idea of wolves threatening humans ridiculous. Then a wolf pack moved into his neighbourhood in the summer of 1999.

"Within three months the deer, geese and ducks we'd seen in the meadows were huddled around houses and barns," Geist said. "All the other wildlife, such as ruffled grouse, pheasants and swans, disappeared. The landscape looked empty, as if vacuumed of wildlife." The wolves ran after quads, tractors and motorcycles trying to get the dogs accompanying them. On occasion, they cornered dogs under porches, attacking and sometimes killing them in front of their shouting owners. Spooked by wolves, cattle broke through fences in a desperate race to the barn.

Two cows were killed and another so seriously injured that it had to be put down. One day a farm employee raced out in a quad to rescue a newborn calf. He scooped it up and dashed to the barn with the wolf lunging at the calf and following them inside the building.

Sheep were a major draw, leading Geist's neighbour to invest in five large livestock guardian dogs, which resulted in night-long howling sessions between predators and protectors. In October 2002, Geist and his neighbours watched the last member of the wolf pack, a male, fraternizing with the LGDs. "The three border collies were on their backs with legs in the air, they and the wolf were all wagging their tails. The wolf was a little bit shy around the two bigger white dogs," he said. "The only problem was the wolf was still killing sheep." In March 2003 the owner of the dogs shot and killed the wolf as he sat among his new canine friends. Altogether, thirteen wolves from the first pack and four from another that showed up in early 2007 were killed, all within 1.5 kilometres (1 mi) of Geist's home.

What was most disturbing was the wolves' boldness around humans. "They didn't run away from people the way larger mainland wolves did," said Geist. People walking or riding horses were followed or approached in an investigative way. Sometimes wolves ran by them closely or sat and watched them intently. They barked or howled at people from 10 to 15 paces away. One did so as Geist's wife, Renate, and 11 visitors walked a short distance from their home. Another vocalized and moved at Renate when one of their dogs was in heat, forcing her to run into the house. "One of the largest wolves tried to dominate me," said Geist. "I was walking in the forest near the house when the wolf stuck its head up then ducked back in. He howled and came closer several times then stepped out on the road about 50 paces off, clearly interested. It was a challenge, he wasn't treating me as prey; he was testing me as if I was another wolf, trying to learn about me. When our eyes met, he fled."

Geist was startled by the canid's behaviour. "Along with my neighbours, I repeatedly saw wolves showing interest in humans and I know from studies of wolves in captivity that they are observation learners," he added. "Nothing in my previous studies had prepared me for this. These wolves were acting more like Russian wolves than North American ones."

The most alarming incident happened about 320 metres (350 yds) from Geist's home in March 2007 when his neighbours went out one morning to inspect their dairy herd. "Their old dog ran in front of them as they entered the forest and five wolves attacked it," said Geist. "My neighbour grabbed a branch and advanced on the wolves, which turned on him, snarling. His wife jumped into the caboose of their nearby excavator. My neighbour's energetic attack freed the dog, and intimidated all but one wolf, which came toward him. However, he too reluctantly withdrew. The next morning when the couple went out to check their cows, the wolves charged and my neighbour shot the most aggressive, a male weighing 74 pounds."

The wolves had been gone for more than five years when I talked to Geist, yet he was still surprised at the way they had focused their attention on dogs, then livestock and humans. That sort of behaviour was unheard of on southern Vancouver Island in the 1990s. Wolves were so rare that, in 1978, when a vehicle hit and killed one on the outskirts of Port Alberni, the RCMP had to call a park warden to identify it. There had been a healthy wolf population on Vancouver Island in the past but by the mid-1960s, a vigorous government predator control program had wiped them out. Sometime in the 1970s, smaller wolves from BC's central coast swam to northeast Vancouver Island and slowly recolonized the island. Geist's "misbehaving packs" were the descendants of those wolves. He suspects they'd come from nearby Strathcona Park looking for new territory and that a low prey base may have prompted their interest in domestic animals and people.

From Port Alberni a narrow road winds through forests, skirts Sproat and Kennedy lakes and climbs Sutton Pass en route to Vancouver Island's west coast, approximately 95 kilometres (60 mi) away. Turn left at the T-junction and it's about a 10-minute drive to Ucluelet, go right and in 20 minutes you're in Tofino. Located on two narrow peninsulas, the communities bracket the Long Beach unit of Pacific Rim National Park Reserve (PRNPR). Around the same time wolves appeared in Geist's neighbourhood, others were causing problems in PRNPR and neighbouring communities.

"Their arrival was very dramatic and there was a significant increase in human-wolf conflicts in a short period of time," says Bob Hansen, who was employed by Parks Canada from 1974 to 2012. He started at PRNPR in 1991, serving the last 16 years as the park's human-wildlife conflict specialist. In addition to filling various roles with Parks Canada, Hansen's volunteer and paid employment includes raising appreciation of the ecological and cultural roles of large carnivores, human-wildlife hazard assessment and risk management, and two years as a wildlife deterrent specialist for Nunavut, working on ways to reduce conflict with polar bears. He's currently a member of the West Coast Regional Coexistence with Wildlife Working Group and the Coexisting with Carnivores Alliance.

"Prior to 1997 there are only 6 human-wolf interactions in PRNPR records going back to the 1970s," he notes. "The winter of 1998–99 was like someone flipped a switch. Within 18 months we had 44 human-wolf interactions within the park and 6 dogs had been attacked."

All of a sudden it seemed like wolves were everywhere in the region and they weren't behaving like the seldom seen, wary North American creatures they were supposed to be. They "escorted" people on trails, either following them or moving beside them a few steps away, and sauntered through campgrounds indifferent to the presence of humans. Two campers spent several hours locked in an outhouse late one night on Clarke Island in the Broken Group Islands when two wolves positioned themselves near the entrance. A person walking alone on Long Beach reported "a wonderful experience of a lifetime" when two wolves aligned themselves in front of and behind him so perfectly that it would have been possible to draw a straight line through all three of them. Over time, reports from all PRNPR units (Long Beach, Broken Group Islands and the West Coast Trail), as well as islands in the nearby Clayoquot Sound UNESCO Biosphere Reserve, suggested encounters with wolves and cougars were increasing in frequency and intensity. "Before, we'd just had to deal with human-bear management challenges," says Hansen. "We had a good handle on that and had brought the number of serious incidents down to zero. That was a bonus as all of a sudden there were all these new situations."

In an effort to understand what was driving the dramatic increase in interactions between people, their pets and resident wolves and cougars, Hansen consulted with First Nations, academics, Parks Canada human-wildlife conflict specialists and others near and far. He discovered that similar events were occurring in North America but not at the sustained intensity of what was taking place on the central west coast of Vancouver Island. Eventually he brought together a diverse group of natural and social science researchers, field biologists, town planners, Indigenous people, kayak guides and knowledgeable local residents to study the links between predators, prey, people and landscape dynamics in an effort to find ways large carnivores and humans could coexist. This collaborative consultation, along with field studies and other data, resulted in PRNPR working with EKOS Communications to produce "Learning to Live with Large Carnivores: WildCoast Project Primer & Guidelines."

"The situation was very complex," Hansen says. "The new wave of recolonizing wolves coincided with a growing appreciation of the importance of predators in healthy ecosystems, and wolves were no longer being persecuted as they had been in the past. The change in human behaviour when encountering wolves seemed to almost foster less wariness in wolves around people. There was also the socio-economic implication of tourism and the outward growth of local communities. There was definitely a much larger human-use footprint on the landscape than there had been in the past."

As in other parts of North America where wolf populations have increased in recent years, much of Vancouver Island had been heavily logged. While the resulting clearcuts create new forage for deer in the short term, as the forest regenerates, taller trees shadow out the understory, leaving nothing for deer to feed on. To compound the problem, the logging of old-growth forests removes the lichen deer depend on for winter feed. Due to the lack of lichen and new lush growth in clearcuts, deer, a primary prey of wolves, began moving closer to and even into communities in search of food—and the predators followed. The island had also experienced a human population explosion and with it came more interest in walking, jogging and mountain biking. Trails for these activities are often built in greenspaces just outside towns on what were originally game trails. Improved road access and vigorous marketing programs have boosted PRNPR into a tourism hot spot, making "Ukee" and "Tuff City," as they're sometimes called, world-class tourist destinations. Sandy beaches, ancient rainforests and the open Pacific Ocean offer endless opportunities to experience nature. These, along with trendy shops, gourmet restaurants and a variety of accommodations, now bring more than one million visitors to PRNPR and adjacent areas each year.

Although there weren't as many visitors in the late 1990s, there was still an increase in human-predator encounters. Some key insights as to why this was happening came from analyzing the diet of resident wolves and discovering that the shoreline served as their travel and food corridor. Similar to what Geist noticed when wolves moved into his neighbourhood, research revealed a huge drop in the amount of raccoon and river otter sign within three years of the wolves' arrival in PRNPR. "Much of what wolves in the park area eat comes from the shoreline," explains Hansen. "Finding a seal pup on the beach is an incredibly rich package; their high fat count packs a big punch nutritionally. Raccoons hang out in the intertidal zone and deer tracks are often seen along freshwater creeks running into the ocean. And almost all human infrastructure in the area, such as communities, trails, beaches, campgrounds and other facilities, are built within 500 metres of the ocean. All this overlaps the primary hunting corridors of wolves."

Dogs are a common element in negative human-wolf confrontations in the area and around 1999, wolf attacks on dogs became more frequent. A woman with a small dog off-leash was confronted on the Goldmine Trail by three wolves. She picked up her dog, screamed and broke sticks against tree trunks but nothing fazed them. She began making her way to the parking lot 15 minutes away with her dog in her arms. The wolves walked on each side of her, eyeing her dog and taking turns running ahead and then racing back, until she reached her vehicle. A guest at the Raven Motel in Ucluelet let their dog out and a wolf carried it away. In April 2012, two dead wolves were discovered in a Tofino dumpster. A resident, who asked to not be identified, says that a woman had been feeding the wolves but when they killed a couple of dogs, someone shot the predators. "It's common knowledge that people in Tofino and Ucluelet have fed wolves," he says. "It's not constant but it does happen."

"People say wolves go after dogs to protect their territory, which is true," notes Todd Windle, human-wildlife coexistence specialist at PRNPR since 2012. "But they also attack and consume dogs and cats as prey, which is what we see most often in our area." Windle volunteered with the WildCoast Project before becoming a Parks Canada employee in 2005. Since then he's worked at Quttinirpaaq

National Park on Ellesmere Island in Canada's Arctic and Cape Breton Highlands National Park in Nova Scotia. He's dealt with human-wildlife interactions involving wolves, cougars, moose, eastern coyotes, and black and polar bears. The wolves of Vancouver Island and how people interact with them are of particular interest. "People drastically underestimate what a huge attractant dogs and cats are to wolves. They may go after garbage but they're much more interested in pets as an easy source of food. Including outlying areas, we average six to twelve wolf attacks on dogs a year, as well as some cats. Not all are reported in the news; it's much more common than people realize." Although wolves are usually wary of people, like any wild animal, that changes if they become habituated or food-conditioned. "If an animal is habituated it's very easy for it to become food-conditioned," explains Windle. "Food conditioning is almost impossible to change. For a wild animal it's just too tempting to obtain those easy calories. It's challenging, but we can work at changing the behaviour of a habituated animal. There aren't many options once they become food-conditioned.

"More people live in cities these days and they want to experience the wilderness," he continues. "They often don't think to scare wildlife away. They allow and even encourage them to come closer. For the person it's a once-in-a-lifetime experience. It can feel very spiritual to be close to a large carnivore. But while a person might have a once-in-a-lifetime experience with a wolf, the wolf may have a similar encounter with another person an hour later, the next day and the next week. It doesn't take long to become habituated. Wolves are incredibly charismatic, that makes it difficult to step back and look at the big picture, to view the situation with the mind, not the heart."

The arrival of a new five-member pack on Long Beach near the end of 2013 was the beginning of a series of events that would build to a climax over the next four years. Seemingly unperturbed by humans right from the start, the wolves lounged at the side of the road and on beaches, allowing people to watch them for long periods of time. By March 2015 they'd attacked three dogs in Ucluelet. Later that month, a couple walking with their child and two off-leash dogs at Wickaninnish Beach watched in horror as two wolves attacked the large dog. The small one darted in to help and was carried off. That fall three wolves visited the village of Ucluelet at midday and had to be chased off by members of the RCMP. "That's not normal behaviour for wolves, to be in town in broad daylight with people around," says Hansen. "People should have been honking their vehicle horns and yelling at them so they learn that's not appropriate behaviour. But these days, often the first instinct is to take a photograph. Everyone has a phone with a camera. That sort of technology wasn't available before so people didn't have an incentive to prolong their contact with a wild animal."

In early November 2016, Brent Woodland was on his normal after-work run with his two dogs at Wickaninnish Beach when he saw a wolf come out of the sand dunes just ahead. The 36-year-old faced the wolf, made himself look as large as possible and yelled as loud as he could. He also kept a tight grip on the leashes of his approximately 36-kilogram (80 lb) dogs. Whenever the wolf backed off a few steps, Woodland inched his way toward the Kwisitis Visitor Centre, all the while maintaining eye contact, yelling and throwing rocks. He saw another wolf moving along in the tall grass and felt like he and his dogs were being corralled. In a short cell phone video he took of the wolf following him, you can hear the dogs barking and Woodland shouting repeatedly, "Get out of here!" in a hoarse voice. It took 30 minutes to cover the 400 metres (437 yds) to the visitor centre. It was closed for the season so Woodland took his dogs up the outside stairs to a balcony where he continued shouting at the wolves as he called 911. The wolves left when the RCMP pulled up with sirens blaring.

"It was a very intense situation," says Windle. "Luckily, Brent did a great job by yelling, maintaining eye contact and making himself appear large. People often think a wolf won't attack a big dog but that's not true. There were numerous human interactions with this wolf over a period of time. Six fairly close encounters had occurred within four days. They all involved dogs that the wolf was hunting for food. In one, a man was trying to get close to the wolf to take a photo with his cell phone."

Since spring, reports of wolves approaching tents and campsites with people in them had been trickling into Parks Canada headquarters. "A big problem is that not all encounters are reported," explains Windle. "Lots of people are afraid that if they report a wolf incident, the animal will be killed. But if we know about it early enough we can try hazing the animal to discourage it from hanging around humans. It's important for everyone to report all predator encounters to Parks so we can track and monitor the animals. People need to realize that they're not saving a wolf by not reporting an incident. They may actually be contributing to its death if it's acting inappropriately."

By March 2017 a pack of seven wolves was seen cruising the beaches, sightings near Tofino and Ucluelet were increasing, and social media posts mentioned wolves in backyards. Early one evening Isabel Flood was walking her large dog while her nine- and twelve-year-old sons played at the other end of the beach near Wya Point Resort, a short drive from Ucluelet. When a wolf attacked her dog and tried to drag it off, nearby campers came to the rescue. The dog survived but Flood was badly shaken, as she often let her children run and play on the beach alone when they visited the area.

There are signs in PRNPR stating that all dogs must be leashed. But those long stretches of sand are dog heaven and it seems cruel not to let your four-legged companion enjoy them. I know because I've done it in the past. I did have an air horn and pepper spray but now realize that if something had happened, chances are I wouldn't have been close enough to save my dog. As Bob Hansen says, "When your dog is off-leash in the park, it's playing on the dinner table of cougars and wolves." On a visit to Wickaninnish Beach in 2016, I watched a park employee ask people to leash their free-running dogs. Not everyone complied, even when told that off-leash dogs had been attacked and killed there. As an incentive, the Parks person sometimes added that a wolf had never attacked a leashed dog in the park's history.

Then in March 2017, a black-faced wolf attacked an on-leash Jack Russell terrier. It took multiple people almost 30 minutes to fend off the wolf—one man even hit it with a piece of driftwood—and for everyone to get back to the parking area. People attempted to block the wolf from going back to the dog after the owner had it in her arms. The wolf followed them all the way to the parking lot, where it lingered for a while after the woman and dog left. Parks intensified their tactics to make wolves wary of people and increased public education. But in late May the same wolf attacked an on-leash golden retriever on the beach below the Green Point Campground. During the scuffle, the owner fell to the ground, where she kicked at the wolf and shouted until help arrived. That day park staff tracked the wolf to Florencia Bay, where it was killed that evening. The BC wildlife vet's report said the wolf was thin but otherwise healthy. This was only the second wolf destroyed by staff in the 47-year history of PRNPR. The first occurred in 2004 when a young food-conditioned wolf was showing increasingly bold behaviour around humans in the Broken Group Islands. A park warden had hazed the animal and was sitting on a log with a clear view of the beach and forest waiting to see if it would return when he heard a noise and turned to see the wolf right behind him with a plastic jar of mustard in its mouth. It had flipped the lid off his lunch cooler. Due to the wolf's persistent boldness around humans, the warden shot it.

A few weeks after the wolf was destroyed in Florencia Bay, another was killed by the BC Conservation Officer Service after showing up at the Ucluelet elementary school while classes were in session. Officials had been tracking it for several days as locals used social media to chart its appearances outside the drugstore, community centre and beer and wine shop. This wolf was also lean but had no signs of health problems or disease.

All the wolf activity prompted Windle to organize public information sessions in communities adjacent to PRNPR, inviting prominent officials, the BC Conservation Officer Service, wildlife officials and others. At some point, Dianne St. Jacques, the mayor of Ucluelet, came up with the phrase "Scare, don't stare" regarding the hazards of allowing wildlife in communities. People began to get the message; one Facebook post by a local woman described how she scared a deer out of town, much to the consternation of tourists. Parks Canada hired 10 wildlife ambassadors as part of a university student summer jobs program to talk to people visiting PRNPR about the importance of leashing dogs, maintaining distance between people and wildlife, and properly managing attractants. It's estimated that non-compliance in leashing dogs dropped from 50 to 25 per cent. "With more people leashing their dogs and the destruction of two wolves, interactions with wolves have been minimal," Hansen told me in September 2017. "They're still there, we see their tracks and see them on wildlife cams in the area, but they're very wary of people."

None of the people whose dogs were attacked in PRNPR wanted the wolves responsible killed. *We're in their territory*, they said. *They're beautiful animals. It wasn't their fault.* They're right on all counts. But the danger goes further than just an injured or dead dog and a bad scare. Dogs are usually found where humans are: on a trail, a beach or in the backyard. What would have happened if other people hadn't been around when the woman fell when a wolf attacked her dog? Would it have shifted its attention to her as vulnerable prey? Or possibly to a nearby child who screamed, ran or fell? Each time a wolf approaches a dog or human and doesn't receive strong negative feedback, it becomes bolder. At some point, it loses its fear of humans and becomes dangerous.

"People need to be super-aggressive immediately if a wolf approaches them or their dog," advises Hansen. "Yell and stamp your feet as you move towards them. That sends an important message that you're human, not prey." Jim Barr told me about a time he was hiking in the mountains behind the Comox Valley and suddenly saw a pack of wolves on the trail ahead of him. He threw a rock and yelled but they just looked at him. When he threw another rock, he took a few steps forward and the wolves left. In addition to bear spray and an air horn, Hansen always uses a hiking stick. This can be waved overhead to make him look larger and used as a weapon if need be. "Always maintain eye contact too," he says. "That's a sign of dominance wolves will recognize. It's important to send a strong, clear message immediately. Everything may happen in a 10-second interval, so you need to be prepared to escalate your aggression quickly. Unfortunately, that seems to be difficult for many people to accept."

Park officials don't like killing wildlife but human safety must come first. And PRNPR staff are very aware of how serious a human-wolf encounter can be. Seventeen years earlier, Sandra Ross, her husband, Bob, and three friends were celebrating the 2000 Canada Day long weekend at Dick and Jane Beach on the northwest side of Vargas Island. Known for its sandy beaches and close proximity to Tofino—about three kilometres (less than two miles) away at the closest points—Vargas is a popular destination for kayakers and day-trippers. Sandra and Linda Hiney were cleaning up after the first night's dinner when they glanced up and saw a wolf. "It was at the treeline with its front paws on a log, chest out, surveying our campsite," says Sandra. "It was incredible the way the sunset highlighted his fur." Torn between grabbing cameras or sticks, the women knew they would never forget the sight. The group had seen the wolf advisory signs but knew the drill: food was stored in the kayak hatches down the beach and a net bag with drinks was stashed in a creek some distance away.

Three wolves visited the camp the next evening but they shooed them away. One member of the group wasn't happy about the wolves coming so close but Bob assured him that, to his knowledge, there had never been a case of a healthy wolf attacking a person in BC. That evening, two sets of campers arrived and set up down the beach. Bob walked over and told the couple and the group of University of Victoria students that wolves were in the area. Everyone was cool, they knew what to do. The 18 students, originally on their way to nearby Flores Island, had decided to spend the night on Vargas due to strong winds and tidal currents. They told Bob they had some bear bangers if there was any trouble.

Around 1:30 a.m. one of the students, Wes Yung, woke to find a wolf sitting on the end of his sleeping bag. He kicked at the wolf and yelled. The wolf moved away but didn't leave until another student made some noise. Yung tried to wake Scott Langevin, who had also chosen to sleep outside, but when the 23-year-old didn't respond, Yung gave up and moved into his tent. Screams woke everyone up 30 minutes later. A wolf had pulled Langevin, still in his sleeping bag, away from the fire pit. When Langevin woke up and shouted at the wolf, it released its grip and stepped back. Then it lunged forward, attacking Langevin's upper body. Encumbered by his sleeping bag, Langevin fought back as best he could, yelling and trying to roll back toward the fire pit. But as he struggled, the wolf jumped on his back and started biting his head. By this time, everyone was awake and a clamour of yelling and bear bangers added to the racket. The wolf took off and help was summoned via a marine VHF radio. Tofino residents Dave LeBlanc and Doug Leys overheard the call to the coast guard and raced to the site. Langevin was bleeding and in shock but conscious when they loaded him into the Zodiac and whisked him to Tofino General Hospital. The injured man was stabilized and transferred to a Victoria hospital where he was treated for wounds to his hands and back, and 50 stitches were required to reattach his scalp.

"We woke up when the bear bangers went off," says Sandra Ross. "It wasn't long before a couple of students came over to tell us what had happened. The next morning the students and couple left. Two conservation officers showed up later that day and asked us to leave but it was too late to kayak back to Tofino so we stayed the night."

The conservation officers set traps at each end of the beach and built a fire not far from the remaining camp. At dawn they checked the traps. The first was empty but as they approached the second, three wolves came running across the rocks straight toward them. "We heard 'Bang! Bang!'" says Ross. "Two wolves were dead. Not the magnificent one we saw the first night, two others. We were sad but understood why it had to happen." Shortly after the shooting, men from Ahousaht arrived by boat, upset that the conservation officers had killed their spiritual brothers. As traditional territory of the Nuu-chah-nulth, Vargas was where many members of the Ahousaht First Nation lived until they relocated to more sheltered land on Flores Island. Wolves and the sacred Wolf Society and ceremony are a vital part of their culture, which prohibits killing the canids.

Helen Schwantje, a wildlife veterinarian with BC's Ministry of Forests, noted that the two wolves were healthy, sexually immature and approximately 14 months old. The male weighed 37 kilograms (82 lbs) and the female 29 kilograms (64 lbs). They were identified as the two that had interacted with people at different locations on Vargas over the summer, and one was linked to the attack on Langevin by fur on his sleeping bag.

The July 2000 mauling and the subsequent shooting of two animals was not the beginning or the end of wolf problems on Vargas. And although it was the first confirmed wolf attack on a human in BC in 100 years, it wasn't the last. In February 2008, 68-year-old Marilyn Maple, who lives on a farm north of Fort St. John, heard one of her goats screaming. When she entered the barn, a crushing force gripped her by the upper arm and she found herself staring into the eyes of a wolf. Maple tried to chase it away with a pitchfork but when it refused to give up the goat, a neighbour shot it. A conservation officer noted that the animal was old and skinny with broken, worn-down teeth. A more serious attack took place on the Anderson Islands, 125 kilometres (78 mi) north of Bella Bella on BC's central coast, in 2007. A 31-year-old kayaker was setting up camp when he noticed movement in his peripheral vision. It was a female wolf charging from about 15 metres (50 ft) away. The wolf latched on to his thigh, repeatedly biting the man on the hands and legs as he tried to escape. He managed to drag the wolf to his kayak where he grabbed a 10-centimetre (4 in) knife and stabbed it repeatedly in the throat and chest. The wolf stumbled off and the man called for help on his marine radio. Rescuers shot the wolf and took it and the wounded man to Bella Bella. After the necropsy, Schwantje said the wolf was old and thin and tested negative for rabies. In each case, the reasons for the aggressive behaviour were obvious: both wolves were old and starving and one attacked while defending its prey, while the other was possibly predatory. The backstory to the Vargas Island attack, however, is much more complex.

About two weeks before Langevin was attacked, Jacqueline Windh and Adrian Dorst, both professional photographers based in Tofino at the time, heard there was a grey whale carcass that wolves were feeding on at a Vargas beach. They planned to camp for a few nights, hoping to get some good photos. For Windh, it was just a normal wildlife shoot. She planned to set up her tripod and camera with a long lens and train it on the dead whale while she hid in the woods. She'd take a chair, a good book, sit still for long periods of time and hope a wolf showed up.

Dorst headed to the island in his speedboat while Windh paddled over in her kayak. As she landed on the beach she saw a wolf walking toward her from the other end. She quickly got out of the kayak and started taking photos. The wolf was moving briskly but not running. Windh kept adjusting her lens for distance and then realized she was looking down and, following her photographer's instinct, squatted. "It all happened so quickly," she says. "One minute the wolf was down the beach, the next I was crouched down face to face with a predator. I felt very vulnerable." The wolf was sniffing the air. Not sure what to do, Windh put her hand out, similar to what she'd do with a strange dog, but with a closed fist. "The wolf sniffed my hand then gently put her mouth around it, clearly expecting food. It was obvious it had been fed by people. When it realized I didn't have anything, it left."

When Dorst met Windh, he told her he'd seen people who lived on a nearby island feeding a wolf on Vargas earlier that day. As the photographers sat and talked at the edge of the woods, two wolves approached. The female was lighter in colour and super friendly while the male was larger and wilder. "They played and ran together, shoulder to shoulder, and were almost certainly brother and sister," Windh says. As she and Dorst set up camp they realized that they didn't need to hide to take photographs, as the wolves were coming right up to them. That night the female curled up and slept between their tents. "I thought it took thousands of years for wolves to become dogs," Dorst told Windh, "but it looks like it could have happened overnight."

Windh felt something bump her tent early the next morning and looked out to see three wolves playing on the beach. When they noticed her, one slipped off into the trees while the others came closer.

These wolf siblings lived on Vargas Island. Over the course of a year or more they became extremely habituated to people and food-conditioned. Sometimes they found food at messy campsites, while other times people fed them. They were hanging around two campers and acting very friendly when suddenly the male wolf lowered his head and came at them in an aggressive manner. Two weeks later, one of the wolves attacked and seriously injured a camper. Photo by Jacqueline Windh

The female stole Dorst's belt and both wolves tried to cart away big juice jugs Windh had filled with water. "The female would dig in the sand in front of me and then crouch down with her bum in the air like a dog wanting to play," she recalls. "It tore me apart—I really wanted to play with her. I had such mixed feelings, the joy of being with wolves and the deep disturbance that they were so habituated. These were wild wolves and this was not normal behaviour. We knew something bad was going to happen, we just didn't know how soon it would be."

They got a hint that morning. "While the female was trying to entice us to play, suddenly the male put his head down and started coming toward us in a more aggressive way—the whole tone changed right then," Windh says. She had on old sweatpants with a tear in the knee, and open-toed shoes. The male wolf started lunging and snapping at the bare skin exposed at her toes and knee. Windh and Dorst knew the situation was becoming dangerous. Standing close together

they slowly backed up the beach toward an area with rocks. By this time the female was involved, circling around and approaching from the rear as the male continued to press forward. "He was clearly testing me," says Windh. "I knew if I ran he would chase me and if he nipped me and tasted blood, I would be prey."

Windh had a stick but didn't want to use it on the wolf—even though she felt threatened, she didn't want to hurt him—and she wasn't sure how he would respond if she was aggressive. "Adrian and I were both yelling," she says. "I was shouting, 'No! No!' then realized that's how I would talk to a dog and asked myself, 'How do wolves communicate?' So I growled, and then the male got really aggressive. By this time we'd reached the rocks. I threw one and it went past the male. He turned to it, obviously thinking it was food, and that somehow defused the situation." Knowing they were putting themselves and the wolves at risk, Windh and Dorst left the area immediately. "A couple of months later I visited an IMAX set in Idaho for a bear film," Windh says. "It was on a game farm with captive wolves. They were way more skittish around people—even their handlers—than the two wolves on Vargas had been."

That same month, Bob Hansen received a marine radio call at 4 a.m. from a kayak guide on Vargas Island with 11 paddlers. She said a wolf kept approaching them and even ventured into a tent vestibule. They'd been up all night trying to scare it away but weren't having any success. Hansen told her to get everyone to raise their paddles over their heads and walk closely together toward the wolf yelling as loudly as possible. While doing so, one of the kayakers threw a stick at the wolf in an effort to scare it away but the wolf ran up thinking it was

Wolves work hard to obtain their food and are more than willing to scavenge a free meal if it's available. For coastal wolves, that includes any dead animal that washes ashore. This whale carcass on Vargas Island was an incredibly rich resource for the wolves that discovered it. Photo by Jacqueline Windh food. Concerned about safety, and since it was already light out, the guide decided to break camp. After everyone had safely launched, she was sitting in her kayak waiting for a wave to lift it off the beach when the wolf came up within a couple of metres (six feet) of her. Tired and angry, she growled at it. The wolf bared its teeth and growled back just as the ocean carried her away.

The wolf attack on Scott Langevin was a flashpoint in human-wolf interactions fuelled by rumour and speculation. Some suspect area residents were being paid to feed wolves to set up photo ops for professional photographers; others heard that people were making contact with the wolves because the animals had a message for humankind and it was their duty to receive it. It's no secret that for at least a year before the Langevin attack, wolves were approaching humans and being fed. One day a German tourist had looked up from his lunch to see a wolf behind his wife. Instinctively he threw something to scare it away. Unfortunately, it was a sausage. Members of the Ahousaht First Nation went to Vargas and cut pieces of meat from a

whale carcass and left it in piles for the wolves. Photographs of kayakers feeding hot dogs to wolves on Vargas made the rounds in Tofino. A woman told my partner about a visit to the island where a wolf spent the entire day with her family. She called the experience "spiritual and mystical" and said that while one of the group was sitting on a log with his shoes off, the wolf came up and put its mouth over his bare toes.

Feelings still run high when it comes to wolves and Vargas. Depending on who you talk to, the attack is blamed on this person or that group. The reality is that the situation was the result of numerous human-wolf interactions that happened over time. It also occurred when deer numbers in the region had declined to historically low numbers. While there's no doubt that the wolves were strongly habituated to humans and food-conditioned, what is debatable is whether the July 2000 altercation began as an attack.

Wolves throughout Canada and Alaska appear to have a high level of curiosity about and fascination with human belongings. In "A Case History of Wolf-Human Encounters in Alaska and Canada," Mark E. McNay documents many cases of wolves stealing shoes, clothing and camping gear. While Paul Paquet was studying wolves in southwest Manitoba in 1984, an older female wolf snatched a camera lens cloth he'd left on the ground. He was surprised to see her still carrying it around when he returned the following year. This attraction to non-food novelty items suggests some wolves may view human belongings as toys, trophies or souvenirs. Camp robbing by wolves has been reported throughout North America since the 1880s. It occurs in remote areas where it's unlikely the wolves are habituated to humans and also where animals have shown high levels of habituation. When I asked Paquet about it, he replied, "I'm not sure other than that they are cognizant of their surroundings and are perhaps attracted to novel objects as part of the psychological mapping of the environment they do."

Langevin isn't the first person to sleep outdoors and wake up to the unwanted attentions of a wolf. As mentioned in the previous chapter, at Algonquin Provincial Park in 1996 a wolf seriously injured a child in a sleeping bag and also snatched a pack being used as a pillow from under a person's head. A man sleeping outside at Tibbles Lake near Quesnel, BC, in the summer of 1988 woke up when a wolf bit him in the side. As he shouted and waved his arms, the wolf moved off, then approached again, leaving only after the man rose to his knees and continued to make noise. Seven years earlier, at BC's Mount Robson Provincial Park, a wolf bit into a sleeping bag and dragged it and the occupant some distance before the camper yelled and the wolf ran away.

In two of the above events, the wolves were known camp robbers and highly habituated to humans. One was old with worn teeth, while the condition of the others is unknown. It's possible the sleeping bags or people in them smelled of food. Of the two cases involving serious human injury, the Vargas attack was classified as predatory but the Algonquin attack raised some questions. Tears in the boy's sleeping bag indicated that the wolf, which had a reputation as a camp robber, tried to pull the bag and the weight of the boy caused the fabric to rip. Officials speculated that the wolf may then have attempted to move the bag by biting into the boy's head. The boy's multiple wounds could mean the wolf was releasing and re-gripping in hopes of getting a better hold or that the boy's cries and frantic movements may have triggered a defensive/aggressive response.

The shooting of two wolves on Vargas didn't end the problems between humans and wolves on the island. Students in the Georges P. Vanier Secondary School Explore Program on central Vancouver Island have camped on the island every spring since 2001. "The caretaker of a house on Dick and Jane Beach where we stay used to scare wolves off with a gun," says Grayson Pettigrew, a science and biology teacher at Vanier. "He didn't hurt them, just shot over their heads to instill fear. Since he left, we've been seeing more wolves the last few years, but always at a distance. They usually disappear when they see us or stick to their end of the beach so there's no interaction."

The first night of the May 2016 trip, Pettigrew and another adult heard a noise at 3 a.m. and found food spread all over the beach. The trail cameras Pettigrew always sets up showed two wolves visiting their camp four times between 11:30 p.m. and 3 a.m. One peed on a kayak, an action typically interpreted as territorial. On one trip through, a wolf easily flipped off the rubber top to a kayak hold while the other undid the buckles on another hold and slid open the hard cover. Despite all that activity, they were extremely quiet and no one heard them until their 3 a.m. foray. "One of our teams lost all their food; we're lucky there were enough of us to share," says Pettigrew. "Also, a spray skirt to one of the kayaks was ripped; it's just a fluke that we had an extra one with us."

A few days before the Vanier trip, BC Parks had posted an alert on the Vargas website warning people not to store food in kayaks

with rubber hatches due to problems with wolves breaking into them. The Vanier group followed those guidelines but no one guessed that the wolves would learn how to get into kayaks with hard hatch covers.

The metal food cache at the campsite wasn't large enough for the group's food supplies so the following three nights, some of the adults built a big fire and kept watch. "We had to run wolves off the first two nights but they didn't come back after that," Pettigrew says. "Several times I had to chase wolves down the beach in my sock feet. They ran away but would kind of look over their shoulder at you like, 'Are you really coming after me?'" The group also used bear bangers and air horns, finding the latter more effective as they produced noise more quickly. The incident was especially disheartening as Pettigrew's trail camera footage from 2014, showing wolves sniffing kayak hatches and then leaving, was being used by BC Parks as an example of the right way to store food in wolf country. BC Parks now recommends removing everything from kayaks and storing all food and toiletry items in the food caches, or the old-fashioned way, using a rope and pulley system high on a tree branch, commonly called a bear hang.

"In the past, people who kayaked wanted to get out into the wilderness," says Liam McNeil, general manager at Tofino Sea Kayaking. "They were usually very experienced and knew what do to. But the increased popularity and lower cost of equipment has changed things. People can go into a big box store, buy a plastic

For many years, kayakers were encouraged to keep all their food supplies in their kayak hatches when camping. When wolves learned how easy it was to break into rubber kayak hatch covers, people were told to store food only in hatches with hard-sided covers. But wolves can smell food from a great distance and have figured out how to undo buckles and flip off hard covers. The only safe way to store food while camping is to use a food safe or bear hang. Photo by Liam McNeil kayak, put it on their car, drive to Tofino and head out. Wolves are very intelligent; sometimes it only takes a single incident to change their behaviour." After wolves began breaking into kayaks with hard hatch covers, the company increased their education about wildlife and provided complimentary bear hang kits with every kayak rental. McNeil also spearheaded a campaign to install two more food caches on Vargas. Ocean Simone, general manager at Ocean Outfitters in Tofino, organized a group letter with other organizations to send to the Clayoquot area supervisor for the BC Ministry of Environment and the Conservation Officer Service, requesting that they honour the Ahousaht First Nation's request for a no-kill policy for wolves on Vargas Island and zero tolerance for improperly stored food. BC Parks also installed additional food caches and increased public education. Meanwhile, on nearby Flores Island, the Ahousaht are worried about wolves coming into the community and taking dogs in broad daylight. But their concerns for the safety of residents and pets clash with their spiritual view of wolves and their cultural protocol of not killing them.

Wolf attacks differ from cougar and most bear attacks. Attacks by cougars and bears can usually be clearly defined as defensive or predatory. A situation arises—people are near a bear's cubs, or a cougar sees a person as prey—and they attack. Wolf attacks can be defensive or predatory, but they seem more willing to interact with humans and it is common for attacks by healthy wolves to follow a lengthy progression of becoming less fearful around people.

Over the course of two decades, the relatively close regions of Port Alberni, Vargas Island and PRNPR and adjoining communities have experienced a level of human-wolf conflict that was unheard of in the past. At times, wolves seemed to innately have no fear of humans; at others, the lack of wariness escalated over time. In some instances the backstory was extensive. There are many contributing factors and some, such as changes to the landscape and an increase in both wolves and people on the land, cannot easily be controlled. Enhanced public education and additional food caches appear to have turned the situation around for the time being, but until more people understand how important their actions are for the safety of both humans and wildlife, chances are more wolves may have to be destroyed.

CHAPTER 11

LIVING WITH WOLVES

The best wolf is a wild wolf.
—DAN STRICKLAND

I WAS PULLING ON MY RAIN PANTS AS UNA LEDREW AND DAVE Ratcliffe's herring skiff nudged up against the Fourth Street dock in Tofino. The couple bought acreage on Vargas Island in the late 1970s and have lived there pretty well full-time since 2007. I heard about them when I visited a walk-in medical clinic on the other side of Vancouver Island. Dr. John Fitzpatrick recognized me as the author of *The Cougar* and asked what I was working on. When I said "wolves," he grabbed a prescription pad and scribbled the couple's names, saying, "You *must* talk to Una and Dave." A couple of emails and phone calls later, Rick and I were on our way to spend a few days with people we'd never met.

My biggest surprise while researching this book was discovering how many people hate wolves so intensely. And it's not just in the past—it continues today. At a public meeting held in Spooner, Wisconsin, two years ago, one family arrived wearing T-shirts emblazoned with the words, "Don't discriminate, kill all wolves." When a woman at the meeting stated, "The only good wolf is a dead wolf," more than half the audience applauded. A few years ago, organizations in several US states attempted to arrange predator-killing derbies, some specifically targeting wolves. The three-day, no bag limit events welcomed participants as young as 10, offering cash prizes for killing the first, largest and smallest animals. An attempt to hold a similar wolf-only contest in northern BC in 2012 was cancelled. Video clips from Eurasia show cheering villagers encouraging their dogs to attack a restrained wolf and men deliberately running over an injured wolf with a snowmobile and then laughing while they beat it and stick lit cigarettes up its nose. Hunting with golden eagles has long been an honoured tradition in Mongolia but I've also viewed video clips that show men using one or more of the large eagles to attack a tied-up wolf.

Wolves aren't a problem when they're way out on the tundra or in the wilderness far from human habitation. There are no livestock, pets or unsecured garbage to tempt them, no hikers accidently dropping energy bar wrappers, no messy campsites and no one trying to lure the canids in for the selfie of a lifetime. It's only when wolves live near human-use areas that there's conflict. But amid the brutality, confusion, ignorance and controversy surrounding *Canis lupus*, coexistence with wolves is possible and I didn't have to travel far from home to find two examples.

Ledrew and Ratcliffe's home sits on a rocky outcropping overlooking Clayoquot Sound. Windows wrap around nearly every side of the upstairs living area, allowing golden light from the rising sun to spill into the space in the morning and silvery light from the stars and moon to fill it at night. Ledrew's ready laugh and Ratcliffe's laid-back manner erased any awkwardness immediately and, dogless at the time, Rick and I enjoyed the company of Powak, the couple's three-year-old labradoodle that never stopped wagging his tail, and Frankie, their adult daughter's French bulldog. An old-timer now, Frankie, lower body snugly wrapped in a brightly patterned piddle diaper, spent most of his time dozing. When his feet twitched, I imagined him dreaming of the dawn long ago when he chased a wolf and, rousted out of bed by the commotion, members of his human family chased after

Frankie and the wolf dressed in their usual sleeping attire, which was nothing at all.

A day of exploring took us to a nearby beach via the herring skiff and a path that required some serious bushwhacking. Even with Ratcliffe breaking trail, by the end of the day, my legs looked like I'd lost a shin-kicking contest and Powak, the three-legged wonder dog, had run circles around us all. We discovered old wolf scat, a single paw print in the sand and remnants of former wolf meals in the form of a large bird skeleton and a pile of seal bones. Ledrew and Ratcliffe had hardly seen any wolves over the winter and thought there might only be one or two left. Wolves haven't always inhabited Vargas. As far as the couple knows, the canids showed up sometime in the 1980s. They were very shy, seen one moment and gone the next, more often heard howling out of sight. "I think they saw us more than we saw them," Ratcliffe says, recalling a time he walked by a bush and noticed a wolf behind it, watching him. At a rough estimate they think the highest number of wolves on Vargas peaked at seven to ten, with two packs, one on the southern end of the island and the other on the northern. Most years there were fewer and some years, as far as they could tell, none. Ratcliffe noted that the island used to have lots of deer, mink and river otter but thinks the wolves ate them all. Ledrew suspects they eat a lot of mice, just like Farley Mowat said in *Never Cry Wolf*.

The couple spent the summer of 2000 tuna fishing, so they weren't on Vargas when the wolf attacked Scott Langevin. They were shocked and saddened by the news, especially since they work so hard to avoid any problems. They're scrupulous about not leaving any food scraps outside, they burn their compost and if their dog or a visiting

Wolves that are not habituated or food-conditioned will pass through human-use areas in the middle of the night or when they think no one is around. With its tail tucked between its legs and head down, this wolf is almost tiptoeing through the yard in an effort not to be noticed. Photo by Una Ledrew dog chases a wolf off the property, they add to the unwelcome committee with air horns, whistles and shouting. They've trained Powak to come to a whistle and he never seems eager to chase a wolf beyond the edge of the clearing. "Having our family dog on the island with us is something we take very seriously," Ledrew explains. "It's a big responsibility and a lot of work. We've clicker-trained Powak to stay close when we're out hiking and he's never left outside alone. We've learned to recognize his bark when a wolf is in the area and immediately leash him or bring him inside."

Ledrew and Ratcliffe usually saw wolves about once a month in the summer and more frequently during the winter and spring. The wolves passed in front of their home on the shoreline rocks or occasionally through their yard to access the stretch of beach adjacent to their property. The spring of 2013 was different, however. A pack of five showed up and stayed for three months. They might have felt comfortable doing so since the couple didn't have a dog at the time. The adult male wolf was black while the adult female and yearling pups had a reddish tinge to their coats. Ledrew and Ratcliffe saw or heard

the wolves every day. "We're on their travel corridor," says Ledrew. "They don't have an option; they have to go by to eat on our beach. There are a limited number of places on Vargas where wolves can turn over rocks and get crabs and gunnels. At low tide they'd eat chitons off the reef just out from our place. You could tell from their scat what they were eating."

The couple quietly observed the wolves from their second-storey windows or deck. The wolves jumped and played on the beach like dogs and one always seemed to be on watch when the others slept. When a dead seal washed up on the beach, the adults waited on the rocks while the youngsters pulled it higher up, then they all chowed down. Ledrew and Ratcliffe never approached, interacted with or fed the wolves, yet sometimes they were nearby when the couple was outside. The wolves liked to lie in the freshly dug earth of the garden and once, when Ledrew put her work gloves on the steps while she went for lunch, she returned to find them in the garden bed where she'd been digging. Sometimes the wolves paralleled the couple in the bush

when they walked island trails. One time when she was alone, Ledrew saw the male coming toward her on the trail from the opposite direction. "I think he was old then. He was walking slowly with his head hanging down. I yelled at him, 'Get out of here, get off my trail, this is my space, go away!' He looked up and then slipped into the bush." The biggest puzzle was the rope. "They were chewing on and swallowing rope of all kinds, plastic rope, big thick rope we used to tie up the skiff," Ledrew says. "You'd find pieces of it a couple of inches long in their scat."

"I told Una that if a wolf ever threatened anyone, I'd have to deal with it," Ratcliffe says. But there were only two incidents, and Ratcliffe felt that the first was his fault. "I was walking up a bank and all of a sudden the big black male was running straight toward me. I yelled and waved my arms and it backed off. I think the way the wind was blowing, it didn't hear or smell me and suddenly this disembodied head appeared. A few minutes later I heard all the wolves whimpering like, 'Wow, that was scary!'" On another occasion, a wolf chased a dog and they both ended up running around Ratcliffe, who kicked out and yelled. "Those were the only two times I wondered if a wolf was too comfortable around humans," he says.

When asked about coexisting with wolves, the couple noted that visitors to the island have really increased since the western portion became a provincial park in 1995. They wish people were required to take a wilderness camping course before visiting places like Vargas and that everyone would follow the regulations requiring campers to use bear hangs or food caches. The couple has backpacked throughout Canada and always practises the "if they don't leave, we do" approach

Coastal wolves often eat a lot of clams, marine-oriented animals and fish. This wolf is lifting rocks in search of food. Vargas Island resident Una Ledrew has often seen wolves eating gunnels (small fish) they've found under rocks. Photo by Una Ledrew to problem wildlife. "If an animal is coming too close or acting aggressive, we just leave them alone and go somewhere else," Ledrew says.

Ledrew and Ratcliffe live on the opposite end of the island from where a wolf attacked Scott Langevin in 2000 but lots of people have camped and interacted with wolves on beaches near their home. The reason they haven't had any problems is because they don't allow wolves to come close, don't leave any attractants out and never feed them. Also, the wolves that spent a few months around their property showed up 13 years after the attack, so they could have been from a totally different pack. For more than 30 years, the couple has lived on Vargas with wolves and dogs, yet managed to avoid conflict. It requires thought and planning but, for Ledrew and Ratcliffe, their love of wild places, and the animals that inhabit them, makes the effort worthwhile. I was impressed by their dedication and commitment. I could see two people making a decision to coexist with wolves but could a community pull it off? In early spring, I headed to Cortes Island to find out.

It was a cold blustery day for two ferry trips and the last ride was rough enough to remind me of the few times I've been seasick. It wasn't my first visit to Cortes, located at the northern tip of the Strait of Georgia, but I'd forgotten its charm. Lakes, forests, sandy beaches, a stunning lagoon and Hollyhock, an adult learning centre that focuses on wellness, leadership and wise social change, attract visitors throughout the summer. During the off-season, the population drops to about 1,000 full-time residents.

The first afternoon I explored narrow, winding, hilly roads tunnelling through tall evergreens with peekaboo gaps showing the water beyond. I passed driveways that looked like goat trails, some appearing impassable without four-wheel drive. It was April and the air was redolent with the scent of skunk cabbage, the bright yellow flowers lining the ditches in a stinky spring display. Later, on a walk, I heard a sound and turned to see a raven flying level with my head within arm's reach. It looked into my eyes, then soared high to circle above me before taking off. The next morning I woke to the sound of rain pelting the metal roof of the little cabin in the woods I'd rented. It also sounded like I was surrounded by a sea of frogs.

Wolves have been on Cortes for as long as anyone can remember and were known to take some sheep in the old days. In the 1970s a vigorous eradication program ended the problem but it wasn't long before new wolves swam over, most likely island-hopping or swimming from the BC mainland a short distance away. Cortes is about 24 kilometres (15 mi) long by 13 kilometres (8 mi) wide. You can draw a line horizontally across the island and more or less isolate the northern part as a large, unfragmented landscape. Most people live on the southern portion of Cortes, so for many years it was wolves in the north, humans in the south. In the past, residents knew wolves were around from the paw prints sometimes found on the edges of clearings or beaches and suspected they were the reason the occasional dog disappeared. On the whole, wolves were heard and not seen. That all changed in 2008.

All of a sudden, wolves were trotting down driveways during the day and walking down the road looking at cars and bikes and sometimes following them. Sheep and chickens were being killed and hikers were sometimes escorted along trails. Members of a pack of about eight wolves were running toward people as they dug clams or walked on beaches. Energetic yelling and rock throwing prompted a retreat but the wolves often came back two or three times, only breaking off when people reached the safety of a boat. Cortes has a large shellfish industry so, depending on the tides and season, people can be working the beaches day or night. There were about eight beach incidents, some involving wolves coming very close to people. For decades it was rare for anyone to see a wolf, and now it seemed like every second person had a wolf story. No one understood what was going on or knew what to do about it.

Instead of getting guns or asking government officials to conduct a cull, a group of residents created the Cortes Island Wolf Project. They arranged for Bob Hansen, employed as a Parks Canada human-wildlife conflict specialist at the time, and Ben Yorke, then-supervisor of conservation officers in the Cortes region, to give a presentation at the community hall. Hansen and Yorke made it clear that, under the right circumstances, wolves will attack humans, and that they had done so on the coast in the not-too-distant past. They stressed that some of the behavioural flags of the wolves that had to be destroyed on the west coast of Vancouver Island were present on Cortes. If Cortes wolves didn't learn to be wary around humans, the threat to people could increase and conflicts leading to wolf destruction would definitely increase.

This meant a radical shift in thinking for many. Fences needed to be mended, livestock and pets brought in at night, chickens fenced, garbage and compost handled appropriately, dogs kept on leash when off property and not left outside for long alone, even during the day. Just as important, wolves needed to be hazed if seen in human-use areas to learn they weren't welcome. If hazing happens soon enough and often enough, wolves can learn to avoid human habitat, as long as the attractants that are drawing them in are also managed.

A database was created to record wolf sightings and descriptions. A "Learning to Live with Wolves on Cortes Island" poster was printed and continues to be displayed on the ferry, as well as at stores, campgrounds and other locations. The highlights of this five-point primer, created in cooperation with Hansen and Yorke and endorsed by the BC Conservation Officer Service, are: never feed wolves; do not feed deer or raccoons; keep yourself safe by hazing wolves when encountered in a residential area; keep your pets safe by leashing dogs or leaving them at home when spending time in wolf territory; and practise good animal husbandry.

One of the first things Cortes residents learned was that the island had two types of wolves. There was one pack with 16 members, easily recognized by their size, colouration and markings; they sometimes roamed together or broke up into smaller sub-groups. There were also transient wolves that swam over from the mainland or nearby islands and left when they realized Cortes already had a resident pack. Initially, biologists and wildlife officials doubted there was enough prey on the island to support a pack of 16, but that was before it was widely known that coastal wolves could survive on a combination of ungulate and marine resources or even marine food sources alone. Like many BC islands, Cortes has a mix of muskrat, deer and Canada geese, as well as rich clam beaches and big haul-outs where seals come ashore.

Hansen and Yorke were invited back for a three-day weekend wolf conference featuring a diverse range of wolf experts. That was a turning point for how Cortes residents thought about wolves. Of course, not everyone buys into the program. Some people still fear wolves, some still hate them and some probably still kill them. But as of 2011, wolf sightings and human-wolf conflicts on Cortes have dropped significantly. Dave Eyer suggested two possible reasons why that may have occurred. As a hunter and trapper who has lived in a remote area of BC for much of his adult life, Eyer has an intimate knowledge of nature and wildlife. Since 2000 he's taught a wildlife safety program for industry and government fieldworkers, which is now a required course for many employees.

"My suspicion is that for some reason the wolves could not or would not utilize all the food resources on the north end of the island," he says. "It may have been easier to move into the human-occupied section of the island to access food. The new territory and behaviour worked for a while but then people changed their behaviour. The easy food that had been available ended or diminished. Without the positive reward, their new territory could not support the pack. In addition, the hazing of the wolves by people, which may have included shooting one or two, taught them that their new territory was being contested by the human 'pack' that was already there."

As well as a change in human behaviour, Eyer thinks there may have been changes within the pack. The wolves had gone from a low, almost extirpated, population in the 1970s, to a high of 16 around 2009 and then, based on fewer sightings, it's assumed that number dropped in 2011. "That's a significant change for a small island, which may have resulted in behavioural changes for the wolves," he says. "Some wolves may have become injured, sick or died, or one or both of the breeding pair may have been replaced, all factors which could influence pack behaviour." Eyer speculated that with a smaller food supply, the big pack may have split into two with one driving the other away. Whatever the reason, he suspects that by 2011, wolf numbers had reverted to a sustainable level and were once again in balance with the food supply at the north end of the island, greatly reducing conflicts with the human population to the south.

All too often, stories featuring angry people protesting against wolves being killed or ranchers detailing recent wolf predation on livestock take precedence in the news. But as I discovered, efforts to coexist are quietly taking place on small islands in BC, ranches in Alberta and Saskatchewan and even in central Idaho, one of the most anti-wolf states in the US. Every year, spring through fall, some ranchers take their livestock out to US Forest Service grazing allotments in Blaine County, Idaho. In the past, they have often experienced problems with wolves. Now in its tenth year, the Wood River Wolf Project is primarily relying on non-lethal means to protect sheep in their allotment. Conservation organizations, along with county, state and federal agencies, are providing education and assistance with resources such as fladry, livestock guardian dogs and range riders. Sheep losses within the project area have been as much as 90 per cent lower than similar livestock grazing areas in Idaho and no wolves have been lethally removed since the middle of the 2016 field season. Respectful collaboration is also taking place in Washington state. Created by Washington's Department of Fish and Wildlife, the Wolf Advisory Group has brought together a diverse group of livestock producers, hunters and others to work together on wolf recovery, conservation and management.

Reducing conflict is key to coexisting with wolves and there are three areas where this can be improved. The first is to call a truce in the cultural divide between the mostly urban environmentalists and the largely rural farmers and hunters. The polarization between these groups is extreme but as Mitch Friedman, founder and executive director of Conservation Northwest, points out, cooperation and collaboration are more likely to produce long-term results than a landslide of press releases backed up by media events and acrimonious lawsuits. Rural residents are on the front line of the return of the wolf and, until their concerns are dealt with, coexistence will be difficult to achieve. And rural residents have to accept that times have changed and seek the help they need.

The urban/rural conflict over wolves in Europe is huge. Yet even though the land mass is smaller, wild spaces fewer and the human population denser, Europe has twice as many wolves as the lower 48 states. This is because some eastern European countries never eradicated their wolf populations and those that did are coexisting whether they want to or not due to strict legislative protection. "Recovery of Large Carnivores in Europe's Modern Human-Dominated Landscapes," published in the journal *Science* in December 2014, notes that countries that don't belong to the EU, which is responsible for most of the legislation protecting wolves, are not experiencing the same rate of wolf recovery as those who are part of it.

The EU model of coexistence clearly shows that government plays a vital role in the protection of large carnivores, as well as providing people with the knowledge and tools they need to understand predator behaviour and act accordingly. This political will, the second component of coexisting with wolves, is not always present in North America. In the contiguous United States, grey wolves seesaw back and forth from federal jurisdiction and protection to state management, usually with a few lawsuits thrown in. Although wolf populations in Canada are, for the most part, healthy and increasing, wolf management plans are often vague and based on old values. BC is a good example. Its current wolf management plan, released in 2014, estimates the province's wolf population at anywhere from 5,300 to 11,600 and states that the number of wolves killed each year by trappers and hunters is not known due to the lack of a mandatory reporting system. The document adds, "Without more reliable estimates of the harvest it is difficult to assess the sustainability of BC's wolf harvest." Despite that, early in 2018, the BC government announced it was considering increasing the number of days wolves can be hunted on Vancouver Island.

The third element necessary for humans to coexist with wolves is educating the general public about the importance of establishing clear boundaries as to what is human habitat and what is wolf habitat. Wildlife officials urge people to keep a minimum of 100 metres (110 yds)—about the size of a football field, counting the end zones— away from wolves at all times. Living-with-wildlife specialist Bob Hansen believes "scare, don't stare" is the right message in any human-wolf situation, no matter how far away the animal is. "It's difficult to find remote areas that only ever receive a handful of human visitors and each kayaker, hiker or yachter that watches a wolf—even from 100 metres—is putting it at risk of becoming habituated," he explains. "Now I scare them away at first sight no matter what the distance. I don't need to see wolves. Finding fresh tracks and knowing that they're living their lives as large, wild predators as they have for millennia is enough of a thrill."

Just seeing wolf tracks disappearing down a fog-shrouded beach is enough to fill the soul with a sense of mystery and awe. Photo by Martin Ryer

Yellowstone National Park is particularly vigorous in their efforts to keep humans and wolves apart. Places where wolves regularly cross roads have signs declaring them no-stopping zones and are patrolled to ensure people comply. If wolves make a kill within view of a road, that area is closed for at least a kilometre (half a mile) and patrolled until the predators move on. "I don't worry about human safety; I worry about humans bothering wolves," says Doug Smith, senior biologist at the park. "In more than 20 years, we have never even come close to a person being injured by a wolf. People are required to remain at least 100 yards away from them. If a wolf moves toward someone, they have to maintain that distance by moving back. We ticket and fine people who don't obey park rules." The park's comprehensive education program includes a website with short wildlife safety videos, including one that explains what bear spray to purchase and how to use it.

"We're very proactive," Smith continues. "If we notice any inappropriate behaviour such as a wolf walking toward a vehicle or people, we haze them. Hazing is very effective if started immediately." Since 1995, six wolves have been hazed and two that did not respond were euthanized. They had not harmed anyone but their fearless behaviour and proximity to humans were considered too dangerous to continue.

Living with wolves also means considering how we want wildlife on the landscape. For a long time, we've focused on numbers: how many of this animal are present, how few of that creature can be found. The ecological health of a region has been a serious consideration only since the second half of the twentieth century. Wolves, perhaps more than any other animal, frequently serve as pawns on the chessboard of wildlife management. They've been imported to curb elk populations in Yellowstone National Park, culled to save caribou in BC and Alberta, and may be reintroduced to Isle Royale in Lake Superior to curtail the burgeoning moose population. But in our efforts to set things right, we sometimes forget that nature is constantly changing and that for a variety of reasons, wildlife populations can experience dynamic swings from many to a few or none.

Closely observed but, as of 2017, not managed in any way, the wolf-moose dynamic on Isle Royale is a telling example of the vagaries of nature. Ecologist John Vucetich, head of the Isle Royale Wolf-Moose Project since 2006, sums it up well on their website: "If we see Nature as a system whose future we can predict, then we will be confident in our efforts to control and manage Nature. If, in Nature, we are more impressed by its essentially contingent, and hence unpredictable, character, then our relationship will be more strongly rooted in striving to live within the boundaries of Nature's beautifully dynamic variation ... The wolves and moose of Isle Royale show how it is not so difficult to be proud for all that we've learned about Nature, yet humble for knowing how limited our understanding of it really is."

Managing wildlife will always be a finicky business fraught with disagreement and conflict, especially when it comes to wolves. The ones that live far from people can be left alone but for the ones living near humans, compromise is needed between those who love them and those who hate them. All wolves can't be saved, just as all wolves can't be killed. "People can coexist with wolves in wild lands and semi-wilderness so long as people accept that in most semi-wild areas, some wolves may have to be killed to minimize conflict with humans," Dave Mech of the US Geological Survey says. "A more balanced view of wolves would lead to better, more normal management with fewer extremes, and a greater chance of reducing conflicts with humans."

The how and why of wildlife management will always be up for debate. Decisions, however, can be based on science, not emotion, with wildlife approached in a thoughtful, compassionate manner. "There's an important distinction between management of wildlife and management for wildlife," points out large-carnivore expert Paul Paquet. "The first is from a human perspective and reflects what we want. The second is more difficult as it requires making decisions based on a concern for the wellbeing of wildlife. There is a lack of concern regarding quality of life for wolves. Their strong family relationships and emotional attachments are real. People see that in their dogs but not everyone sees it in wolves."

In addition to science-based, ethical management, the biggest gift we can give wildlife is space. In the 1980s, Stephen Herrero, a professor at the University of Calgary recognized worldwide for his studies on bear behaviour, began investigating the concept of large carnivore conservation in the Rockies. Eventually Paquet and others became involved in more detailed planning and mapping. The Yellowstone to Yukon Conservation Initiative (Y2Y), a joint Canada-US organization, was founded in 1997. Their grand vision is attempting to preserve and connect as many intact temperate and boreal forest ecosystems between southern Wyoming and northern Yukon as possible. The idea followed advances in GPS technology that revealed the vast territory wildlife move through.

Momentum for the project really took off when a five-year-old wolf was collared as part of the Central Rockies Wolf Project in 1991. It was raining so Graham Neale named her Pluie, the French word for rain. Pluie amazed everyone by travelling from Alberta's Peter Lougheed Provincial Park to BC, Idaho, Wyoming and Washington state. At one point, she was moving so fast they thought she'd hitched a ride on a truck. In 1993, someone found her collar battery and turned it in. When the research team saw the bullet hole in it, they were convinced she was dead. But in 1995, Pluie, collar intact except for the battery, as well as an adult male and three pups, were legally killed by a hunter near Invermere, BC. Pluie's 100,000-square-kilometre (40,000 sq mi) journey shone a light on the need for conservation corridors where wildlife would be protected. Twenty years on, Y2Y has doubled the park and conservation land within its designated habitat highway. The concept has caught on globally, with numerous countries around the world participating in a similar conservation program called Nature Needs Half.

Modern technology is allowing humans to observe previously unknown wildlife behaviour. When I visited Tofino in October 2015, Bob Hansen told me about a camera in the woods near his home and Wickaninnish Community School. It was part of the Connecting Students with Wildlife program that Hansen and Kelty Minton started at local schools. The goal was to teach students how to identify wildlife tracks, sign and game trails and, as Hansen says, give them a glimpse "behind the curtain of the forest" with motion-sensor cameras. The hill behind the school is a network of trails and Hansen felt confident they would record some animal activity. "We recorded a wolf the first week," he says. "Wolves were playing on the school field at night and bears and cougars were passing through." What Hansen hadn't expected was the amount of human activity—mostly dog walkers and joggers—the camera picked up. "What really amazed me was that the most often used wolf trail was also the most commonly used human trail," he says. "People were on it throughout the day and evening and the wolves were on it from 2 to 4 a.m." All the activity was taking place in a residential area a couple of blocks from "downtown" Tofino.

Parks Canada has used cameras to detect wildlife for some time. Long periods can go by without any reports of people seeing wolves, yet they show up on the cameras on a regular basis. "This tells us that wolves actively avoid people and have strategies to avoid being seen by us," explains Hansen. "They're in our communities way more than people realize. We could expect more conflict but most of the time, they're doing their bit to coexist with us, but humans aren't always doing theirs."

Coexisting isn't easy. Most of the time people don't even think about it until something happens and then they're upset if a wolf has to be killed. Feeding wolves may seem like a kind thing to do. What we often forget is how adaptable they are. If we haze them out of our communities and campsites during the day, they learn to stay away or pass through only when humans aren't around. If we stop wolves from coming close, as people are doing on Vargas and Cortes islands, we prevent conflict and possibly save their lives.

"Most people want carnivores on the landscape but they have to connect the dots for humans and carnivores to coexist in the long term," Hansen says. "People don't realize or give any thought to the consequences of how they act around wildlife. We need to train wolves how to behave and to set boundaries. Animals behave the way we've taught them to. It's a two-way relationship. We're the teachers and wolves are our incredibly astute students. We create the reality they adapt to."

CHAPTER 12

CHASING THE MOON

Wolves are what they are, not
what we think they are.
—KEVIN VAN TIGHEM,
The Homeward Wolf

IT ALL BEGAN WITH A DISCUSSION ABOUT HAIR. GARY ALLAN WAS WOR-
ried my black fleece jacket would be covered in it if I wore it into the
backyard to greet his four-member wolf-dog pack. I wasn't concerned
as I'd visited the pack several times over the last couple of years and
that had never happened before. I knew the routine: I'd go into the
backyard and Tundra and Meshach would come up to me and Nahanni
and Mahikan would fade into the background. Still, Allan insisted I
wear his old red raincoat. He's almost 30 centimetres (1 ft) taller than
me so it hung below my knees and the super-long sleeves meant he
had to zip up the front for me. All the wolf-dogs bounded onto the deck
the instant we stepped outside. Two-year-old Nahanni and Mahikan
hung back a bit but were still closer than normal. Tundra, age nine,
started lightly jumping up on me and Meshach, the stocky elder of
the crowd, gently mouthed my arm. None of this had ever happened
before. All the wolf-dogs seemed excited so I carefully moved to the
edge of the deck and sat down.

Then I was surrounded. No, that's an exaggeration. All the action
was behind me, with vigorous sniffing vibrating my eardrums in a symphony of loud whispers. It felt like each inhalation lifted tendrils of
my hair straight out into a static-shock halo. Snouts and paws nudged

235

my head and shoulders forward as hairy bodies jostled for position. Coarse tongues tousled my hair and left wet smears on the back of my neck and occasionally my face. "It tickles! It tickles!" I said between bursts of laughter. Allan provided a running commentary on who was doing what. Mahikan was the most vigorous sniffer but even the wary Nahanni pressed his nose against my neck. One of the wolves placed its front paws on my shoulders and stood up as another nibbled my hair. I tossed pieces of European wiener to the wolf-dogs behind me until one of them, probably Tundra, pawed my head, inadvertently scratching my scalp.

Back inside, Allan said he'd never seen such unusual behaviour before, especially from Nahanni. The pack had met me numerous times so probably recognized me. But after some discussion, we decided that the jacket—covered in Allan's scent—was most likely the reason for the effusive greeting. When I stopped by the next morning, Tundra barely opened an eye at the sound of my voice. "You must be considered a member of the family now," Allan said when she didn't

get up and come over to greet me. Even though I knew Allan's scent had a lot to do with it, I was startled and flattered by the wolf-dogs' enthusiastic greeting and acceptance. I'd visited them off and on for about two years so it wasn't a sudden event like meeting someone and feeling like you know them right away. In addition to Allan's jacket, this stage of our acquaintance had taken time. I wonder if time and understanding wolf behaviour is what's needed for people to accept wolves? By acceptance I mean moving beyond the perception of the wolf as poster animal for the wilderness or savage killer, and looking at the animal in a more holistic way. I'm still shocked by the polarization of opinion and unwillingness for many to find or even approach a common ground of understanding. I expected differences, sure, but not of the magnitude I encountered. People love wolves. People hate wolves. It's that simple.

Dave Mech has studied wolves for 60 years so I asked him about it. He says, "I believe folks tend to have such extreme views of wolves because, being so familiar and emotional about dogs, they see the wolf as a form of dog, which, of course, it is. Then, being emotional about their pets, they transfer those feelings toward wolves. They then become defensive in the extreme about farmers and ranchers who hate wolves because of their depredation on livestock. Each extreme view exacerbates the other."

I suspect that commonalities between wolf and human behaviour have something to do with it too. Wolves mate for life but sometimes have sex with other wolves. As family groups they raise and play with their young, work together to obtain food and mourn the loss of pack members. Yet they also bicker, sometimes seriously, fight with other packs over territory and kill one another. There are bullies, flirts and

Wolves lead extremely active lives. They travel long distances, hunt large prey and sometimes fight each other or rival packs. And sometimes they just relax. Photo by Cheryl Alexander strong leaders, wolves that mind their own business and those that get into trouble. I think it's difficult to escape the love/hate dichotomy when people are faced with an animal that looks like their pet and possesses some human-like traits yet, under the right circumstances, can be dangerous to pets, livestock and occasionally humans.

Following the rise and fall of wolf populations is like chasing the moon. At times it's fat, round and brilliant in a star-studded sky; at others, a thin sliver that's barely noticeable. Although the waxing and waning of wolf populations occurs both through natural and human influences, often wolves survive only because humans allow them to. Now the wolf is returning to its ancestral territories, in many areas after an absence of one to two hundred years. Accepting them is easy for some and a huge challenge for others. Perhaps as Doug Smith, senior biologist at the Yellowstone Center for Resources, once said, tolerance is the best we can hope for.

I've learned a lot about wolves but know only a fraction about them. Every question I asked led to five more and that could probably continue forever. Once when I was talking to long-time wolf researcher Paul Paquet, he said, "I love the not knowing. Animals deserve and are fine with us not knowing everything." He's right, of course. That said, I think I figured out why four-month-old Nahanni deposited a turd on the deck where I'd been sitting during my first visit. Wolves urinate and defecate in conspicuous spots throughout their territory to let other wolves know they claim that space. I suspect that when they poop and pee on tents, kayaks, people's footprints and where humans have been sitting, they're doing the same. Nahanni had just met me and was letting me know I was on his turf.

I'm not sure what the prolonged eye contact with the wolf on Quadra Island was about. In the wolf world, eye contact is a sign of dominance. Maybe that's why the wolf kept moving back to a more secluded position. On the other hand, some people believe wolves show themselves to humans only when they have something to tell them. Was there a message I was supposed to receive? The wolf's eyes were piercing and direct. Like Troy Bennett, I felt mesmerized and could not look away. The details of the encounter are clear in my memory. We came around a corner and the wolf was starting to cross the road. When it saw us, it turned around and went back the way it had come. I sometimes wonder if it was simply waiting for us to drive on so it could continue its journey. Either way, I know now we should have just taken a quick glance, perhaps honked our horn, and been on our way.

I think of wolves differently now than before. I see the beauty but also the beast. It's somehow humbling to have an icon of the wilderness reduced to four paws on the ground. But it's much more realistic. I like Louise Liebenberg's practical attitude: wolves are here and unless we kill them all again, it's up to us to come up with strategies to deal with them. By keeping her livestock safe, she keeps wolves safe too. Wolves, like all animals, do what's easiest for them to survive. It's up to us to teach them that being around humans does not result in a reward, and to enforce the boundaries of our human territory.

My journey with wolves has made me more aware of the relationships wolves and all wildlife have with their own species, as well as other creatures. Their alliances, emotions and thought processes may be more significant than most of us realize. The same holds true for the ebb and flow of their presence across the landscape and the way that affects other animals and the land we share. No matter where humans go, we leave a footprint—and sometimes it's the equivalent of a size 17 gumboot. Even if our feet never leave the sidewalk, we influence the natural world by the votes we cast, the items we purchase, how we dispose of our garbage and in a multitude of other ways. What we do matters a great deal in the endless loop of cause and effect.

In *Are We Smart Enough to Know How Smart Animals Are?* author Frans de Waal explores the social behaviour and intelligence of a variety of wildlife. As a biologist with doctorates in zoology and ethology (the science of animal behaviour), his discussions about animals, cognition and culture are insightful and thought-provoking. In one section he writes about how animals shape their reality based on their perceptions of what is occurring in their environment. Humans are no different. The wolf that lopes across the human psyche is a beast of our imagination and experience. It is what we believe and want it to be: devil, werewolf, spiritual messenger or legendary symbol of all that is wild and free. Yet its essence remains shrouded in a mist of speculation, fairy tales, rumours, righteousness and sometimes truth.

Toward the end of the film *Cave of Forgotten Dreams*, the narrator presents three possible scenarios for the prints of a young boy and wolf found side by side in the Chauvet-Pont-d'Arc Cave: that the wolf was stalking the child, that they were walking together as companions or that the tracks were made thousands of years apart. I consider them all possible. Wolves sometimes look upon humans as prey. We have walked side by side with some form of wolves as they became dogs. Or the tracks could have been made at two very different times.

I like the third interpretation best. Not the thousands of years part but the idea of distance, that humans and wolves could see each other occasionally from far away and then go about their lives without disturbing each other. There would be problems from time to time but I hope that for the most part we can see the landscape as large enough for wolves and people and do what is necessary to make and keep it that way.

One night in the fall of 2016, our next-door neighbours heard wolves howling from across the nearby railway tracks. They had probably trotted down the Royston to Cumberland Trail, once a railway line used to bring coal from Cumberland mines to the deepwater port of Union Bay. I missed that night's chorus but now open the window a crack when I go to bed. Yes, even in winter. I'm hoping to hear the wolf's song. I want the cascade of notes to send shivers up my spine and touch my soul. I want to hear the wolves but I don't want them to come too close. For their safety, not mine.

Wolf pups learn to howl by listening to their elders. Howling is a bonding experience that the entire family group can participate in.
Photo courtesy of US Fish and Wildlife Service

WOLF SAFETY CHECKLIST

- Never feed wolves or wildlife that may attract them.
- Manage attractants such as pets, pet food and livestock, as well as human food and garbage.
- Be aware of your surroundings and wolf activity in the area.
- Supervise young children when outside. Teach them what to do if they see a wolf.
- Keep your dog leashed or leave it at home if visiting wolf country.
- Carry an air horn, pepper spray and a fixed blade knife (or firearm if you're licensed and they're not restricted in the area). Check the expiry date on pepper spray, know its range and learn how to use it.
- Keep pets and livestock in secure enclosures at night.
- Enjoy the outdoors in groups of two or more. If a wolf approaches, act together to scare it off immediately.
- Keep a clean campsite. Store food, toiletries and garbage in a food safe, cache or bear hang. Cook and store food away from sleeping areas and pack all garbage out. Do not leave any items out when away from camp. Dispose of dirty dishwater away from camp.

- Use the outhouse or pack it out as wolves have been known to eat human feces.
- Avoid camping near a carcass.
- Always sleep in a cabin, RV, tent or vehicle, not in the open.
- Always use the buddy system for after-dark trips to the outhouse.
- If you want a close-up view, use binoculars or the zoom lens on your camera. If you can take a photo with your cell phone, you're *way* too close.
- Report wolves that approach or appear interested in people, their belongings or garbage to the appropriate wildlife agency as soon as possible.
- If you come across a kill, den or rendezvous site, remain calm and slowly back away from the area immediately. Be prepared to act aggressively or find a safe place if the wolves show undue interest.
- Keep a minimum of 100 metres (110 yds) away from wolves when on foot or in a motor vehicle, boat or kayak.
- Aggressively haze wolves if they're near people or human-use areas (including your tent on a remote beach). Hazing means making loud noises, throwing rocks or sticks and anything else that lets wolves know they are not welcome.
- If a wolf approaches, make yourself look big, yell and wave your arms, stamp your feet and move toward it.
- Never run from or turn your back on a wolf.
- Maintain eye contact. Remove sunglasses.
- If a wolf acts aggressive, back away slowly.
- Avoid growling at wolves, which appears to provoke aggression.
- If the situation escalates, prepare to defend yourself with rocks, sticks or whatever you have.
- Try to find a safe place such as a car or building, or a tree to climb. Be prepared to wait for the wolf to lose interest.

- If multiple wolves are approaching and you cannot scare them away, try to place your back against a big tree or rock in case one attempts to circle behind you.
- If you're on a bike, stop, dismount and try to scare the wolf off. Be prepared to use the bike as a shield or weapon.
- If a wolf attacks, fight back as hard as you can. Focus blows on the eyes and nose.

SELECTED
SOURCES

INTERVIEWS, CONVERSATIONS AND PERSONAL CORRESPONDENCE

WILDLIFE/WOLF-DOG SPECIALISTS

Cheryl Alexander, wolf researcher

Gary Allan, Who Speaks for Wolf: Wolf Advocacy and Education

Troy Bennett, wolf specialist/nature guide

John Benson, Assistant Professor of Vertebrate Ecology, School of
    Natural Resources, University of Nebraska

Chris Darimont, science director at Raincoast Conservation
    Foundation and Raincoast Chair in Conservation Science,
    University of Victoria

Tristan Donovan, author of *Feral Cities: Adventures with Animals in
    the Urban Jungle*

Dave Eyer, wildlife safety consultant, owner/operator of Eyer
    Training Services

Valerius Geist, professor emeritus of environmental science,
    University of Calgary

Michael Grandbois, Clayoquot area supervisor, BC Parks

Will Graves, author of *Wolves in Russia: Anxiety Through the Ages*

Bob Hansen, living-with-wildlife specialist

Mark Hebblewhite, professor of ungulate habitat ecology, University of Montana

Bob Jamieson, systems ecologist and environmental consultant

David LeGros, natural heritage education specialist, Algonquin Provincial Park

Louise Liebenberg, rancher and co-owner of Grazerie, Canada's first wildlife- and predator-friendly ranch

Liesl Lockhart, rancher and co-owner of Candll Lamb & Cattle Co.

Ian McAllister, author, photographer and executive director of Pacific Wild

L. David Mech, senior research scientist, US Geological Survey

Regina Mossotti, director of animal care and conservation, Endangered Wolf Center

Paul Paquet, senior scientist, Raincoast Conservation Foundation and Raincoast Conservation Science Lab, University of Victoria

Rolf Peterson, former lead, current co-investigator, the Isle Royale Wolf-Moose Project

Helen Schwantje, wildlife veterinarian, BC Ministry of Forests, Lands, Natural Resource Operations and Rural Development

Barbara M.V. Scott, wolf researcher

Doug Smith, senior biologist at Yellowstone Center for Resources and head of the Yellowstone Wolf Project

Wendy Spencer, executive director, Wolf Haven International

Jonathan G. Way, founder of Eastern Coyote/Coywolf Research

Brad White, professor of environment and life sciences, Trent University

Jesse Whittingon, wildlife ecologist, Banff National Park

Todd Windle, human-wildlife coexistence specialist, Pacific Rim National Park Reserve

Kim Young, director of communications, Wolf Haven International

ADDITIONAL SOURCES

Wayne Barnes

Gary Flath

William "Mac" Hollan

Marcus Jais

Una Ledrew

Liam McNeil

Grayson Pettigrew

Dave Ratcliffe

Sandra Ross

Marg Selkirk

Ocean Simone

James Swan

Jacqueline Windh

GOVERNMENT AGENCIES

Alberta Energy and Parks

BC Ministry of Forests, Lands, Natural Resource Operations and
Rural Development

BOOKS

Bekoff, Marc. *The Emotional Lives of Animals: A Leading Scientist Explores Animal Joy, Sorrow and Empathy—And Why They Matter.* Novato, CA: New World Library, 2008.

de Waal, Frans. *Are We Smart Enough to Know How Smart Animals Are?* New York: W.W. Norton & Company, 2017.

Donovan, Tristan. *Feral Cities: Adventures with Animals in the Urban Jungle.* Chicago: Chicago Review Press, 2015.

Haber, Gordon, and Marybeth Holleman. *Among Wolves: Gordon Haber's Insights into Alaska's Most Misunderstood Animal.* Fairbanks, AK: University of Alaska Press, 2013.

Hyde, John. *Romeo: The Story of an Alaskan Wolf.* Piermont, NH: Bunker Hill Publishing, 2012.

Lopez, Barry. *Of Wolves and Men.* New York: Scribner, 1978.

McAllister, Ian. *The Last Wild Wolves: Ghosts of the Great Bear Rainforest.* Vancouver: Greystone Books, 2007.

Mech, L. David, and Luigi Boitani, eds. *Wolves: Behavior, Ecology, and Conservation.* Chicago: University of Chicago Press, 2003.

Mech, L. David, Douglas W. Smith and Daniel R. MacNulty. *Wolves on the Hunt: The Behavior of Wolves Hunting Wild Prey.* Chicago: University of Chicago Press, 2015.

Mowat, Farley. *Never Cry Wolf.* New York: Dell Publishing Company, 1963.

Niemeyer, Carter. *Wolfer: A Memoir.* Boise, ID: Bottlefly Press, 2010.

Safina, Carl. *Beyond Words: What Animals Think and Feel.* New York: Henry Holt & Company, 2015.

Van Tighem, Kevin. *The Homeward Wolf.* Victoria, BC: Rocky Mountain Books, 2013.

White, Howard, ed. *Raincoast Chronicles First Five, Collector's Edition.* Madeira Park, BC: Harbour Publishing, 1976.

Young, Stanley P., and Edward A. Goldman. *The Wolves of North America* (Part 1). New York: Dover Publications, 1944.

ARTICLES AND REPORTS

"Learning to Live with Large Carnivores: WildCoast Project Primer & Guidelines." EKOS Communications, Inc., and Parks Canada Agency, 2010.

Linnell, John D., et al. "The Fear of Wolves: A Review of Wolf Attacks on Humans." Trondheim, Norway: Norwegian Institute for Nature Research, 2002.

McNay, Mark E. "A Case History of Wolf-Human Encounters in Alaska and Canada." Alaska Department of Fish and Game Wildlife Technical Bulletin 13, 2002.

Penteriani, Vincenzo, et al. "Human Behaviour Can Trigger Large Carnivore Attacks in Developed Countries." *Scientific Reports* 6, article 20552 (February 2016).

Tarlach, Gemma. "The Origins of Dogs." *Discover* (December 2016), pp. 32–36.

ONLINE RESOURCES

Eastern Coyote/Coywolf Research: www.easterncoyoteresearch.com

Mission: Wolf—Education vs. Extinction: www.missionwolf.org

Who Speaks for Wolf: www.whospeaksforwolf.com

Wolf Haven International: www.wolfhaven.org

The Wolf Is At The Door, Inc.: www.wolf-to-wolfdog.org

Wolf Science Center Austria: www.wolfscience.at/en

Wolves and Moose of Isle Royale: www.isleroyalewolf.org

FILMS

Cave of Forgotten Dreams. Director: Werner Herzog, 2010.

Meet the Coywolf. Director: Susan Fleming, 2014.

Wolf Hunter. Director: James Morgan, 2016.

Wolves Unleashed. Director: Andrew Simpson, 2012.

ACKNOWLEDGMENTS

WHILE WORKING ON THIS BOOK I OFTEN JOKED THAT I SPENT ALL MY time alone locked in a room with a wolf. But the truth is I had countless conversations, email exchanges and visits with people who have studied, lived with and loved wolves, as well as those who have been challenged by their presence. Their knowledge and stories, so generously shared, are the backbone of *Return of the Wolf*.

A thousand thank yous to all the experts who took time out of their busy lives to talk to me. Bob Hansen and Todd Windle were invaluable contacts for information and discussions about human-wolf conflict and coexistence. Dave Eyer, as always, was informative, encouraging and insightful. Talking to Paul Paquet influenced my perspective on the way humans treat all wildlife.

Gary Allan gets a giant thank you for early research leads, welcoming me into his home and letting me hang out with the pack as often as time allowed. My visit to Wolf Haven and discussions with Wendy Spencer and Kim Young contributed greatly to my understanding of captive wolves and wolf-dogs. Valerius Geist was generous with his personal observations about wolves, as was Will Graves with his reflections on wolves in Russia. BC wildlife vet Helen Schwantje answered every question quickly, measured wolf teeth and took photos for me, and delivered it all with a great sense of humour. Thanks also to Cheryl Alexander for providing insider knowledge about a unique wolf. And to Liesl Lockhart and Louise Liebenberg for their insights on livestock predation.

Thank you, Ken Gibson, for letting me stay at your beach cabin while researching wolves in Tofino. And to the Access Copyright Foundation for a research grant. A huge thanks to Una Ledrew and Dave Ratcliffe for taking strangers in and filling them up with good food, great hikes and info about wolves, and for becoming friends. And to all who contributed fantastic photos—wow! Especially Rooobert Bayer, for finding a way to make the impossible possible.

Words are not enough to express my gratitude to the terrific team at Douglas & McIntyre who take a manuscript, turn it into a book and then do an excellent job of introducing it to the public. A heartfelt thanks to Pam Robertson (substantive editor) and Cheryl Cohen (proofreader) for their diligence. I'm also grateful for all the book reps who pound the beat, bookshops that stock my books and, of course, people who purchase them.

I wish I could thank every one of you personally but these few words will have to suffice. It's been a wild ride with the wolf—an experience that has deepened my knowledge and appreciation of all nature and one that I will never forget.

INDEX

Page numbers in **bold** indicate images